Gift and Promise

Gift and Promise

The Augsburg Confession and the Heart of
Christian Theology

Edward H. Schroeder, author

Ronald Neustadt and Stephen Hitchcock, editors

Fortress Press
Minneapolis

GIFT AND PROMISE

The Augsburg Confession and the Heart of Christian Theology

Cover image: Erstausgabe der Augsburger Konfession mit Vorstücken und Anhang in lateinischer Sprache, Confessio fidei exhibita invictiss. Imp. Carolo V. Cesari Aug. in Comicijs Augusta. Anno M.D.XXX. Addita est Apologia

Cover design: Ivy Palmer Skrade

Library of Congress Cataloging-in-Publication Data

Print ISBN: 978-1-5064-1068-5

eBook ISBN: 978-1-5064-1069-2

The paper used in this publication meets the minimum requirements of American National Standard for Information Sciences — Permanence of Paper for Printed Library Materials, ANSI Z329.48-1984.

Manufactured in the U.S.A.

This book was produced using Pressbooks.com, and PDF rendering was done by PrinceXML.

Contents

Introduction

Elizabeth Eaton, presiding bishop of the Evangelical Lutheran Church in America (ELCA), wants everyone to understand that what defines Lutherans is their theology. Bishop Eaton states that it is not Jello or "hot dishes" or any of the ethnic or cultural characteristics we may chuckle over when we listen to Garrison Keillor.

"We have a very particular way of understanding the Jesus story," Eaton writes. "It's the story of God redeeming us from sin, death and the devil, setting us free from our bondage to sin so that liberated and alive, we may serve God by serving the neighbor. And it's not about our effort or goodness or hard work. It's about God's gracious will to be merciful."[1] That "particular" theology, presented in the Augsburg Confession, is the subject of this book.

The premise of this book is that the theology expressed in the 1530s by Luther and the other Reformers in Saxony, Germany, is as relevant today—and as necessary today—as it has ever been. The current de facto theology of many (including even heirs of the Reformation) is a theology that assumes we have a transactional relationship with God—if I do this, then God will do that. The sad result is that the work of Christ—in particular his death and resurrection—is wasted and human beings are left with burdened consciences or with self-destructive pride. They are left with the realization that the good they do is never really all that good and never really good enough—and that the good they do does not undo the selfish and hurtful things they have done or said. Or they end up deceiving themselves into thinking they are better than they really are, setting themselves up for the critique of God who commands us to love God with all our heart, soul, and mind—and our neighbors as ourselves.

In contrast, the Augsburg Confession offers the promise that we are

1. *The Lutheran*, October 2015, 50.

justified by faith in the crucified and risen Christ. This promise sets burdened consciences free and liberates us from sinful self-centeredness. In the midst of our existential dread and pervasive anxiety, the Augsburg Confession and the writers of this book invite us to find joy in the promise that God makes to us through the death and resurrection of Jesus.

Dr. Edward Schroeder began to write this book forty years ago. But the controversy that had ruptured the Lutheran Church—Missouri Synod in the 1970s (and had cost him his job) resulted in his delaying its completion.

Now nine of Schroeder's students have finished what their teacher began. They, too, believe that the theology of the Augsburg Confession speaks to our time as it articulates the law and the promise that are at the heart of the scriptural Word of God.

The first three chapters are revisions of Schroeder's original work. They establish the core of the Augsburg Confession, articulated in article 4 of that confession. That core, of course, is the gospel itself. It is the good news that God has reconciled sinners to God's self through the death and resurrection of Jesus, and that those who trust this good news already have, by that very trust, what God offers them in Christ. The core, in short, is a promise—a promise we have as a gift.

That realization, Schroeder points out, came to Luther as an "Aha" (or perhaps as a series of "Ahas"). For Luther, the promise of the gospel had gotten lost in medieval theology and preaching. That promise is always in danger of being lost (even today), given the sinful nature of human beings. The writers hope this book helps keep that gospel "Aha" alive.

Schroeder demonstrates how Luther's "theology of the cross" stands in sharp contrast to the "theology of glory" that so agitated Luther—and why. The "theology of glory" that did not proclaim the gospel as a promise failed to make full use of Christ or his benefits. It wasted them. And the result was that troubled consciences remained troubled. The "theology of the cross" that informs the Augsburg Confession makes use of Christ's death and resurrection *and* brings consolation to troubled consciences.

In the first three foundational chapters, Schroeder demonstrates how Luther's intense study of the scriptures informed his theology of the cross. Schroeder invents a new metaphor to illustrate the Augsburg Confession's way of evaluating theology to determine if it is "theology of the cross." The term is "double dipstick," sometimes also called the "two-sided measuring stick": (1) does the theology being presented make full use of Christ's benefits, and (2) do we receive maximum comfort and consolation "in the midst of earthly life"? Faith that trusts Christ's full benefits—faith that "has Christ"—enables us to live with joy and hope in the face of the evil, sin, and death that are present in "earthly life."

The nine chapters that follow Schroeder's, written by his students, discuss the other "articles of faith" contained in the Augsburg Confession. They show how these articles "articulate" the one doctrine the church has—justification by faith alone.

Throughout this book, we use a visual illustration that Schroeder himself gave us, Illinois farm boy that he is. The Augsburg Confession is like a wagon wheel. The hub is justification by faith alone (articles 3 and 4). The spokes articulate that doctrinal hub in various contexts. The rim is the proper distinction between law and gospel that is necessary for the gospel to be heard and trusted.

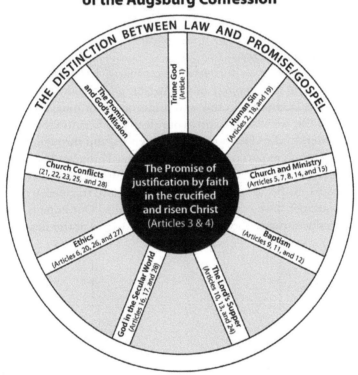

Gift and Promise: the Theology of the Augsburg Confession

THE DISTINCTION BETWEEN LAW AND PROMISE/GOSPEL

The Promise and God's Mission

Triune God (Article 1)

Human Sin (Articles 2, 18, and 19)

Church Conflicts (21, 22, 23, 25, and 28)

The Promise of justification by faith in the crucified and risen Christ (Articles 3 & 4)

Church and Ministry (Articles 5, 7, 8, 14, and 15)

Ethics (Articles 6, 20, 26, and 27)

God in the Secular World (Articles 16, 17, and 28)

The Lord's Supper (Articles 10, 13, and 24)

Baptism (Articles 9, 11, and 12)

The Spokes: Articulations of the Promise, the one and only doctrine of the Gospel.

The Augsburg Confession, of course, has twenty-eight articles. We have grouped some of them together to end up with nine spokes.

The writers of this book have a variety of vocations and write in a variety of styles. Some are parish clergy; one is a bishop; one is an attorney; four are professors. In this book they write, not for the academy (although they could have, being scholars themselves), but for a broader readership. Our hope is that this book will help students, laypersons, and scholars alike to gain insight into the theology of the Augsburg Confession and its "up-to-date-ness" for our times.

You will find treasures in this book: Schroeder's discussion of the radical difference between Luther's and Anselm's atonement models; Repp's discussion of Trinity and science; Felde's insight into marriage. You will also discover how timely the theology of the Augsburg Confession continues to be, especially as you read Kleinhans's chapter on original sin or Failinger's treatment of the current debate about affirmative action. As an added bonus, Kääriäinen's Augsburg perspective on mission is a significant contribution to current discussions in missiology.

We believe all our writers have contributed, not just to a clearer understanding of the theology of the Augsburg Confession, but also to a greater appreciation of its value and importance for today. In bringing this book to life, we wish to express our deep appreciation for the gift of Ed Schroeder. In the classroom, at conferences, and through hundreds of online postings as part of Sabbatheology and Thursday Theology (see www.crossings.org), he has patiently and persistently presented the gift of the gospel. As he (and his email messages) have traveled around the world, thousands have experienced Luther's "Aha." Our hope is that this book introduces many more to the promise that is at the heart of this theology.

Ronald C. Neustadt
Stephen Hitchcock

Foreword

The 500th anniversary of Martin Luther's Ninety-five Theses, whose publication in October 1517 marks the traditional starting point of "The Protestant Reformation," is leading many to ponder: "Who was this Luther? What trouble did he create? What impact, both negative and positive, has he had on our world? Does Luther still have anything to teach us today?" The Jubilee year of 2017 has become an occasion for people within and beyond Christendom to study his life and work with renewed intensity. What is the ecumenical significance of Luther's theology and reforms?

Although this book is not about Luther's famous theses or even about Luther himself, it does attend to themes that were central to him and received their classic articulation in the Augsburg Confession of 1530. To study these themes is to be taken to the heart and center of Christian teaching: the unconditional mercy and forgiveness of God that is given in and through Jesus Christ for all sinners.

Luther himself—a university professor and occasional preacher, it should be remembered—became convinced the scriptures teach that a person is "justified" or "right" before God through grace, solely as a gift, for Christ's sake, by faith alone (*sola fide*), apart from human "good works."

This Christian gospel or "good news" has a central importance, not merely for the justification of the individual sinner. It is also crucial for one's theological understanding of other issues: the proper distinction between God's demands and gifts, the nature of repentance and faith, the church and the means of grace, the freedom of the baptized, and the importance of good works. Included in this mix are the relation between scriptural teaching and church traditions, the nature and condition(s) for true unity in the church, the mission of the church, and authority in the church.

Of course Luther did not want people to focus on his life or to celebrate his achievements. He had a realistic sense of his own limitations and placed the focus elsewhere:

> I ask that people make no reference to my name; let them call themselves Christians, not Lutherans. What is Luther? After all, the teaching is not mine. Neither was I crucified for anyone. St. Paul in First Corinthians 3 would not allow the Christians to call themselves Pauline or Petrine, but Christian. How then could I—poor stinking maggot-fodder that I am—come to have people call the children of Christ by my wretched name? Not so, my dear friends; let us abolish all party names and call ourselves Christians, after him whose teaching we hold. (*LW* 45:70–71, trans. slightly modified)

The Wittenberg professor likewise suggested an additional label, in place of the pejorative "Lutheran," namely, "evangelical." Luther understood that term to mean "oriented to the gospel" ("evangel" = "good message" or "good report"; cf. Mark 1:15-16, 1 Cor. 15:1ff.).[1] Already in the Ninety-five Theses Luther pointed in this direction: "The true treasure of the church is the most holy gospel of the glory and grace of God" (*LW* 31:31).

The conflict that ensued after October 1517 between the authorities (both political and ecclesial), on the one hand, and Luther and his supporters, on the other, developed into a far more significant disagreement. Eventually Luther would be excommunicated, in early 1521. As this conflict unfolded, Luther saw more clearly just how central the promise of the gospel really is. He gradually learned that this promise really was his sole concern as a professor of the Bible and that it was the true issue at stake in his theological disputes.

This gospel promise alone had brought comfort and peace to his own troubled soul, and it had given him the most profound solution to the most perplexing and vexing of spiritual trials and tribulations he had encountered. No longer would the biblical phrase, "the righteousness of God," frighten him, as it had when he had pondered it as God's just demand and the divine judgment against him, the sinner. Instead, Luther came to understand the gospel promise as the righteousness that God freely gives the sinner as a *gift*, as a *promise* that is received solely *by faith*. In the promise, God declares that our sins have been taken from us and transferred to the crucified Christ and that this Christ's righteousness is now predicated to us sinners. What an amazing transfer!

---

1. The term "evangelical," as it was used by Luther and his followers, meant something different from how that word is used today to describe a subset within American Protestantism (e.g., nondenominational American evangelicalism, the National Association of Evangelicals, conservative American politics, etc.). Since the sixteenth century, many Lutheran churches and some other Protestant churches have understood the word to be synonymous with "Protestant" or "Lutheran," especially in Germany, and yet even then the earlier connection to a gospel-oriented theological perspective is not entirely absent.

When that gospel "sense" of that biblical phrase, "the righteousness of God," entered Luther's head and heart, it was as if he had been brought to the very "gates of paradise." It was, to use Edward Schroeder's catchy descriptor, Luther's "Aha Moment" (or series of insightful epiphanies, since Luther seems to have come to this teaching rather slowly, with fits and starts, between 1514 and 1518).[2] Gift, promise, by faith alone—together these terms clarify what is truly "good" about the "good news."

The author of the Augsburg Confession, Philip Melanchthon (1497–1560), who was Luther's friend and younger colleague, experienced his own "Aha Moment" when he crafted that confession's twenty-eight articles and then responded to its critics in the Apology to the Augsburg Confession. Crucially, Melanchthon came to see that the gospel promise is central to *all* of the articles of faith.[3] Of the twenty-eight articles in the Augsburg Confession, the fourth—on justification—articulates the "chief article of faith" that informs and shapes all the others, including those on "abuses that have been corrected" (for example, distribution of only the Eucharistic host, forced celibacy of clergy, the mass as human work and sacrifice, satisfactions, monastic vows, and the exercise of ecclesial oversight). That gospel of justification by faith, apart from works of law, is the key that not only unlocks the scriptures—by identifying their one true purpose, to create and sustain faith in the triune God—but it also properly orients every church doctrine. This is the evangelical dogma that those Augsburg confessors proposed to the church catholic as the norm of orthodoxy and catholicity.

Robert Bertram (1921–2003), whose influence is evident throughout the following chapters, referred to Melanchthon's "Aha Moment" as his discovery of "the hermeneutical significance of Article IV."[4] According to Bertram, Melanchthon's "Aha" was his recognition of the deep and abiding connection between "reading the Bible" and "articulating the biblical teaching of salvation." How one reads the Bible is inseparable from the question of how people get saved biblically, and how one understands biblical salvation is inseparable from how one reads the scriptures. This basic Bertramian-Melanchthonian insight was later expanded and clarified by Bertram's student, friend, and collaborator, Ed Schroeder (see the first three chapters below). Now some of their

---

2. See Edward Schroeder, "Some Thoughts on the Augsburg Aha! The Augsburg Confession Itself," http://www.crossings.org/some-thoughts-on-the-augsburg-confession-itself/. Accessed 3/28/2016.
3. Ibid.
4. Robert W. Bertram, "The Hermeneutical Significance of Apology IV," in *A Project in Biblical Hermeneutics*, ed. Richard Jungkuntz (St. Louis: Concordia, 1969), 124–26.

students have added their voices to that duet in order to "fess up" evangelical expansions and clarifications of their own.[5]

One needs to underscore that the authors of these chapters do not see the Augsburg Confession as a sectarian document. Its intended purpose is not to set forth "the Lutheran" faith over against "the Catholic" one. Nor is it to define "Lutheran Protestantism" over against some other ism. Rather, the Augsburg Confession's own explicit and rather audacious claim is that it sets forth the one, holy, catholic, and apostolic faith, that it teaches the "evangelical faith," which is also "the catholic faith." The intent of the document and of those who sign(ed) it—as Luther himself did (despite his private protestations that his drinking buddy's confession was too pacific in places)—is thus an ecumenical and catholic intention in the broadest and best sense of these terms.

Given its original ecumenical aim, the Augsburg Confession invites repeated examination and testing in inter-Christian and interreligious contexts as well as in both ecclesial and academic settings. Does the Augsburg Confession in fact set forth the catholic faith? Is its exhibition of doctrine "biblical," that is, truly "evangelical"? Can one recognize within this confession a "catholic" consensus? Moreover, do this confession's articulations of doctrine have an abiding significance for contemporary theology? Can this sixteenth-century "source" serve as a useful "re-source" for twenty-first-century theological teaching and preaching? To answer these questions, one has to return to the text itself (*Ad fontem*! Back to the source!), to engage its claims and to test them against what the scriptures themselves set forth in the context of our contemporary world.

Each of the ensuing chapters insists on an affirmative answer to the above questions. Each essay returns to the originating spring of that 1530 confession in order to discern in it "the evangelical pattern of doctrine" and to identify gospel clues for how to go about addressing contemporary theological problems and issues. A key question always is: "How is one to confess the one sufficient gospel at the present time?" The authors, each in his or her own

---

5. Both Bertram and Schroeder first taught at Valparaiso University and then later at Concordia Seminary, St. Louis (a seminary that went into "exile" in 1974). For Bertram's use of "fessing up," see Robert Bertram, "Confessional Movements and FC-10," an address delivered in Munich in July 1977, http://www.crossings.org/library/bertram/ConfessionalMovementsFC-10.pdf. Accessed 3/28/2016. See also idem, *A Time for Confessing*, ed. Michael Hoy, Foreword by Edward H. Schroeder, Lutheran Quarterly Books (Grand Rapids: Eerdmans, 2008). Dr. Bertram's comments and suggestions to the editors and translators of the most recent scholarly edition of the Lutheran Confessions in English had a significant impact on the final draft of that book. See *The Book of Concord: The Confessions of the Evangelical Lutheran Church*, ed. Robert Kolb and Timothy Wengert (Minneapolis: Fortress Press, 2000).

way, demonstrate the difference that the "Augsburg Aha" makes for the central and traditional topics of the Christian faith and for professing that one gospel faithfully (often, like Luther, even over against the established authorities of one's time and place). While the dogma of Augsburg is the jumping-off point for each of the following chapters, the overall goal is to allow that evangelical orientation to speak to a contemporary audience, whose questions and problems, issues and complexities may (or may not) be different from those in that earlier era.

Perhaps I can be permitted a personal word of gratitude as a conclusion to this Foreword. For a first-year student at a college of the Lutheran Church—Missouri Synod, studying the published essays of Bertram, Schroeder, and their colleagues brought about an "Aha moment" that was not dissimilar from Luther's own. Those essays came bundled together under the title, "The Promising Tradition: A Reader in Law-Gospel Reconstructionist Theology."[6] By the time I read them, their authors had long been "exiled" from the Missouri Synod—the church body that had nurtured them in the faith, the same church body that had nurtured me.

When I first read those essays, I had been wrestling with the nature of biblical authority and the challenge of understanding those parts of the Bible that cause the most problems and difficulties for many young university students—especially after they have sat through a few science, philosophy, and history courses. What a liberation it was to encounter confessional Lutheran theologians who employed historical-critical resources and methods in the most rigorous of ways, and yet did so entirely in service to the evangelical *promissio* and as a prophetic *confessio* against that which is anti-gospel, "another gospel," or no gospel at all. What a blessing it was to discover the hermeneutical significance of article 4 of the Augsburg Confession and the corollary article 4 in Melanchthon's Apology, and to learn about the proper distinction between law and gospel.

I also discovered how making that distinction properly—for the sake of the solely sufficient "one gospel-and-sacraments"—leads away from all sorts of theological dead-ends. That "aha moment" included a recognition of how one's theology could be both "faithful to its confessional legacy" and yet "responsible to its time."[7] That same

---

6. *The Promising Tradition: A Reader in Law-Gospel Reconstructionist Theology*, 2nd ed. (St. Louis: Concordia Seminary in Exile, 1974). See also the June 1987 issue of *Currents in Theology and Mission*, which offers essays on the same theme by students of Bertram and Schroeder.

7. Jaroslav Pelikan, Foreword, *The Structure of Lutheranism*, vol. 1, by Werner Elert, trans. Walter A. Hansen (St. Louis: Concordia, 1962), xi.

"promising tradition" comes forward to our time and place in the chapters of this book. The one who reads them should be prepared for his or her own "Augsburg Aha."

Matthew Becker
Professor of Theology
Valparaiso University
The Resurrection of Our Lord 2016

Introduction to the Writers

The Rev. Steven E. Albertin, STM, DMin, is a pastor of the Evangelical Lutheran Church in America, currently serving at Christ Lutheran Church, Zionsville, Indiana. He has served various Lutheran congregations in Indiana for more than thirty-five years.

Dr. Matthew Becker is associate professor of theology at Valparaiso University. He is the author of *Fundamental Theology: A Protestant Perspective* (2014), *The Self-Giving God and Salvation History: The Trinitarian Theology of Johannes von Hofmann* (2004), "F. H. R. Frank" in *Nineteenth Century Theologians*, which he edited, as well as numerous scholarly articles.

Professor Marie A. Failinger is a professor of law at Hamline University School of Law. She is the former editor of the *Journal of Law and Religion*. She received her LLM from Yale Law School and, recently, she was awarded an honorary Doctor of Laws degree from Valparaiso University, where she had received her BS and JD degrees. She teaches and writes in constitutional law, law and religion, and other areas of law.

The Rev. Dr. Marcus Felde serves as pastor of Bethlehem Lutheran Church in Indianapolis, Indiana. He has served the church as a missionary in Papua New Guinea for fourteen years and as the pastor of congregations in Indiana for twenty-two years.

Dr. Michael Hoy is a teacher, author, and editor who has served as the pastor of congregations in Wisconsin, Ohio, Missouri, and Illinois. He has edited two works by his mentor, Dr. Robert Bertram—*A Time for Confessing* and *The Divorce of Sex and Marriage: Sain Sex*. He is currently writing a book on the theology of hope.

The Rev. Dr. Jukka Kääriäinen serves as a missionary and assistant professor of systematic theology at China Lutheran Seminary, Hsinchu, Taiwan. He has pastored Lutheran churches in New York City, Long Island, and Princeton, New Jersey.

The Rev. Dr. Kathryn A. Kleinhans holds the Mike and Marge McCoy Family Distinguished Chair in Lutheran Heritage and Mission at Wartburg College, Waverly, Iowa, where she has taught since 1993. A fifth-generation Lutheran pastor, she served a parish in Atlanta, Georgia, while engaged in doctoral studies at Emory University.

The Rev. Dr. Steven C. Kuhl is a pastor of the Evangelical Lutheran Church in America and lives out his vocation in a variety of callings: rector of St. Mark's Episcopal Church in South Milwaukee, Wisconsin; adjunct professor of religious studies at Lakeland College; and executive director of The Crossings Community.

Catherine Lessmann is a lay theologian in St. Louis, Missouri. She works and writes for The Crossings Community; is chairperson of Lutheran School of Theology in St. Louis; and is a licensed lay minister in the Central States Synod of the Evangelical Lutheran Church in America.

The Rev. Dr. Marcus C. Lohrmann is the bishop of the Northwestern Ohio Synod of the Evangelical Lutheran Church in America, an office he has held since 1998. Prior to his election as bishop, he served as a pastor of congregations in Missouri and Ohio.

The Rev. Dr. Arthur (Chris) Repp is a pastor of the Evangelical Lutheran Church in America and a board member of The Crossings Community. His doctoral work in Russian history led to service with the ELCA as a seminary instructor in St. Petersburg, Russia, prior to his current congregational call in Champaign, Illinois.

The Rev. Dr. Edward Schroeder, developed a passion for the theology of the Augsburg Confession during his early years of theological study in the USA and in later post-graduate work in Germany. He kindled that passion in hundreds of students during his decades of teaching at Valparaiso University, Concordia Seminary (St. Louis), Christ Seminary-Seminex, and within The Crossings Community, which he co-founded. In post-retirement years he accepted invitations to teach at venues in all continents except Antarctica. He still doodles in cyberspace, inviting others to share his passion and mentoring those who already have it.

Acknowledgments

A community of co-confessors has helped give birth to this book. Thanks to the board of directors of The Crossings Community for initiating the project, and to Cathy Lessmann in particular, for encouraging us along the way.

Of course, this book would not have been possible without Edward Schroeder. For nearly fifty years, he has taught us well, beginning at Valparaiso University and later at Concordia Seminary and Seminex. We are grateful for permission to proceed with this project, his collaboration in revising the first three chapters, and his encouragement along the way.

Thanks also to Marie Schroeder for patiently and carefully transcribing handwritten manuscripts, for graciously providing helpful suggestions, and for offering affirmation and support. We are also grateful to Anne-Marie Bogdan who, with her editorial expertise, reviewed the entire manuscript.

Thanks to Michael Hoy for so carefully proofreading the entire manuscript numerous times, for providing citations and updating footnotes, for developing the index, and for providing expert counsel from his own experience as a scholar and editor.

We are grateful to those co-authors who joined Michael Hoy in writing the chapters of this book. They graciously took time from their teaching and ministerial responsibilities to bring new insights and fresh perspectives to the "gift and promise" of the Augsburg Confession.

Thanks to Matthew Becker for commending this book as he does in his Foreword and for his invaluable assistance in getting it in front of the eyes of a publisher. We are honored that someone with such vast and deep knowledge of Lutheran theology and history has contributed to this effort. His experience as an author and his generosity in guiding us through the process was a gift.

Thanks to William Burrows for his frequent encouragement, his solid counsel, and his commending this book to others as a "worthy manuscript."

Thanks to Fortress Press for recognizing the value of this book and to their editorial staff.

Finally, thanks to our wives, Debra Neustadt and Janice Hitchcock, for their patience during the times we were preoccupied with this endeavor, and for their loving support and understanding throughout the process. We delight not only in them and their support of us but also in their evident trust in the gift and promise that is the heart of the theology of this book.

Ronald C. Neustadt
Stephen Hitchcock

Martin Luther and the Augsburg Confession

The Augsburg Confession is the major document that sets forth the theology of what would become the Lutheran Church. It came about because Martin Luther and other reformers in the early sixteenth century were concerned that people were not hearing or trusting the life-giving word of promise God was speaking to them in Jesus Christ.

Martin Luther and his colleagues at Wittenberg University taught, preached, and wrote about hearing this word of promise—God's good news, the *euangelion*—and so were labeled evangelical. As the early chapters of this book make clear, it was Luther's intense study of the scriptures—in preparation for his classroom lectures—that drove him to this new understanding.

This new understanding led to reforms in church practice and brought the evangelicals into conflict with the religious authorities. This conflict upset the political order in the rule of Emperor Charles V of the Holy Roman Empire, which included Germany, France, and Italy. As early as 1519, in his Leipzig Disputation, Luther had appealed for a general council of the church to resolve the doctrinal issues he had raised. Instead, Emperor Charles, at the Diet of Worms in 1521, outlawed Martin Luther and his teachings.

Throughout the 1520s, in various diets or assemblies, the representatives of Pope Clement VII challenged the new evangelical teaching. At the same time, the Holy Roman Empire was under intense pressure by the invading Turks, who had laid siege to Vienna in 1529.

Fearing the political upheaval caused by these controversies and wishing a united front to oppose the Turkish onslaught, Emperor Charles, with the backing of the pope, convened the Diet of Augsburg in 1530. He called on the evangelical theologians to give a public explanation of their theology before an imperial audience.

As an outlaw, Luther could not take the risk of appearing in Augsburg. As a result, the delegation from Wittenberg was headed by Philip Melanchthon, a colleague of Luther's at Wittenberg University. Luther himself was in protective custody in the Coburg Castle, from where he could receive news and send notes to his colleagues appearing at the diet.

In Augsburg, Melanchthon was confronted by a document produced by John Eck, one of the leading papal theologians. Citing Luther and others, Eck condemned the reformers as heretical. Rather than presenting the defense demanded by the emperor, Melanchthon chose to prepare a Confession. In assembling the Confession's twenty-eight articles, he used material from recent conclaves of evangelicals as well as from Luther's "Confession of Christ's Supper" (1528).

On June 25, 1530, the Confession was read aloud in German before the imperial audience, and a Latin version was presented in writing.

Eck prepared a Confutation or rebuttal to the Augsburg Confession, but the Confessors did not receive a written version of this confutation, nor would the emperor permit them to present any response to it. However, Melanchthon did prepare a written response, published in spring 1531, which he called the Apology to the Augsburg Confession. Once back in Wittenberg, and having read a transcript of the Confutation, Melanchthon—in collaboration with Luther—produced a revised version of the Apology, published in autumn 1531.

This 1531 edition of the Apology was also signed by theologians who assembled in Smalcald in 1537, where Luther presented his Smalcald Articles. Those articles along with the Augsburg Confession, the Apology, and Luther's catechisms were used as the basis for teaching and practice by those territories that accepted the Reformation as part of the Peace of Augsburg in 1555.

At the end of the Reformation era, these documents along with the three ancient creeds, the 1531 edition of the Apology (and not any of the oft-edited versions Melanchthon produced over the years), and the Formula of Concord (1577) were published as the Book of Concord on June 25, 1580, the fiftieth anniversary of the presentation of the Augsburg Confession.

Today, the constitution and bylaws of Lutheran church bodies around the world along with those of individual congregations affirm the value of these confessions. In their ordination vows, Lutheran pastors pledge to uphold the teaching of the Augsburg Confession and the Apology.

Abbreviations

AC   Augsburg Confession. Unless otherwise noted, all quotations from the Augsburg Confession are from *The Book of Concord*, Robert Kolb and Timothy Wengert, eds. (Minneapolis: Fortress Press, 2000).

Apol   Apology of the Augsburg Confession. Unless otherwise noted, all quotations from the Apology of the Augsburg Confession are from *The Book of Concord*, Kolb/Wengert, eds. (Minneapolis: Fortress Press, 2000).

BoC   *The Book of Concord*, Kolb/Wengert, eds. (Minneapolis: Fortress Press, 2000).

LCC   *Library of Christian Classics*, John Baillie, John T. McNeill, and Henry P. van Dusen, eds. (Philadelphia: Westminster, 1961).

LW   *Luther's Works*, Jaroslav Pelikan, gen. ed., vol. 1–30 (St. Louis: Concordia, 1955–) and Helmut Lehmann, gen. ed., vol. 31–55 (Philadelphia: Fortress Press, 1955–).

SWML   *Selected Writings of Martin Luther*, Theodore G. Tappert, ed. (Philadelphia: Fortress Press, 1967).

WA   *D. Martin Luthers Werke, Kritische Gesamtausgabe, "Weimarer Ausgabe"* (Weimar: Hermann Böhlaus, 1883–2009).

Preach One Thing:
The Wisdom of the Cross

Edward H. Schroeder

In the first three chapters of this book, Edward Schroeder describes the heart of the theology of the Augsburg Confession, the hub of the Augsburg "wheel" to which all articles of the Confession are necessarily connected. In this first chapter, he makes the case that the cross is both form and content for that theology.

"Eck does not even have an inkling of the theology of the cross."[1]

"Ever since the scholastic theology . . . began, the theology of the cross has been abrogated, and everything has been completely turned upside down."[2]

"A theology of glory calls evil good and good evil. A theology of the cross calls the thing what it actually is."[3]

These three comments from Luther in 1518 summarize what he himself had learned in his first years as professor at the University of Wittenberg:

1.) The scholastic theology[4] dominating the life and teaching of the late

---

1. *WA* I, 290, 38f. Edward Schroeder's personal translation.
2. *LW* 31:225.
3. *LW* 31:53.
4. Scholasticism is the name for the teaching and learning that dominated European universities during the late Middle Ages (1100–1600 CE), including Luther's own education at University of Erfurt. A major source of medieval scholasticism was the rediscovered fourth-century BCE Greek philosopher Aristotle. As scholasticism—and Aristotle along with it—moved into the medieval university, theology too was taught in scholastic fash-

medieval church was in conflict with the Bible's message centered in the cross of Christ.

2.) This conflict was fundamental, not trivial. Theology of the cross and theology of glory—now as in the time of the apostles and prophets—constituted an either/or alternative.

3.) Scholastic teachers contemporary with Luther had no antennae for perceiving there was a conflict because they were ignorant of the word of the cross at the center of biblical theology.

Scholars continue to debate what events triggered this learning on Luther's part. The locale for his learning, though, is clear: his daily work as professor of biblical theology. *Doctor in Biblia* was his professional degree granted on October 19, 1512. That was what he was called to do at Wittenberg, from then on to the end of his life. The very terms "theology of the cross, theology of glory" had come from the scriptures, especially from St. Paul. Yet those words were not Paul's alone. The "word of the cross," the message of the crucified Lord and Savior, was at the heart of the entire New Testament and even of the Old, for those who have eyes to see.

The scholars' debate noted above refers to the question of Luther's "break" with Western (or Roman) catholicism. Scholars have tried to find out what the decisive breakthrough was and when it occurred. Luther's reminiscences in his later years suggest there was something akin to a Damascus experience in his blinding-flash understanding of the "righteousness of God." One of those reminiscences about those early years, this one from the Table-Talk, goes as follows:

> For a long time I went astray and didn't know what I was about. To be sure, I knew something, but I didn't know what it was until I came to the text in Rom. 1:17, "He who through faith is righteous shall live." That text helped me. There I saw what righteousness Paul was talking about. Earlier in the text I read "righteousness of God." I related the abstract ("righteousness of God") with the concrete ("the faith-righteous human") and became sure of my cause. I learned to distinguish between the righteousness of the law and the righteousness of the gospel. I lacked nothing before this except that I made no distinction between the law and the gospel. I regarded both as the same thing and held that there was no difference between Christ and Moses,

ion. After Luther's breakthrough to the "theology of the cross," scholastic theology became for him the very opposite of that theology. In taking its signals from Aristotle, Luther said, scholastic theology became an attempt by sinners to reach God through human wisdom rather than receiving God's wisdom, namely, the gift of mercy in Christ crucified and risen. The opening chapter of 1 Corinthians, where St. Paul contrasts God's wisdom with the wisdom of the world, was Luther's anchor text for setting the theology of the cross against scholasticism.

except the times in which they lived and their degrees of perfection. But then when I discovered the proper distinction—namely that the law is one thing, and the gospel is another—I made myself free. [German: *Da riss ich her durch* = That was my breakthrough.][5]

As dramatic as Luther makes this discovery sound, most scholars have abandoned the search for a Damascus experience—a singular, private, internal, isolated, existential event—and looked instead for evidence of a steady growth sequence rooted in Luther's job of studying and teaching the Bible. This suggests an unfolding series of "Aha's" rather than the "eureka" of the blinding flash.

A winsome case for that point of view is Leif Grane's *Modus Loquendi Theologicus: Luthers Kampf um die Erneuerung der Theologie, 1515–1518*.[6] Grane takes the daily workplace where Luther prepared his lectures and the classrooms where he delivered them as the locale for the renewal. And the chief agent for the renewal was not some blinding flash, even less some psychological need or theological idea that mesmerized Luther. Much more ordinary and low-key, it was the apostles and prophets, the writers of the Old and New Testament, who pushed Luther from scholasticism to the Bible, from Aristotle to the apostles and prophets, from theology of glory to theology of the cross.

Grane picks 1515 as his opening date, when Luther began his lecture series on Romans. Although Luther had been lecturing on the Psalter for most of the two previous years, it was not until the Romans lectures that he moved into direct attack upon scholastic theology and became fully aware of his own opposition to it. Such sharp and unmistakable conflict with scholasticism is not apparent in Luther's Psalms lectures, although these lectures do include expressions of the theology of the cross.

For his Romans lectures, Luther made use of Augustine's anti-Pelagian writings as a help for his understanding of St. Paul. That combination—Augustine and Romans—provided the basis for Luther's reflection on the theological presuppositions implicit in trying to coordinate St. Paul with the late medieval scholastic heritage. Grane shows that there is growing clarity from the Romans lectures onward about the two modes of language for theology: scholasticism's theology of glory in contrast to the Bible's theology of the cross.

At first we might think that this contrast was nothing more than two different modes for handling the same material. However, the key terms cross and glory signal here at the outset that the conflict is over the substance(s) as well. Method (mode) and substance—form and

---

5. *LW* 54:442f.
6. Leif Grane, *Modus Loquendi Theologicus: Luthers Kampf um die Erneuerung der Theologie, 1515–1518* (Leiden: E. J. Brill), 1975.

content—are corollary to each other. New wine needs new skins.[7] Scholastic theology "abrogates" theology of the cross. Try to put the latter in the skins of the former and one or the other will be "completely turned upside down."

Luther Sharpens His Attack on Glory Theology

It is not our concern to trace the development, the series of "Aha's" leading up to the 1518 quotations with which we began. But a bit of chronology may help for seeing the trees as well as the forest.

1.) After getting his degree, Luther's first biblical course began with the Psalms. "They kept him busy for two years, from the beginning of the summer semester 1513 until the end of the winter semester of 1515."[8]

2.) For the next three semesters he lectured on Romans—Easter 1515 until early September 1516.

3.) Next, he taught the letter to the Galatians (winter semester 1516–1517) followed by the Letter to the Hebrews (summer semester 1517 and winter semester 1517–1518). Then he went back to the Psalms for a second time.

Teaching biblical courses was Luther's bread and butter. But during the months that he was lecturing on Hebrews (March 1517 to March 1518) Luther also drew up several sets of theses for purposes of academic disputations. These disputations were the serious "fun and games" of sixteenth-century academic life. With them, students were tested for their mastery of their disciplines and here professors also proved their mettle. On September 4, 1517, Luther put Francis Gunther of Nordhausen on the stand to earn his "baccalaureate in the Bible" by responding to ninety-seven theses that Luther had composed as a "Disputation against Scholastic Theology." The next month, October 1517, Luther composed the much more famous Ninety-five Theses, the "Disputation on the Power and Efficacy of Indulgences."

In the spring of the next year, 1518, toward the end of April, came yet a third set of theses as Luther joined his fellow Augustinians at Heidelberg for the general chapter meeting. There he and his fellow Wittenberg Augustinian Leonhard Beier presented the arguments for the forty-nine Heidelberg Theses, which Luther had composed to inform the brothers of what was going on in Wittenberg.

These three sets of theses—along with Luther's "Explanations of the Ninety-five Theses" (170 pages in *LW* 31)—reflect what he had been learning in his lectures on Romans, Galatians, and Hebrews. For

7. Ibid., 17f.
8. *LCC* 15:xix.

example, Heidelberg theses 9 and 10, which rehearse the deadly-ness of good works done without faith in Christ, are lifted nearly verbatim from his lecture notes on Heb. 9:14: "How much more shall the blood of Christ . . . purify your conscience from dead works to serve the living God." The same is true of the other earlier disputation theses. In each instance the theses reflect the exegetical work Luther was doing for his classroom lectures.

Luther Presents Cross Theology as an Alternative to Scholastic Theology

The ninety-seven theses against scholastic theology juxtaposed Aristotle's dominant role in that theology against Paul's theology in Romans. According to Luther, Aristotle's optimistic view of human potential for redemption contradicted Paul at every point. The "glory" at the center of such scholasticism was the presumed human potential to meet the demands of moral law. Yet the biblical truth is that the human will at the center of human potential and the law of God "run counter one to another." Luther noted, "In relation to God's law the [human] will is always perverse. . . . What the law wants the will never wants," for the law wants the death of the sinner! Thus "the law is a tyrant over the will, and is never conquered save by 'the little child born for us.'"

The ninety-seven theses expose scholasticism's contrariness to the theology of the cross, but they do not yet construct the cruciform alternative. That comes a few months later in the Heidelberg theses. Luther was working on his "Explanations" to his ninety-five indulgence theses at the same time that he was composing the agenda for Heidelberg.

It was also when, as part of the winter semester of 1517–1518, the Letter to the Hebrews was Luther's regular classroom assignment. For the first time in any set of theses, the Heidelberg theses present the substance of theology of the cross, Luther's proposal for replacing scholastic theology. The Bible's alternate *modus* for its alternate theology of the cross—drawn from Romans, Galatians, and currently Hebrews—is at the center of the presentation.

Luther seemed to be unhappy that the Ninety-five Theses against indulgences had created such a fuss. Eck had launched his own counter-charge with a set of theses against Luther's ninety-five. The publicity media of the day had quickly cast Luther as an angry young man attacking indulgences. Yet the jugular that Luther was going for was the theology behind the church practice of indulgences. Even though the practice of indulgences did merit a hefty critique, it was scholasticism's

Pelagianism that was cooking on Luther's front burner. When Luther chides Eck for not having "even an inkling" of the theology of the cross, Luther is also saying even such a first-rank theologian as Eck is unaware of what the real issue is that has surfaced in the university theology from Wittenberg.

Since the themes of cross and glory do not surface explicitly in the text of the Ninety-five Theses, it is not surprising that Eck and other respondents do not notice the larger issue at stake in Luther's critique of indulgences. So the "Explanations of the Ninety-five Theses" make the connection.

These themes from the "Explanations" reappear in the Heidelberg theses, but in a revised form. The first eighteen theses contain Luther's attack upon the scholastic teaching about an individual's natural powers, namely, the human's free will and the scholastic favored formula *facere quod in se est* (i.e., to do [at least] that which you are able to do). Scholastic definitions and distinctions, says Luther, only serve to conceal the human's need to despair of oneself in order to desire grace (thesis 18).

In his classroom lectures at this time and in Heidelberg, Luther is out to destroy the security that scholastic theology elicits no matter which of the several schools of scholasticism it comes from. Luther responds to the objection that he thereby leaves human beings in despair. Such an objection, Luther says, misses its target. For not until one learns from the law that one is a sinner does any space for hope even appear; the one who does despair of self has nothing left but grace on which to set his hope and trust.

The way Luther uses the terms "the visible and invisible things of God" in theses 19, 20, and 22 must genuinely have struck his contemporaries as *paradoxes* (which was the actual word Luther used for his theses in the title he gave them). Concerning the invisible things of God that a theology of glory seeks after, the words of Paul in Rom. 1:19ff. apply: "They are without excuse, did not honor God, futile in their thinking, claiming to be wise, they become fools. Therefore God gave them up."

In contrast, the theologian worthy of the name is the one who according to 1 Cor. 1:21ff. knows God via God's *visible data*, namely, via God's human presence in Jesus. Here the data are not only visible; they are reprehensible: foolish, weak, low, despised. "Therefore in Christ crucified is the true theology and the knowledge of God."[9] In the offensive weakness of the cross, not in his majesty and glory, we come to know God.

With this assertion, Luther mounts his attack on scholastic or

---

9. *LCC* 16:291.

philosophical (i.e., Aristotelian) theology. There is no doubt that he identifies scholastic theology with glory theology, although he does not explicitly say so as he had in the "Explanations." For Luther, the speculative theology that had created the medieval systems is linked with the morality of works-righteousness. Consequently the theologian of glory calls evil good and good evil. He prefers works to suffering, glory to the cross. In a nutshell he loves what is lovely and thereby proves himself to be an enemy of the cross of Christ. "Unless he has first been deflated and destroyed by suffering and evil, it is impossible for a person not to be puffed up by his good works."[10]

The theology Luther opposes consists not merely of a false teaching, but of a false approach, a false starting-point, that cannot lead to theology. It winds up with a pseudo-theology instead.

Luther Exposes the "Ladder" in Glory Theology

The thesis of this book is that the cross gives both form and content to Luther's theology. The cross is the paradigm for his hermeneutics and for the subject matter of the theological enterprise. Of course, the clash with glory theology is more than verbal. It's not as though glory theologians never treat the cross and vice versa for cross theologians. "Glory" is in the vocabulary of cross theology—the glory of the crucified Messiah. And, yes, glory theology treats the cross, but it wastes it, turns it upside down. Commenting on thesis 62 of the Ninety-five Theses, Luther says, "The true treasure of the church is the most holy gospel of the glory and grace of God. . . . The (cruciform) gospel is not very well known to a large part of the church . . . [but] the true glory of God springs from this gospel."[11]

The cross of Christ as proclaimed in the scriptures gave Luther a picture of what biblical theology is in its entirety—and how that theology stands against the scholastic tradition. In the crucified Christ, say the apostles, God acts contrary to the reasonable expectations of seriously religious people. The cross exposes the rule of opposites which is God's basic ground rule. In the crucified Christ God exposed his secret—mercy through judgment, life through death, exaltation via humiliation. But note well, it is not simply *my* exaltation via *my* humiliation at God's hands, *my* achieving life via *my* going through death—although that is true. The greater paradox is that I receive mercy via Christ's undergoing judgment, life for me through Christ's death under God's law, my ultimate exaltation via Christ's humiliation. In

10. *LW* 31:53.
11. *LW* 31:230f.

fact the prior sentence is true only because of the latter: my death, my humiliation, my condemnation are not salutary per se, but *only if I am linked to the Christ* in his humiliation and death. As Luther puts it, "therefore in Christ crucified is the true theology and knowledge of God."[12]

Glory theology in its scholastic forms is different all down the line. Taking a cue from Aristotle, not from the scriptures, it presupposes continuity between God and humans, between God's ways and human ways, especially between the human will and the divine will. Not so, says cross theology. Contradiction and conflict is the state of humanity's normal situation with God. Scholastic theology fudges on the primal situation of original sin and the enslaved human will. For cross theology, our dilemma with God is not spatial separation of two otherwise compatible partners. Instead it is that, though spatially very close (God has not departed the planet), we are at enmity with God and, consequently God, too, with us. It is this "bad" situation that glory theology calls "good," while the cross theologian calls it what it really is.

When glory theology starts with this spatial notion of separation between the human and divine, there is already implied an entire picture of what salvation for such a person would entail. She must move across the gap that still exists between her and God—using the god-like resources that are in her (*facere quod in se est*) to meet God who is graciously working from the other side. The visual picture is that of a ladder. The task is to climb the ladder either via moral or mystical or ascetic or rational performance. Apart from the God visible in the crucified one, we are teased by the invisible things of God to do just that. Thus such ladder-climbing attempts are not impossible.

In fact, says Luther, the yen to get to God via ladder theology is itself a sin-symptom of the ladder-climber. The worst thing that could happen to such a climber is success. If, as the scriptures claim, God has acted in the crucified Christ to come "down to earth" to work out our salvation (in the visible, lowly sin-saturated realm of the law of sin and death), then it is rank rebellion on my part to try any ladder theology. Were I to succeed in finally encountering God atop my ladder—bereft as I would have to be of the crucified Christ since he is at the opposite end of such ladders, yes the opposite of all ladder theologies—God would simply overwhelm me. First Corinthians 1 and Romans 1 have just such a person in mind with their words of categorical condemnation. Yet glory theology calls such ladder-topping achievement "good." Cross theology calls it what it really is, "bad."

12. *LW* 31:53.

Scholasticism did incorporate Christ into its theology, even the grand finale of his ministry in Good Friday and Easter. But even when scholasticism used the cross of Christ, it was "abrogated," was turned "upside down." It's no wonder that this was the case. Scholasticism—by holding on to the anthropology of Aristotle—always had an open door to the whole ladder scenario. The handles to the door—better yet, its hinges—were the free will it ascribed to humanity and the ethic of performance-righteousness it proposed. A door swinging open on such hinges automatically stimulates our yen to achieve by performance. So it fits: I am free enough *facere quod in se est* (to do [at least] what one is able to do). I have the yen to achieve righteousness by performance. Performance is the way that righteousness comes. Righteousness equals salvation.

Cross Theology Necessitates Repentance

Central in scholasticism's knowledge of God was its perception of God's relationship to humans in metaphysical terms: causality—first cause, unmoved mover—and our correspondence with the divine in terms of the *analogia entis* (God's being is like our being refracted by the metaphysical differences between divine and human being). God is pure reason, and so humans are reason creatures. God is (or has) free will; so too—with modification—do humans. God acts and achieves his own proper destiny; so do humans.

But does such a God and such people actually exist? The scriptures claim that such a God cannot be correlated to Christ crucified and also that no such humans exist on the planet either. Scholasticism affirmed the contrary and led all those who were so convinced into the damnable *securitas* of medieval salvation schemes. Salvation, though difficult, was workable.

The concluding theses of Luther's Ninety-five Theses on indulgences give the response of cross theology to scholasticism's salvation scheme: "(92) Away then with all those prophets who say to the people of Christ, 'Peace, peace,' and there is no peace! (93) Blessed be all those people who say to the people of Christ, 'Cross, cross,' and there is no cross! (94) Christians should be exhorted to be diligent in following Christ, their head, through penalties, death, and hell; (95) and thus be confident of entering heaven through many tribulations rather than through the false security of peace."[13]

The failure here of glory theology is not merely its invented deity and fictitious human beings—not even its erroneous built-in model of

13. *LW* 31:33.

performance-righteousness. Worst of all, it hoodwinked the populace and provided them with no practical resources for dealing with the realities of human lived experience: the tyrants of devil, conscience, death, sin, doubt, and God's own accusing law.

For Luther, God is indeed creator, but that is more than cause. Day in, day out, with no time off, sons and daughters of Adam and Eve live their lives *coram deo* (face to face with God). That means being called to account. The one who donates our existence to us unceasingly also calls us to give an account of our stewardship of this gift. Since all humans have a de facto link with their creator from the very beginning, the truth about themselves and about God (where scholasticism was wrong on both counts) will come only by God speaking first. The theology of the cross demonstrates and embodies this link between us and our creator when it lifts up the crucified Christ and draws from his "true theology," that is, the truth about God and about us.

If human beings are chronic glory theologians, as cross theology affirms, then there needs to be a change in the theologian before "true theology" can be done. The hermeneutics of the cross put the *theologian's own repentance* as the prolegomena for theologizing. The mind that is doing the theology is never a neutral entity. The cross theology itself needs to take the theological mind captive so that the theologian does not simply use the theological method that is automatic and natural with every human being. Constant contact and conversation with the biblical writers and their alternative theology was Luther's program for contrasting cross theology and glory theology. This approach is not sacrificing one's intellect by affirming what I know to be untrue. It is rather "having this mind in you which you have in the mind of Christ." So for the theologian too, cross theology is the hopeful (not despairing) self-confession that says: "O wretched man that I am. Who shall deliver me from this body of death? Thanks be to God through Jesus Christ our Lord!" That's a "true theologian" doing "true theology."

Cross Theology: Both Law and Gospel

Our chapter began with citations that used two different paired sets of opposites—law and gospel, glory theology and cross theology—as Luther's own key for what was new in his exegesis of the scriptures. The two paired sets, however, are not completely synonyms. Yes, glory theology is always a proposal for salvation by the law, and cross theology is salvation by the gospel. At that point they are synonyms.

Yet both law and gospel properly distinguished belong to cross theology—always and only, of course, with the proper distinction (*discrimen* is the term from the Table Talk). The absence of the distinction was one, if not *the*, fundamental defect in Luther's own earlier scholastic glory theology before his breakthrough. After his breakthrough, law and gospel properly discriminated are the heart and soul of the theology of the cross.

Chapter 2 of this book will delve more deeply into Luther's distinguishing of law and gospel. Here, though, we note that Luther saw that glory theology (scholastic theology) had no inkling that there even was such a discrimination to be made within the scriptures. Thus scholastic theology with this cardinal defect was *unable* to let God's law and God's gospel work as God intended. As Luther says: "God makes a man a sinner that he may make him righteous."[14]

In contrast, glory theology took all the words and actions of God to be qualitatively the same stuff. Moses and Christ were both spiritual. Law and gospel, moral instruction and holy absolution, God's judgment and God's forgiveness, God's preserving and God's redeeming were all of a piece—all "godly." The godly quality distinguished them from things earthly, human, natural, secular. Yes, glory theology does make a distinction, but the distinction in glory theology is *between human and divine*, secular and sacred, nature and grace, finite and infinite—in short, the Chalcedonian categories of the ancient church's christological debates. But if the work of God is "to make a man a sinner (the law's *alien work*) so that God may make him righteous," how does the divine-human distinction of glory theology help?

One way to pinpoint the difference between cross and glory theologies is to look at where they locate the fundamental *distinction*, the fundamental either-or. Glory theologies located the either-or at the divine-human dividing line. Luther's cross theology found it *within* the divine component itself—and as a corollary, within the human component as well. God speaks two qualitatively different words to a human being, resulting in two qualitatively different people. Luther distinguishes two opposite God-human *relationships*, not between two opposing—divine versus human—realms of being. Because of God's odd propensity to be operating *"auf die Erde nieder"* ("down on the ground"), I am always in some sort of linkage with God. Being a creature at all is existence *coram deo*, living "in front" of God, inescapably linked to God. What is crucial is the kind of linkage, the type of relationship we have with God: is it based on law (God my critic, I God's rebel) or on gospel (God my merciful Father, I God's forgiven sinner)?

The divine-human distinction of glory theology is the standard in

14. *LCC* 16:289.

the rhetoric of Christian history up to the sixteenth century and down to our time. Even in our allegedly secularized atheistic age, the terms "divine" and "human" continue to be the dominant theological currency of conversation. Thus the God in whose existence most Western atheists don't believe is the god of the supernatural, the infinite, the nonmaterial spirit, the god up there or out there in some other world. In keeping with spatial imagery, then as now, God was at the top of the ladder we have yet to climb.

Luther Affirms God as Creator and Always Present in Human Life

Luther's eventual dismay with this standard vocabulary and visual picturing for God does not come from some skeptical strain within him. Luther was no logical positivist born too soon. Rather his skepticism comes from his work with the Bible. The Bible does not present God and humans this way. Luther frequently chastised the scholastics for their basic vocabulary of newfangled terms that obliterated the plain meaning of scripture. His "Answer to Latomus, 1521" is replete with such critique of the current theological terminology.[15] And not just the newfangled words of the recent scholastics, but even the shibboleth of Nicea, *homoousios* ("same substance, of one being"), gets its comeuppance from Luther as a nonscriptural word that brings a mixed blessing.

Why did Luther rail against these key terms and concepts themselves, instead of confining the critique to the mis-managers of the vocabulary storehouse? Answer: the new wine of the Bible's cross theology can't be contained in such skins. The vocabulary of glory theology aided and abetted the yen to move from earth to heaven, from the human to the divine—away from the creaturely world where the creator placed us, "up" into the creator's realm where he did not, away from work and pain and suffering to leisure and power and limitless existence. This yen is the original sin of Genesis 3—to vacate our location in creation and "be like God," that is, moving into God's habitation. This is the sin of not trusting (*sine fiducia*) that *where God has put us* is good for us—and that in that very locus, *God* is good for and to us.

Luther, of course, continued all his life to use the inherited terminology of the theological tradition and to do so without qualifications: body and soul, divine and human, God up in heaven and we down on earth. But the fundamental dualism of Greek antiquity—divine and human as the blueprint for Christian theology—Luther would consciously revise and even turn on its head.

---

15. *LCC* 16:308–64; *LW* 32.

So in 1539 (*On the Councils and the Church*) he reflects on the impassibility and immortality of God (i.e., divinity by definition cannot suffer or die). Luther writes, "For God in his own nature [by Greek definition?] cannot die; but now that [in the crucified Christ] God and man are united in one person, it is called God's death. . . ."[16] The word of the cross turns the classical predicate of God's immortality upside down. For Luther, the grounds for claiming a god who can suffer and die are the grounds of salvation. "If it cannot be said that God died for us, but only a man [died], we are lost."[17]

Thus the primary defect of the dualist universe of nature and super-nature—with God's abode above and ours below—is finally a soteriological defect. The Bible's Good News of salvation won't fit. God is separate from us not by space but rather because God is God and we are not. Worse yet, the normal pattern of such a two-story universe leaves our bottom story normally devoid of God just by the very nature of the case. In the dualistic universe of glory theology, God is present in the bottom story only by choosing to cross the dividing line, the metaphysical line of two qualitatively different and even mutually exclusive beings. This crossover—in principle impossible for us—is not going to be easy for God either.

No, counters Luther, ever since the creation began God has remained inside this created hemisphere. God never vacated it.

The glory theologian works from created things (our lower hemisphere) to the invisible things of God (the upper hemisphere). Thus the glory theologian never hears the criticism addressed to humans by God in the data of our lower hemisphere. The glory theologian mishears the law data which really are God's condemning call to repentance, and perceives that data to be invitations to climb the ladder. He sidesteps the law's *opus alienum* (alien work), with the even more tragic result that the gospel's *opus proprium* (proper work) then passes him by. Lacking the law-gospel discrimination, he loses both works of God. That is a big loss.

The Resurrection Certifies Cross Theology

It is perhaps easier to see triumphalism rather than legalism as the enemy of cross theology, especially in the recent history of the West with its ostensible mastery, technology, and economic and managerial control of the planet. Surely that suggests hubris as the besetting sin of the race. Against this hubris, cross theology proclaims the alternative

16. *SWML* 4:296.
17. *SWML*, 4:295.

of weakness, defeat, and the foolishness of Jesus Christ to be the very power, victory, wisdom of God for salvation.

This perspective (cross theology vs. triumphalist hubris) trademarks much of the renaissance of cross theology. Thus these contemporary cross theologians walk a very tight rope when it comes to the resurrection. These theologians—most notably Douglas John Hall—are wary of giving quarter to the triumphalism they have just abolished with the suffering-servant mode and posture of the cross. As a result, they have difficulty working with the resurrection. Attempting to follow the rubrics of the New Testament, they suggest that the resurrection of Jesus does not displace cross theology, but completes and clarifies what the word of the cross is all about—for those who have eyes to see.

The second *discrimen* in Luther's Heidelberg theses (law and gospel) would help here. Remember, it is not glory per se, victory per se, wisdom per se, strength per se that is the antithesis of cross theology. Rather, it is cross-less glory—victory, wisdom, strength without the cross. The cross-less-ness refers not only to Christ's cross, but also to the crucifixion of the ones whom Christ's cross is to save.

The crucifixion of that one to be saved (as also of the crucified One who saves us) is the work of God's law. The cross-less preaching of God's law is invariably a legalist preaching of that law, one that contradicts Heidelberg thesis 23: "The law works wrath: it kills, curses, makes guilty, judges and damns everyone who is not in Christ." Scholasticism when compared with the hefty biblical texts supporting thesis 23 (Gal. 3:13; 3:10; Rom. 2:12, 23; 4:15; 7:10) was simply law-shy—not allowing God's law to work such harsh operations as are predicated to it in those biblical verbs of thesis 23.

Thus it is not merely the chronic legalism that barricades one from the work of the gospel of the glory and grace of God. *God's law itself is the sinner's nemesis.* The law aims to kill the sinner. The folly of the legalist is that "[w]hosoever glories in the law as being wise and learned glories in his own shame: he is glorying in being cursed, he is glorying in the wrath of God, he is glorying in death."[18]

The cross-theology renaissance—represented by Douglas Hall, Stanley Hauerwas, Jürgen Moltmann, and others—could use a fuller dose of Luther's own cross theology to counteract its inclination toward law-shyness. The corollary to their law-shyness is some timidity about Christ's resurrection. For Luther's exegesis of St. Paul exposes a law of God in operation in the normal interfaces of daily life that is not "good news." The human dilemma is worse than the indisputable data of our

---

18. *LCC* 16:293.

idolatry, our cussed pride in self-justifications. The sinner's life proceeds "under" God's law and its curse. Not just our legalisms, our idolatries need to be overcome. The "unending voice" of God's own law, our constant critic, needs to be silenced. And that is what Easter proclaims.

The crucifixion that cross theology commends to believers is more than the meek and lowly imaging of Jesus the suffering servant in the conviction drawn from his life and work that such is the way of God through the world—although it is that. Even worse (or better) than that, cross theology is the brave reception of the crucifixion of the Adamic self, administered by the law of God itself. The resurrection of Christ certifies not only that God-trusters survive the slings and arrows of outrageous fortune administered by wicked and vain glory theologians. Even more scandalously, the resurrection certifies that gospel-trusters survive the death of the old Adam administered by God's rightful and just execution of sinners.

Thus there is no danger that the resurrection message might supplant cross theology with glory theology. The real "cross" is God's law as it is properly administered to mortify sinners (Heidelberg thesis 23). Preaching and believing the resurrection of Christ as *my* shared conquest of the law of sin and death is prerequisite for preventing my cruciform lifestyle from devolving either into despair or hubris (or even prideful humility). Such a person

> knows that it is enough if he suffers and is broken through the cross, nay rather is utterly brought to naught. But this is exactly what Christ says in John 3:7: "Ye must be born again." If we are to be born again we must first die and be exalted (resurrected) with the Son of Man. I said, "Die," and that means to find death ever present in all experiences.[19]

It is not just any old suffering and weakness that constitutes theology of the cross. What made the suffering and weakness of Jesus salvific was that "*God* was in Christ" doing the suffering and being crucified—"him being made sin for us [i.e., under the powers of sin, death, wrath, and law] . . . so that we might become the righteousness of God." And what finally made that suffering and cross redemptive is again not merely that it was God enduring it. Rather it is that—in the Good Friday finale of that suffering—God breaks through that very law of sin and death that is the mortal enemy of all sinful people. Easter announces that one like us, our friend of sinners, has broken through the law of sin and death. He has directly encountered those powers and conquered them by full and open admission of their claims upon him and the sinners he was befriending.

---

19. *LCC* 16:293 comment on thesis 24 of Heidelberg.

The theology of the cross is not simply a theology of suffering. It is theology of Christ-connectedness in view of the kind of Messiah Jesus really was. What needs crucifying in our old Adam is more than our ethics of triumphalism, of achievement, of pride. True that all is, but the core lies deeper. The deepest fault of glory theologies is *not* that they are lifestyle proposals (ethics), but rather that they are salvation proposals (kerygma and dogma). Cross theology calls for more than discomfort, disestablishment, divestiture, denial. It calls for the death of that Old Adam at the center of the sinner's life.

The death of the Old Adam may or may not occur in the experience of negativity. For it is within the power and skill of Old Adams to utilize suffering and humiliation as moral achievements, moral plusses, on the basis of which to pursue yet another ladder theology. Cross theology calls for the death of the ladder-building and ladder-climbing person by linkage with the Crucified One. Whatever good, grand, glorious consequences follow upon that—and they do—are not theology of glory. They are first fruits from the First-born from the dead, the glory of the crucified Messiah in his people.

2

Necessitating Christ:
The Clue to Handling the Scriptures

Edward H. Schroeder

The rim of a wagon wheel is what keeps all the spokes firmly in the hub of justification by faith in Christ so that the wheel is useful. In this chapter, Edward Schroeder identifies Luther's (and the Augsburg Confessors') insistence on the proper distinction of law and gospel as the rim that makes it possible for us to read the Bible in light of its Source (Jesus the Christ) and thus to understand the scriptures rightly.

> "The Holy Scriptures are a vast and mighty forest, but there is no single tree in it that I have not shaken with my own hand."[1]

In an early sermon fragment from November 11, 1515 (Luther's thirty-second baptism anniversary!) we find a four-word epigram: *Unum praedica, sapientiam crucis* (Preach one thing, the wisdom of the cross). That sermon fragment begins with a statement on how to read the Bible, how to shake the trees of that vast and mighty forest. Luther says:

> If you are going to read the Bible, you must be on guard not to go astray. For the Scriptures are docile and can readily be stretched this way or that. Yet no one should deal with them according to his own feelings. Rather let him

---

1. *LW* 35:227.

lead them to the wellspring, that is, to the cross of Christ. In this way he will certainly not fail to score a direct hit.[2]

Since the theology of the cross commended itself to Luther as the constant message of the Bible, it is no surprise that the same cross of Christ should be the prism through which he read the scriptures. The citation above presents several aspects of that cross-focused hermeneutic.

As Luther says above, the scriptures are "docile." They are not immune to being tugged this way or that by the interpreter. But why should that be true? A text says what it says, one would think. You cannot make it say just anything you please, stretching or twisting it arbitrarily. How could Bible readers go astray if they honestly gave serious attention to what the text actually said?

There are actually two reasons why Bible interpreters might "fail to score a direct hit" in reading the Bible.

One reason lies in the biblical texts themselves. Recall Luther's "breakthrough" statement in the previous chapter: "For a long time I went astray. . . . I lacked nothing except that I made no distinction between the law and the gospel. . . . But when I discovered the proper distinction—namely, that the law is one thing, and the gospel is another—that was my breakthrough."[3]

Thus readers of the Bible find that what the Bible itself presents is not all that homogenous. The law's texts on righteousness are not the same as the gospel's texts on righteousness. To read both of these sets of texts correctly Luther needed what he called the *discrimen*, the discriminator, the distinguishing key that the gospel is something else than the law, even though both are from God. Apart from this *discrimen* the law texts either sound as though salvation is by the law ("Do this and you will live") or they sound like a counsel of despair ("The soul that sins shall die"). In both cases the law texts of the Bible are being read wrongly. Such reading misses the mark, doesn't hit it.

How so? Is it not true that God's law demands that we "do"? Yes. Also, is it not true that if we don't we are marked for death? Yes again. Well then, where is the misreading? It comes from reading such passages (both the performance demands and the condemnation for nonperformance) without any reference to the wellspring, the cross of Christ. That cross constitutes a different lens for reading the demand passages and the condemnation passages. To read any passage—even a good-news passage—without "leading it to the wellspring" is to "fail to hit the mark."

2. *WA* I, 52:15ff. Edward Schroeder's translation.
3. *WA, Tischreden,* V:210.

The law by itself (i.e., read without the appropriate discrimination) leads to a misreading of the law. The undiscriminated law texts of the Bible lead the reader astray intrinsically. Luther's own experience verified this for him.

Yet it is not quite on their own that the law texts do this. They get hefty help from the readers themselves in managing a misreading of the Bible. This is the *second reason* Bible readers might "fail to score a direct hit" in reading the Bible.

The Mindset of the Law Misreads Scripture

Every reader comes to the scriptures with a prior "feeling" (*affectus* was Luther's Latin term) about what the Bible is going to say. No one comes to the text of the scripture neutral. This doesn't mean that the reader knows ahead of time what the texts must say, but that the reader does have an expectation, an anticipation, for the kind of message this religious book will offer. Even with the best of intentions to be objective and open-minded, the reader's companion—an already functioning theological "affect"—always comes along. Who is that reader's companion? The reformers called it the *opinio legis* (the mindset of law, the law-and-order Old Self). That is the same mentality that needed reconstruction in the previous chapter's discussion about theology's form and content.

When Luther admits that he formerly read the scriptures without making the *discrimen*, he is not saying that he read them with no intermediary lenses. He says that he read Moses and Christ as though they were essentially the same with only chronological and quantitative differences between them, and that amounted to having Moses as the one who set the tone. What did that mean as far as righteousness is concerned? Righteousness is what God demands. Performance is the appropriate human response. Performance makes a person righteous. Conclusion: Get busy! That is the mentality of the Old Self. It is pious, no doubt. But to read the Bible with the mindset (*opinio*) of ladder-theology is to misread both the law and the gospel, both the Moses and the Christ texts. Such misreading of the biblical texts is rooted also in the readers' own misreading of themselves.

Not only must the texts themselves, especially the law texts, be led to the cross of Christ in order to deliver up their message to the reader, but also the reader's own *opinio legis* has to be led to the same cross—in this case to be crucified. As Luther says elsewhere in the sermon fragment, it is the cross's "wisdom" that "human beings do not have the resources or the ability and therefore need to learn to despair of self and to hope in

Christ."[4] For Luther, the crucified mind of the theologian is corollary to the crucified Christ. The law-gospel *discrimen* functions as a lens both for reading the Bible and for "reading" the "text." And the text is, in effect, the Bible-reader herself.

The central assertion of the law-gospel discrimination is that salvation is not by ladder (i.e., not by law, even God's law), but by God's coming to us (gospel) in our experience of negativity. That discrimination is always at odds with the law mentality for reading the scriptures. Discovering the *discrimen* and crucifying the law mentality (*opinio legis*) are of a piece with discovering how surprisingly good the gospel's good news really is.

So far we have focused on three elements in Luther's biblical hermeneutics. First, the scriptures are pliable. They can be stretched in different directions to yield diverse fundamental meanings. This is so because God's law and God's gospel are themselves so fundamentally different. Second, the reader comes to the biblical text with an already-functioning mindset (the Old Self's *opinio legis*) that practically guarantees a misreading of the text. Third, both the text and the reader's mindset need to be "led" to the cross of Christ in order for the reader to read the text correctly.

Christ's Cross Is the Wellspring

The picture-word of the wellspring (*Brunnen* in German) gives us a *fourth element*, a most important one, in the hermeneutic. This word is what Luther uses to depict what the cross of Christ is. Christ's cross as the fountain, the bubbling well, is a frequent and favored picture for Luther. He uses it, for example, in his debate with Erasmus on the clarity of the scriptures. Erasmus asserts it is little wonder that people have such trouble understanding the Bible, given the multitude of unclear passages in it. Luther responds with the analogy of the fountain at the center of a medieval town. Even though many passages admittedly are obscure in the Bible, he says, Christ the center is not.

> What solemn truth can the Scriptures still be concealing, now that the seals are broken, the stone rolled away from the door of the tomb, and that greatest of all mysteries brought to light—that Christ, God's Son, became man . . . suffered for us, and will reign forever? . . . Take Christ from the Scriptures and what more will you find in them? You see, then, that the entire content of the Scriptures has now been brought to light, even though some passages which contain unknown words remain obscure. . . . Who will maintain that the town fountain does not stand in the light because the people down some alley cannot see it, while everyone in the square can see it?[5]

---

4. *WA* I, 52:19–22.

The fountain signals centeredness and life-giving energizing action. Christ's cross is the center from which all the meanings of the Word of God (even the seemingly—or genuinely—contradictory words of God's law and God's gospel) flow. In the late medieval towns of Luther's time, the fountain was the center to which all the residential streets finally led. And it served not only as geographical center, but also as energy center, life source for the town. Thus for Luther the cross, in the words of St. Paul, "is the power of God for salvation." The cross is like a wellspring that never stops running day and night.

Of course here too the "rule of opposites" surfaces which is at the center of cross theology. The cross as the signal of weakness, shame, criminal execution, and death appears to be clean contrary to the notion of the bubbling life-giving source of strength, honor, righteousness, and life. Nevertheless, the cross is good news. It is good news, not pessimism nor hopelessness, when a sinner—and a biblical text—are led to Christ's cross. In fact, as John's Gospel claims, this is the avenue whereby the biblical texts will "testify of me (Christ)" so that "you may have life in His name."

Luther Sees Promise in the Hebrew Scriptures

It is a commonplace in Luther studies that Luther is a Paulinist, that is, his hermeneutics is taken from Paul. By his own admission it was St. Paul's words in Rom. 1:17 about the "righteousness of God" and "justification by faith" that figured in his breakthrough. So some would argue that Luther reads the Bible with Pauline glasses and, as a result, succumbs to misreading of non-Pauline scriptures. Not only is Luther alleged to misread (or to give short shrift to) the rest of the New Testament, but also the Old Testament.

In his 1522 translation of the New Testament, called "The September Testament" by virtue of the month of its publication, Luther tacked on a "Preface to the New Testament." Notably, Luther includes John's Gospel "and his first epistle" as among "the books that show you Christ and teach all that is necessary and salvatory." He goes on to say that the New Testament properly ought to "go forth without any prefaces ... and simply have its own say under its own name." However, current circumstances have so befuddled Christians that

> no one any longer knows what is gospel or law, New Testament or Old. Necessity demands, therefore, that there should be a notice or preface, by which the ordinary man can be rescued from his former delusions, set on

---

5. Martin Luther, *The Bondage of the Will*, trans. James I. Packer and O. R. Johnston (Tarrytown, NY: Fleming H. Revell, 1957), 71f.

the right track, and taught what he is to look for in this book, so that he may not seek laws and commandments where he ought to be seeking the gospel and promises of God.[6]

The "nature of the gospel" as "promises of God" is Luther's fundamental canon within the canon, both the Old Testament and the New Testament canon. Although he will frequently contrast the terms "Old Testament" and "New Testament," he is most often not contrasting the older half of the Bible with the younger half. The point of contrast is law and gospel, which is not to say that the ancient Hebrew scriptures are law and the more recent Greek scriptures are gospel. A vivid illustration of that appears again in the "Preface to the New Testament." As Luther seeks to clarify for the befuddled reader what "gospel and promises of God" are, what is the "nature" of the gospel, he takes much of his data from the Hebrew scriptures. To illustrate promises of God he goes to Genesis 3 (Adam and Eve), Genesis 22 (Abraham), 2 Samuel 7 (David), Micah 5, and Hosea 13 (God's commitment to rescue his own from the power of death and hell). And what about gospel?

> For "gospel" (*euangelium*) is a Greek word and means in Greek a good message, good tidings, good news, a good report, which one sings and tells with gladness. For example, when David overcame the great Goliath, there came among the Jewish people the good report and encouraging news that their terrible enemy had been struck down and that they had been rescued and given joy and peace; and they sang and danced and were glad for it. . . . Thus this gospel of God or New Testament is a good story and report, sounded forth into all the world by the apostles, telling of a true David who strove with sin, death, and the devil, and overcame them, and thereby rescued all those who were captive in sin, afflicted with death, and overpowered by the devil. Without any merit of their own he made them righteous, gave them life, and saved them, so that they were given peace and brought back to God. For this they sing, and thank and praise God, and are glad forever, if only they believe firmly and remain steadfast in faith.[7]

Why such "encouraging tidings" should be called a new "testament" Luther explains in the same way as he had interpreted the "new testament in my blood" of the Lord's Supper.

> For it is a testament when a dying man bequeaths his property, after his death, to his legally defined heirs. And Christ, before his death, commanded and ordained that his gospel be preached after his death in all the world. Thereby he gave to all who believe, as their possession, everything that he had. This included: his life, in which he swallowed up death; his righteousness, by which he blotted out sin; and his salvation, with which he overcame everlasting damnation. A poor man, dead in sin and consigned

6. *LW* 35:357.
7. *LW* 35:358.

to hell, can hear nothing more comforting than this precious and tender message about Christ; from the bottom of his heart he must laugh and be glad over it, if he believes it true.[8]

The nature of the gospel as promise of God constitutes God's new testament, God's "new deal" for sinners. This new testament can be traced all the way back to the beginning of the Hebrew scriptures. From Adam and Eve onward, the new testament is in force whenever God promises goodness to the selfsame sinners. For Luther, this awareness of old and new is what the ordinary reader needs to have to be "set on the right track" for reading the New Testament as well as the Old.

Luther Presents a Two-Sided Measuring Stick

"To be set on the right track" sounds like a corollary—the other side of the coin—to Luther's earlier statement about not going astray if one leads a text to the fountain so that one does not fail to hit the mark. Being on the right track, not failing to hit the mark, means hearing Christ come off the pages of the Bible as God's "promise," *and* hearing that promise as good news *for you*.

Thus, the hermeneutical yardstick has two sides corresponding to each other. One is the *christological*, maybe even the liturgical measurement: is the full Christ of cross theology for all that he is as Lord and savior coming off the page to the reader/hearer so that Christ's merits and benefits are not going to waste. That is one side of the measuring stick. The other side is the *pastoral* measurement: Are the intended beneficiaries of this cross-marked salvation actually receiving it? Is it getting through to those for whose comfort and enjoyment it is so "necessary and salvatory"? In short, do actual sinners hear genuine good news from God to supplant the law's no-news or bad-news that otherwise informs their lives?

These two content-tests, the christological-liturgical and the pastoral-salvatory, surface in Luther's well-known negative comments about the epistle of James. Though occasionally understood as evidence of his bull-in-the-china-shop character or his cavalier treatment of non-Pauline texts, his critical evaluation of James is nothing of the sort. It is sober theology based on the distinction between the two testaments, old and new, law and promise.

When Luther reads James he does not find God's promise as good news for sinners there at all. Although James is in the New Testament canon, there is no new testament in James. In a separate preface that

---

8. *LW* 35:358f.

he wrote for James in "The September Testament," we have his famous *"Christum treiben"*[9] statement. "To promote Christ," he says, is the apostolic task to which Christ commissioned his apostles. But James, says Luther,

> does not once mention the Passion, the resurrection, or the Spirit of Christ. He names Christ several times; however, he teaches nothing about him, but only speaks of general faith in God. Now it is the office of a true apostle to preach of the Passion and resurrection and office of Christ, and to lay the foundation for faith in him, as Christ himself says in John 15 (v. 17), "You shall bear witness to me."[10]

James's failure expressed more precisely is on the "apostolic" test.

> That is the true test by which to judge all books, when we see whether or not they promote Christ (*Christum treiben*). . . . Whatever does not teach Christ is not yet apostolic, even though St. Peter or St. Paul does the teaching. Again whatever preaches Christ would be apostolic, even if Judas, Annas, Pilate, and Herod were doing it.[11]

Thus, despite Luther's love for Paul, it is not Paul per se who norms James into second place; it is James's failure to *"Christum treiben."*

James fails on the christological side of the yardstick to promote Christ for all that he is worth. He also fails—necessarily so, one might add—on the pastoral side of the stick. In "ascribing justification to works," James is not only contradicting St. Paul, but he is contradicting Moses himself in Gen. 15:6, "for Moses is speaking here only of Abraham's faith" when it is said that Abraham was justified. The pastoral consequence is that "James does nothing more than drive [people] to the law and to works."

After all this, we might expect that James would disappear from Luther's edition of the New Testament. Not so, for that would amount to a denial, or at least a forgetting, of what was at the center of the "breakthrough," namely, the distinction between law and gospel when one is reading the Word of God. James, according to Luther's reading, is not the word of God's gospel; but James is the word of God. What word of God? The word of God's law. "Though this epistle of St. James was rejected by the ancients [placed among the antilegomena, 'disputed books' of the ancient church], I praise it and consider it a good book, because it sets up no doctrines of men but vigorously promulgates the law of God." However, because that is all that it does, Luther concludes, "I do not regard it as the writing of an apostle."[12]

9. "to promote Christ"
10. *LW* 35:396.
11. *LW* 35:396.
12. *LW* 35:395f.

God's Two Righteousnesses

In recommending John, Paul, and Peter as the standard for what is apostolic—and in criticizing but retaining James in the canon—Luther practices what he preached about his breakthrough. The fact is that his breakthrough is predicated to another discovery. "But when I discovered the *discrimen*, that the law is one thing and the gospel is something else than the law—that was my breakthrough."[13] It was not Paul whom Luther discovered in the breakthrough. But via Paul's words on righteousness, Luther broke through to the perception of the duplex or twofold character of the word of God. God's two testaments are not the two halves of the Bible but the different ways the Righteous One deals with sinners. It would be more accurate therefore to say that this was not the discovery of the righteousness of God, but rather of *the two righteousnesses of the one God and the distinction between them.*

> I learned to distinguish between the righteousness of the law and the righteousness of the gospel. I lacked nothing before this except that I made no distinction between the law and the gospel. I regarded both as the same thing and held that there was no difference between Christ and Moses, except the times in which they lived and their degrees of perfection.[14]

These two righteousnesses of God is the theme of our next chapter, the hub of the wheel of Luther's theology. But we need to touch the matter here briefly since it is at the heart of Lutheran biblical hermeneutics. Once Luther had this distinction in hand he put it into practice, lecture after lecture and sermon after sermon. His "helps" offered to Bible readers are almost monotonous in recurring to that theme. One example we have already seen is in the material cited above from his "Preface to the September Testament." He sought in the preface to take the "ordinary man" and "set him on the right track . . . so that he may not seek laws and commandments where he ought to be seeking the gospel and promises of God."

Luther's repeated insistence on this distinction is because the "yen" of the Old Self's *opinio legis* is to be always listening for law to clarify and implement his ladder theology, his own self-salvation. Even if and when the Old Self's mind catches signals of the life under the gospel, the Old Self either hears those words as a demand for even greater perfection or as an offer of forgiveness that will let the Old Self get to the top of the ladder on the cheap, without undergoing crucifixion—in short, another mode of self-salvation.

---

13. *WA* V, 210:5518 (. . . *quod aliud esset lex, aliud euangelium, da riss ich her durch*).
14. *WA* V, 210:5518.

A second example typical of many other instances of his counsel for Christians reading the Old Testament is his 1525 sermon "How Christians Should Regard Moses."

> Dear friends, you have often heard that there has never been a public sermon from heaven except twice. . . . The first sermon is in Exodus 19 and 20 (Sinai). . . . In the second place God delivered a public sermon through the Holy Spirit on Pentecost. . . . Now the first sermon, and doctrine, is the law of God. The second is the gospel. These two sermons are not the same. Therefore we must have a good grasp of the matter in order to know how to differentiate between them. We must know what the law is, and what the gospel is. The law commands and requires us to do certain things. The law is thus directed solely to our behavior and consists in making requirements. For God speaks through the law, saying, "Do this, avoid that, this is what I expect of you." The gospel, however, does not preach what we are to do or to avoid. It sets up no requirements, but reverses the approach of the law, does the very opposite, and says, "This is what God has done for you; he has let his Son be made flesh for you, has let him be put to death for your sake." So, then, there are two kinds of doctrine and two kinds of works, those of God and those of men. Just as we and God are separated from one another, so also these two doctrines are widely separated from one another. For the gospel teaches exclusively what has been given to us by God, and not—as in the case of the law—what we are to do and give to God.[15]

The consequences of such a discriminating hermeneutic are the following:

> Why then do you preach about Moses? . . . I want to keep Moses and not sweep him under the rug, because I find three things in Moses . . . first because he provides fine examples of laws, from which excerpts may be taken. Second, in Moses there are the promises of God which sustain faith . . . excellent and comforting promises . . . for my weak faith. . . . In the third place we read Moses for the beautiful examples of faith, of love, and of the cross, as shown in the fathers, Adam, Abel, Noah, Abraham, Isaac, Jacob, Moses, and all the rest. From them we should learn to trust in God and love him.[16]

The Crucified Christ as Lord of Scriptures

"Bypassing Christ" was Luther's frequent complaint about scholastic use of the scriptures. On this score Luther saw the scholastics and the "Schwärmer," the "left-wing" radical reformers, to be cut from the same cloth. Neither practiced an exegesis that viewed the Bible as heading for this one sole target. If a text is not led to Christ's cross to be interpreted from this center, it becomes a law book for doctrines (what you must

---

15. *LW* 35:161f.
16. *LW* 35:166–73.

believe) and for ethics (what you must do). Such exegesis takes the biblical texts and seeks to apply them directly to people's lives without first leading the text to the one target and then picking up its meaning, so to speak, on the rebound. Such exegesis presents a text to Christ's people without first presenting it before its own Lord.

When engaged in controversy Luther audaciously asserted Christ's centrality and his Lordship over the scriptures. He can say, "Therefore, if the adversaries press the Scriptures against Christ, we urge Christ against the Scriptures."[17]

Such a statement, however, was more rhetorical than factual. For over and over again Luther's argument with his adversaries was *not* that they did indeed have scripture on their side and he was now forced to "punt" with a leap to Christ. Almost without fail he responded to his opponents that they were not seriously using the scriptures at all. Either they were holding to some segment of the tradition (Eck) or else they were inventing a previously unknown exegesis (Zwingli) that the "clear passages of scripture" (i.e., the clearly cross-gospel-faith passages) themselves refuted. And, in Luther's view, often the very passage for which one of his critics claimed some venerable church father's interpretation was itself the passage that upset the alleged interpretation.[18]

One final Luther axiom for interpretation was the unitary meaning of scripture. In coming to this position, Luther was departing from the fourfold meaning of scripture which he himself, as a product of medieval biblical scholarship, had initially practiced. Especially two of these four meanings, the literal and the spiritual (historical and allegorical), had dominated exegesis in the West ever since Origen. This pattern for the meanings of scripture reflects the scholastics' two-story universe, the double-hemisphere blueprint for reality, discussed in our previous chapter. If one practices leading texts to the cross of Christ, however, and if in the crucified Jesus we have the tangible historical Word of God in person, then the actual, historical, literal meanings of the texts of scripture—unless they tell us point blank to read them allegorically—are the spiritual meanings intended for us to hear. Spiritual meaning is not nonmaterial, trans-historical.

In cross theology, spiritual meaning is that good news that comes from the grubby events of God in Christ reconciling the world. There is no spiritual meaning that is above or beyond or deeper and more concealed than what is announced about and from this one historically crucified

17. *LW* 34:112.
18. See Jaroslav Pelikan, *Luther the Expositor*, LW Companion Volume (St. Louis: Concordia, 1959), 109–34.

Christ with his pre-history in the Old Testament and his post-history in his body, the church. A search for some "hidden God" (*deus absconditus*) allegorically or spiritually behind or beyond this God who is revealed (*deus revelatus*) on the cross can be attempted, but such a search is not faithful. If the Holy Spirit is the Spirit of the crucified and risen Christ, there is no additional spiritual meaning behind or beyond the cruciform Word of God.

In the last analysis the desire to get back through the grubby commonplace elements of manger and stable, suffering and cross, to some spirit behind them amounts to a vote of no confidence in God's chosen revelation medium and substance. At its worst it is an act of hubris wherein we presume to penetrate the communication barrier between God and ourselves in order to grasp God, thus implying that God cannot or did not yet get through to us without our help. This practice of the theology of glory (*theologia gloriae*) is the sinful and inordinate lust to view God apart from the "clothes" God has assumed in our midst in manger, cross, words, and elements.[19] It is the hermeneutical form of original sin.

For Luther, the "mysteries" of God are not hidden *behind* the words. Rather, it is *in* the very words of the texts that "promote Christ" that the Mysterious One has "shone forth in our hearts to give knowledge of the glory of God in the Face of Christ." Not apart from, not behind, but in the face of the crucified Christ is the glory of God. In these very words are Spirit and Life. In words from Luther's favorite evangelist, John, "These things are written that you might believe that Jesus is the Christ, and that believing you might have life in his name."

Luther's Hermeneutic and the Augsburg Confession

The Lutheran hermeneutic received its most public display and most careful articulation during Luther's lifetime in the aftermath of an event in which he did not even participate. At the Imperial Diet of Augsburg in 1530 the Lutheran parties in Germany made their first public confession. Because of the emperor's ban, the Edict of Worms 1521, Luther did not appear at Augsburg. He had been relegated to the category of "public enemy." As a result, the architect for the Lutherans' confession was Philip Melanchthon, Luther's younger colleague at Wittenberg University.

The Augsburg Confession, which finally was presented June 25, 1530, was gentle by comparison with Luther's familiar rhetoric ("I could not have stepped so lightly," he said after reading Melanchthon's text).

---

19. Luther's term is *deus nudus*.

However, Melanchthon did forcefully present the cross at the center of justification entirely by faith (*sola fide*).

The response of the papal theologians, who composed the Roman Confutation while the Diet was still in session, nevertheless took the Augsburg Confession to task for its error on this central affirmation. And the fundamental grounds of their critique was *not* that the Lutheran teaching was at odds with the tradition. What proved the Lutherans wrong was not tradition, they asserted, but rather *sola scriptura!* "It is entirely contrary to Holy Scripture to deny that our works are meritorious."[20] "Their [the Lutheran princes'] ascription of justification to faith alone is diametrically opposed to the truth of the Gospel."[21] Melanchthon in turn rises to respond to the Confutation's criticism with his Apology (or response to the Confutation). Right at the very outset he indicates the field of battle:

> Our opponents boasted that they had refuted our Confession from the Scriptures. Therefore, dear reader, you now have our Apology. It will show you both the judgments of the opponents (we have reported faithfully) and their condemnations of several articles in opposition to the clear writing of the Holy Spirit.[22]

The agenda is the validity of the Lutheran hermeneutic. Melanchthon formulates it, argues for its legitimacy, and puts it into practice in his "apology" of the *sola fide* center of the Augsburg Confession.

> To substantiate our confession and to remove the objections that the opponents raise, we need first to say a few things by way of a preface in order that the sources [*fontes*, wellsprings] of both versions of the doctrine, the opponents' and ours, can be recognized. All Scripture should be divided into these two main topics [*loci*]: the law and the promises. In some places it communicates [*tradit*] the law. In other places it communicates [*tradit*] the promise concerning Christ, either when it promises that Christ will come and on account of him offers the forgiveness of sins, justification, and eternal life, or when in the gospel itself, Christ, after he appeared, promises the forgiveness of sins, justification, and eternal life. Now when we refer to the "law" in this discussion we mean the commandments of the Decalogue, wherever they appear in the Scriptures. . . . Of these two topics, the opponents single out the law . . . and through the law they seek the forgiveness of sins and justification.[23]

What follows is drawn largely from Robert W. Bertram's study "The Hermeneutical Significance of Apology IV" in *A Project in Biblical Hermeneutics* (St. Louis, 1969).[24]

---

20. *BoC*, 120n47 (quoting the *Confutation*).
21. *BoC*, 107n9 (quoting the *Confutation*).
22. *BoC*, 110.
23. *BoC*, 121.

In his Apology, Melanchthon does agree with the Roman Confutators that the scriptures are the heart of the disagreement at Augsburg. But, clearly following Luther's blueprint, Melanchthon argues that it was not the question of literary procedures in reading ancient texts. On that score there was general agreement among the Christian humanists in the debate—agreement about attention to context and historical-grammatical meanings. The theological issue of justification had raised the issue of biblical interpretation. If justification is, as Luther and the Augsburg Confessors claimed, *sola fide*, what does that do for biblical interpretation? Perhaps Melanchthon didn't know it as clearly before Augsburg as he did after: the controversy showed that "it is impossible to ask how Scripture is to be interpreted without constantly asking how people are saved." Biblical hermeneutics is at no point separable from biblical soteriology, the understanding of how one is saved.

Thus the interpreter confronts not just the Bible, but the Bible and the alternate (even antagonistic) interpreters. The interpreter's task is to cope with both. Why not just ignore the alternative, antagonistic interpreters? Answer: they have had a lot to do with framing the question of how to use all that scripture says about good works and merits to keep Christians ethically serious. What Melanchthon does in Apology IV is reformulate the question: how to commend good works without losing the promise. In so doing he interprets "not only Scripture but his opponents as well." In restating their question so that it becomes a question directly about the gospel, Melanchthon interprets their question and the opponents themselves as subevangelical.

Another reason for including the critics in the interpretation of the scripture is that they claimed considerable scriptural support for their opinion. This forced Melanchthon to get to the fountains (the sources) of their objections, to do source analysis. One of their sources was biblical, the biblical law, but another source was not. It was his critics' legal mindset (*opinio legis*). It was their exaggerated opinion of something that was genuinely biblical, the law. That mindset had elevated to a saving truth what, though it is not saving, *is still truth*. And the Bible's law motif does seem to contradict the promise motif. Does that leave us with scripture against scripture?

Melanchthon's final answer is no, but he comes to it only after having worked out the "treacherously difficult operation" of distinguishing the law motif in scripture from its promise motif. The papal critics saw no need to make this distinction, preferring to regard scripture as a self-evident unity. For doesn't the Bible itself combine at important

24. A publication of the Commission on Theology and Church Relations of The Lutheran Church—Missouri Synod.

places both law and promise into a most intricate togetherness? Why put asunder what God had joined together?

Melanchthon's intention was also to rejoin the two, but to do so in the same way as the scriptures themselves make the connection. So his method for that was to make promise dominant. The critics "select the law" and from there move to the promissory material. Their joining of the two with dominance ascribed to the law produced a legalistic mixture that was neither promise nor law.

Sola Fide—Entirely by Faith

But relegating the law to subdominance is not simply a matter of the interpreter's choice. The law is more formidable than that. The law must be led to the fountain, the cross of Christ. Only in Christ is the law given its full biblical due and yet reduced to its biblical position of subdominance. The only way the interpreter has the right to subdue the law exegetically is if she "has" this biblical Christ. And the only way to "have" Christ, his merits and benefits, is *sola fide*, entirely on faith.

The *sola fide* is thus the key for distinguishing what is legal and what is promissory in a text in order to finally relate them back together the way they belong; the law and promise are at odds yet able to coexist effectively in one and the same passage. Beyond this hermeneutical angle, there is also the concomitant soteriological angle: only via *sola fide* can God's law and God's promise be distinguished in order to finally relate them back into effective coexistence in one and the same *sinner*. Biblical hermeneutics is at no point separable from biblical soteriology.

Promises work only when they are trusted. Otherwise they go to waste. So Christ is "used" for what God intended only by faith alone. When God's promise in Christ is not trusted for what he really was (the coming true of sheer merciful promise), then Christ is wasted. Bad exegesis brings about disastrous soteriological consequences.

All that promissory biblical history goes to waste as well. It does no one any good any more. Why then bother to squabble whether it happened or not? Or how much of it really occurred?

But why do we continue to *need* promissory history from God? Because day in and day out God's other motif, God's law, impinges on our lives of inchoate but woefully incomplete righteousness. And there the law does the same job it always does when it catches a partially uncovered (unrighteous) sinner. The law always accuses.

Faced with this accusation, we need some history that could be our history. We need a history we could "have" to hold up against the wrath of God encountered in our historical linkage with the accusing law. As a promissory trump card to the law's continuing criticism, Melanchthon has a corollary phrase antithetical to *lex semper accusat* (The law always accuses). It is: *Christus manet mediator* (Christ continues as mediator). Christ continues, we need him to continue, as the history of promissory mercy "coexisting effectively" (i.e., soteriologically) with the law's history-writing of our own histories. That's why we read the Bible, so that, by the work of Christ's Spirit, we continue to "have" this promissory history.

Luther's law-promise hermeneutic probes the secret of scripture's deepest diversity and its ultimate unity. It realigns the biblical record again and again with what was actually going on there: God subduing God's own law with God's own promise so that good works could freely be commanded and "commended without losing the promise."

This realignment of the biblical record is evident in what Melanchthon offers as a sort of appendix to the hermeneutical model in the Augsburg Confession. In a practice repeated throughout his argument with the Confutators, Melanchthon says that if, in a given text, the accent on promise has been "omitted" (and some biblical texts appear that way), then that accent needs now to be "added" by the faithful interpreter. Is that pious interference or willful rewriting of the biblical history to suit one's own "feelings"? No. It was simply a case of having no evangelical reason for commending anything onto the hearer as word of God without leading it first to the fountain where promise happened in our own history. And the biblical passages most "clear" are those that announced from "the fountain in the center of town" that God was justifying the ungodly in the crucified Jesus *by faith alone*—as God still does.

Scripture's Gifts for Today

If after Luther's shaking the trees of the scriptural forest, we too perceive just what is growing there and how it is effectively "used," we don't need Luther as the only one who can do it for us. We can shake the trees ourselves for the continuing fruits they have to bestow in later seasons to later generations.

And what might be some such gifts for our own church life and present theology if we shake the scriptures expecting a law-promise harvest?

1. The biblical interpreter today—helped with the law-promise distinction—will not be embarrassed by the diversity, even contrariety, of any two or more texts as she works with the troublesome question of scripture's diversity and unity. There is no need to seek for unity in

lowest-common-denominator factors that might still be found between various theologies within the Bible. The unity envisioned in Luther's hermeneutic is something deeper than agreement between different theologies in the Bible. It pushes for unity in the initially contrary words coming from God. In much of the scholarly tussling with scripture's diversity today, a surprising kind of biblicism occasionally surfaces among allegedly "liberal" biblical scholars. While "liberals," of course, prefer "liberal" instead of "conservative" interpretation of texts, the fundamental axiom of both liberal and conservative biblicism is often the same: "If it's in the Bible, no matter how contrary to Justification by Faith alone or how Christless the passage may be, since it's 'in the Bible,' it comes with divine authority." The law-promise *discrimen* opens the door for taking promise-less texts as godly and authoritative, but not giving them soteriological authority, since God's promissory last Word has taken such dominance away from them.

2. Is there in Luther—I speak as a fool—some resource for Jewish-Christian dialogue? Law-promise hermeneutics expects to find both words of God in the Hebrew scriptures. Without question for Luther, as for all Christ-confessors, Jesus is the fulfillment of the "Old" testament of God's law and promises. Yet both are there in the Hebrew scriptures even apart from their fulfillment. They are genuine, they "coexist effectively." The Messianic question would not thereby be avoided, but it might have a better chance if it arose—as it did in Jesus' day—as an inner-Jewish question about the word and work of God *and* whether and how the words and works of Jesus were one with that ancient promising (and Messianic) tradition. The question might be: How does God resource people to live by the promise? How does that promise take on historical concreteness in those human histories? Conflict would be anticipated when the question is raised about the subdominance of the law. However, the Christian's interest in the question comes not just from her own tradition, but to see whether and where law and promise are linked in the Hebrew scriptures so as to "commend works without losing the promise." If participants anticipated from the outset that how one interprets the Bible will be inseparable from how one understands the way one is saved, might that not be an asset, and not a liability, for the dialogue?

3. In the wake of the two-century Western tradition of historical-critical biblical studies, there is still the touchy problem of history, historicity, and facticity. Law-promise hermeneutics does not simply ask the question: Did it really happen? Rather, it asks: Did *what* happen? And in asking that question, it is pressing for evidence of something particular happening, to wit, the promise. History today as well as that

in the Bible is not all of one piece. Luther's observation about the two sermons that were ever preached directly from heaven allows that both of them happened. But two different things happened in those two events. As Luther listens to the Sinai pericope, he hears law happening; Israel's history in that moment is a law event. The sermon on Pentecost is event, to be sure, a happening, but *what* is happening? For Luther, the promise of the Risen Christ is happening in the city of Jerusalem. All history is not alike. It is not a flat plain with events of relative equality. The law's area of historical coverage is vast and territorially immense. The promise's history covers a smaller turf: an ancient pilgrim people, a small band gathered around a teacher finally crucified, and a reconstituted people. This reconstituted people is dispersed in the world and lives by the promise as it confronts the vastly larger territory of the law's history.

Thus the need for history in the Christian faith is not a need for God to enter a mostly God-vacated world, even less for God to do "law" history for us and to us. That we get twenty-four hours a day willy-nilly. What we need is *promise*-history. If *promise*-history doesn't happen, we are not left with no historical encounters with God, but only with encounters with sin and death that is "law's history." The historicity of Sinai and of Jesus' resurrection are different questions theologically (i.e., soteriologically) and remember, that means also hermeneutically. That much at least is clear in Paul's reading of the Easter history in 1 Corinthians 15. If Christ is not risen, our plight is *not* that we are left with no "history" that links us to God's operation. We have a continuing historical linkage. We are yet in our sin—that's a statement of historical linkage to God. As in Adam we all keep on dying.

The promissory history of Good Friday and Easter Sunday subdues the law's history for us and for our salvation. Apart from such promise history, there is only one other history. The "miracle" of Easter is not the abrogation of "secular" history, that is, of scientific cause-and-effect linkages, but it is the abrogation of the otherwise universal *theological* history. It is the end of the law's history with its inexorable linkage of sinners with death. The occurrence in the realm of the law's history of the Easter Christ "is the end of the law [as the final word about a sinner's soteriological prospects in her own history] so that there may be righteousness for everyone who believes."[25]

4. The three contemporary applications of Luther's hermeneutic set out above were offered with theological professionals in mind—seminary teachers, official dialogue participants, and the realm of

---

25. Rom. 10:4.

academe. However, most of the interpretation of the scriptures going on Sunday after Sunday and on the days in between occurs elsewhere: in the preaching and teaching of a Christian congregation and wherever two or three gather together in the Name. The law-promise hermeneutic, though not denigrating the work of the theological professionals, commends itself to the nonacademics as well for their use.

A workable procedure for using the law-promise hermeneutic suggests approaching biblical texts as follows: (1) What is the "bad news" that this text exposes about past and present human history? To make sure the probe gets as deep as the text itself proposes, interpreters—upon getting a first answer—are encouraged to ask, "Is it even worse than that?" This diagnostic probe into the text would not rest until it is as deep as the text's own probe into our history. (2) The next procedure asks the text: What "good news" do you propose in the face of the diagnosis just done? And again a second time, "Is it even better than that?"—and maybe even a third or fourth re-asking until the full promise a text has to offer is out in the open.

With the textual data now on the table—produced by the repeated bad news/good news questioning—the law-promise hermeneutic commends the double-dipstick for evaluating the data: the Christ-quotient and the consolation-quotient. Do the merits and benefits of Christ finally come to the surface to be used as he intends them? If not, were they present in the text but missed in the first exegetical operation? If they are not there in the text itself, then we have a situation that calls for "adding" the promise—just as we saw Melanchthon do in his debate with the Roman Confutators. The other side of the two-sided measuring stick (the "double-dipstick," as we've been calling it) is the consolation quotient. Is this genuinely good news for the present company of listeners/readers? Is it useful? How can they become participants in "using" the merits and benefits of Christ in their own lives for "commending good works without losing the promise"?

The promise—in all its full "good news"—is the fruit we gather as we join Luther and the Confessors in "shaking the scriptural tree." Unless the searcher is overtly probing for promise, the law's hegemony will dominate. The promise test (Christ-quotient and consolation-quotient) is what the Christian community must always apply to new techniques to see how well they help in getting the promise off the biblical page to revitalize the people of God.

3

Why the Cross Is at the Center

Edward H. Schroeder

In this chapter, Edward Schroeder presents the core of Luther's theology and the "hub" of the Augsburg "wheel"—justification by faith alone. Schroeder uses Luther's language ("remarkable dual," "God's two righteousnesses," "the happy exchange," "more than halfway out of death") to show how Christ's death on the cross is such good news for us.

What happened on the first Good Friday that resulted in giving all theology this trademark: "of the cross"? God was doing something here that God had not done before, nor has God done since. On the cross the second person of the divine majesty was suffering and dying, was suffering and dying for sinners, was suffering and dying *as* a sinner.

God's suffering and dying had been the issue for the early church councils that hammered out the trinitarian and christological dogmas. God's suffering and dying troubled those early Christians, who worked with the Greek wineskins of divine immortality (which viewed God as automatically death-proof). But the "one time only" character of the cross and its deepest scandal lies elsewhere. On the cross the Son of God died for sinners *as* a sinner. And to top it all off, *that* very event is *the* Good News of the New Testament.

That Christ the sinner suffered rightfully the sinner's fate—where did Luther get that notion and how could he place it at the center of theology? Answer: the New Testament apostles did it before him, and

Luther's daily work as professor of Bible committed him to say what they said.

As Luther read them, two passages from Paul said this unequivocally: "Christ redeemed us from the curse of the law, having become a curse for us—for it is written: 'Cursed be everyone who hangs on a tree'" (Gal. 3:13) and "God made Him to be sin for us who knew no sin, so that in him we might become the righteousness of God" (2 Cor. 5:21).

Luther's most extensive handling of the Galatians 3 passage comes in his classroom *Lectures on Galatians, 1531* (published 1535). There, Luther cites the Corinthian text over and over again as a solid parallel. Here is his interpretation of Christ being made a curse for us as he dies on the accursed tree: *"Mirabile duellum"* becomes *"jucundissimum duellum,"* that is, "amazing duel" becomes a "very joyous duel."[1]

Luther begins the discussion of "Christ became a curse for us" by noting that St. Jerome, *the* authority on biblical interpretation from Christian antiquity. Jerome had translated the entire Bible, turning its original Hebrew and Greek into Latin, the daily language of his day, and he was "distressed" by the passage "Christ became a curse for us." Jerome thinks that Christ's holiness and righteousness are insulted, and that Paul cannot be serious about such a crass assertion. But, for Luther, the words "for us" signal that Paul is not talking about Christ in his personal innocence. Christ gets entangled in the sinner's fate because he entangles himself with us who are "sinners and thieves." As Luther concludes, "Thus the whole emphasis (namely, of Christ's being accursed) is on the phrase 'for us.'"[2] Just how deep that "for us" takes Christ is already signaled by Isaiah (53:12): "he is numbered among the thieves." On the cross

He is not acting in His own Person now. Now He is not the Son of God, born of the Virgin. But He is a sinner, who has and bears the sin of Paul, the former blasphemer, persecutor, and assaulter; of Peter, who denied Christ; of David, who was an adulterer and murderer. . . . In short, He has and bears all the sins of all men in His body—not in the sense that He has committed them but in the sense that He took these sins, committed by us, upon His own body, in order to make satisfaction for them with His own blood. Therefore this general Law of Moses included Him, although He was innocent so far as His own Person was concerned; for it found Him among sinners and thieves. Thus a magistrate regards someone as a criminal and punishes him if he catches him among thieves, even though the man has never committed anything evil or worthy of death. Christ was not only found among sinners; but of His own free will and by the will of the Father He wanted to be an associate of sinners, having assumed the flesh and blood

1. *LW* 26:164.
2. *LW* 26:277.

of those who were sinners and thieves and who were immersed in all sorts of sin. Therefore when the Law found Him among thieves, it condemned and executed Him as a thief.[3]

In Luther's view, Jerome's tradition in medieval exegesis deprives Christians of the "most delightful comfort" when it "segregates Christ from our sins." To "unwrap" Christ from us and our sins is to make him useless. For then we must cope with our sins and the accompanying curse on our own. If Christ does not take ownership of our sins—in his body, in his own biography—then we remain the owners and are stuck with the consequences. According to Luther, by himself "He is, of course, innocent, because He is the Lamb of God without spot or blemish. But because He bears the sins of the world, His innocence is pressed down with the sins and the guilt of the entire world. . . . They are as much Christ's own as if He Himself had committed them."[4] It is not an insult to predicate the words "sinner" and "curse" to Christ. It is necessary for salvation. "In short, our sins must be Christ's own sin, or we shall perish eternally."[5]

The debate with Jerome about what happened on Good Friday is of a piece with the central Reformation debate about the justification of sinners. When the sophists[6] call for "faith formed by love" (i.e., faith plus works) as the grounds for a sinner's justification, they are ascribing part of sin's removal to our own performance. This portion of their proposal "to remove sins and be justified" comes to nothing short of this: "to unwrap Christ and to unclothe Him from our sins, to make Him innocent, to burden and overwhelm ourselves with our own sins, and to behold them not in Christ but in ourselves. This is to abolish Christ and to make Him useless."[7] Jerome's "diluted" reading of Gal. 3:13, intending to protect Christ's innocence and honor, is linked with a cooperation model of justification that makes Christ useless. To preserve Christ's "moral" honor in his own person leads to dishonoring him as the Savior of Sinners.

The desire to keep Christ clean from the predicates "cursed" and "sinner" is consistent with a view of Christianity as a religion of attainable legal morality. But that of course is the point of debate at Augsburg between glory theology and cross theology. And the debate surfaces in conflicting readings of the scriptures *and* of the human dilemma. The two go together. What happened on Good Friday is corollary to how bad the human dilemma is. The depth of the sinner's

3. *LW* 26:277f.
4. *LW* 26:278.
5. *LW* 26:278.
6. The scholastic theologians of the church.
7. *LW* 26:279.

real trouble is the mirror image of what happens on Good Friday to rescue those sinners from just such trouble. When the sophist objects "But it is highly absurd and insulting to call the Son of God a sinner and a curse!" Luther asks the sophist to reflect on the creed:

> If you want to deny that He is a sinner and a curse, then deny also that He suffered, was crucified, and died. For it is no less absurd to say, as our Creed confesses and prays, that the Son of God was crucified and underwent the torments of sin and death than it is to say that He is a sinner or a curse. But if it is not absurd to confess and believe that Christ was crucified among thieves, then it is not absurd to say as well that He was a curse and a sinner of sinners. Surely these words of Paul are not without purpose: "Christ became a curse for us" and "For our sake God made Christ to be sin, who knew no sin, so that in Him we might become the righteousness of God." [2 Cor. 5:21][8]

All of this would be unnecessary, of course, if sinners themselves weren't so bad off. The bad news for them is that they are under "the curse of the law." And how bad is that? Luther responds, "The curse . . . is the divine wrath against the whole world."[9]

The Remarkable Duel

How does this become good news? "Christ became a curse for us to set us free from the curse of the Law" is Paul's assertion. But how does Christ's involvement in our curse bring about our liberation from the sinner's curse? Luther's answer is to retell the passion story with the main theological participants (law, Christ) as the *dramatis personnae*.

> Paul speaks this way throughout his writings. To make the subject about this remarkable duel (*mirabile duellum*) joyful and clear, he usually portrays the Law by personification as some sort of powerful person who condemned and killed Christ. Christ then overcame death and conquered this person in turn, condemning and killing him. The duelists are Christ and the Law (not Christ and Pilate, nor Christ and the Devil) but Christ and the Law of God, the Law which rightfully says: "Let every sinner die!"[10]

The law, of course, has no claim on Christ in his own person. It is only by virtue of his association with sinners, an association that merits Christ the predicate of sinner, that the law has a rightful claim on him.

Luther got the *mirabile duellum*—the remarkable duel—notion from the ancient Easter sequence hymn "Lauds to the Paschal Victim." "About this wondrous duel the church beautifully sings: 'It was a strange and dreadful strife when death with life contended.'"[11]

8. *LW* 26:278.
9. *LW* 26:281.
10. *LW* 26:279.
11. Ibid.

Here's how Luther narrates what happened at the cross:

> When the merciful Father saw that we were being oppressed through the Law, that we were being held under a curse, and that we could not be liberated from it by anything, He sent His Son into the world, heaped all the sins of all men upon Him, and said to Him: "Be Peter the denier; Paul the persecutor, blasphemer, and assaulter; David the adulterer; the sinner who ate the apple in Paradise; the thief on the cross. In short be the person of all men, the one who has committed the sins of all men. And see to it that you pay and make satisfaction for them." Now the Law comes and says: "I find Him a sinner, who takes upon Himself the sins of all men. I do not see any other sins than those in Him. Therefore let Him die on the cross." And so it attacks Him and kills Him.[12]

So far, that does not sound like much of a duel. The "law of sin and death" already prescribes how such an encounter will end. The law will win and the sinner will lose. But this chief sinner is more than just a sinner. Christ is not less than a sinner—that for Luther, and for Paul too, he thinks, is perfectly clear from his being accursed. If the law can exercise its jurisdiction of death on anyone, that fact itself signals that the victim is a sinner.

But this sinner, the friend of sinners, is more. He is the second person of the Godhead, the incarnate *logos*, "the purest of persons ... God and man."[13] There we have the makings of a genuine duel. This is the person whom the law (and its co-antagonists: sin, death, wrath, curse, devil) attacks.

And lest we be too quick to once more predict the outcome as obvious in favor of the divine contender, we must be clear about the strength of the antagonists. The law is drawn into this duel not at its weakest (as one might deduce from the flimsy Jim Crow justice of the Sanhedrin or the patent political expediency of Pilate) but at its strength. The law has a *bona fide* sinner in the dock. It has a "godly" claim upon this sinner's life by virtue of the divine authority it bears ("The soul that sinneth, it shall die"). Let us not denature the duel with "cheap law." Then there would be nothing very marvelous about the duel. Both contenders are strong.

Living as we do after Easter, we can anticipate how the duel will end. The blessing of God will overcome the curse of the law. "For if the blessing in Christ could be conquered, then God Himself would be conquered. But this is impossible."[14]

Yet before the Holy Week events occurred, Luther contends that God's victory over the curse is not such a foregone conclusion.

---

12. *LW* 26:280.
13. *LW* 26:287f.
14. *LW* 26:282.

Now let us see how two such extremely contrary things come together in this Person. Not only my sins and yours, but the sins of the entire world, past, present, and future, attack him, try to damn Him, and do in fact damn Him. But because in the same Person, who is the highest, the greatest, and the only sinner, there is also eternal and invincible righteousness, therefore these two converge: the highest, the greatest, and the only sin; and the highest, the greatest, and the only righteousness. Here one of them must yield and be conquered, since they come together and collide with such a powerful impact. . . . He [sin] attacks Christ and wants to devour Him as he has devoured all the rest. But he does not see that He is a Person of invincible and eternal righteousness. In this duel, therefore, it is necessary for him to be conquered and killed, and for righteousness to prevail and live.[15]

So righteousness trumps sin, blessing trumps curse, and life trumps death. "Therefore Christ, who is divine Power, Righteousness, Blessing, Grace, and Life, conquers and destroys these monsters—sin, death, and the curse—without weapons or battle, in His own body and in Himself."[16]

Here lies another marvel of the remarkable duel. "Without weapons or battle, in His own body," this is where the duel is fought. There is no external battlefield, and yet a "strange and dreadful strife" . . . where (finally) "the victory remained with Life," as the Paschal Victim hymn proclaims. "This circumstance, 'in Himself,' makes the duel more amazing and outstanding; for it shows that such great things were to be achieved in the one and only Person of Christ."[17]

Christ as Lord of the Law

Both sets of contraries—the human sinner and divine righteousness—had to be really Christ's, "in Himself." Why? To draw the Law into its own demise. Had they been separable, the law could have avoided its dilemma (and eventual blasphemy) by cursing the one and not the other. Christ's willing self-incrimination with sinners was the same decision of the "indescribable and inestimable mercy and love of God." Thus the law could not do what it had to do against the one without attacking the other. In short, it was the very will of God the Father, as well as of the Christ, that this union of divine righteousness with sinners in one person took place: "Of His own free will and by the will of the Father He (Christ) wanted to be an associate of sinners."[18] The law then—in rightfully cursing this sinner par excellence—found itself cursing its own author and Lord, whom to curse is sheer blasphemy.

Luther goes on to describe Christ's duel with the Law:

15. *LW* 26:282.
16. Ibid.
17. Ibid.
18. *LW* 26:278.

He Himself is Lord of the Law; therefore the Law has no jurisdiction over Him . . . because he is the Son of God. He who is not under the Law subjected Himself voluntarily to the Law. The Law did everything to Him that it did to us . . . eventually it sentenced Him to death, even death on a cross. This was truly a remarkable duel, when the Law, a creature, came into conflict with the Creator, exceeding its every jurisdiction to vex the Son of God with the same tyranny with which it vexed us. . . . Because the Law has sinned so horribly and wickedly against God, it is summoned into court and accused. . . . Here the Law . . . has nothing with which to defend or cleanse itself. Therefore it is condemned and killed in turn, so that it loses its jurisdiction not only over Christ . . . but also over all who believe in Him.[19]

Christ's conquest of the Law is not via a divine power play. Luther describes Christ's decision:

I could have overcome the Law by My supreme authority, without any injury to me; for I am the Lord of the Law. . . . But for the sake of you who were under the Law, I assumed your flesh and subjected Myself to . . . the same imprisonment, tyranny, and slavery of the Law under which you were serving as captives. I permitted the Law to Lord it over Me, its Lord, to terrify Me, to subject Me to sin, death, and the wrath of God—none of which it had any right to do. Therefore I have conquered the Law by a double claim: first, as the Son of God, the Lord of the Law; secondly, in your person, which is tantamount to your having conquered the Law yourselves.[20]

Christ's double claim against the Law is rooted in all this having happened "in his own body and in himself," "in the one and only person of Christ"—simultaneously a sinful human (not just human) and the Son of God. The Law has done its duty in putting Christ to death as a sinful human being. Now it is "case closed," the Law's case against us. At the same time, the Law's rebellion against Christ as the Son of God has abrogated the Law's right to continued accusation and condemnation of sinners. Thus the case of the Law's Lord against the Law has also been adjudicated against it and it too is "case closed." The consequence of this "remarkable duel" that renders it a "very joyous duel" is, Luther says, that "He has granted us the victory. Therefore the Law has gone out of existence for us permanently, provided that we abide in Christ."[21]

Thus, what is remarkable about the remarkable duel is the marvel of the incarnation at the root of that duel: that the incarnation is not simply the unity of the Son of God and human being, but the Son of God *and human sinner.*

19. *LW* 26:369f.
20. *LW* 26:370f.
21. *LW* 26:369–71.

The Remarkable Duel: Luther and Paul's Exegesis

Conceiving of Good Friday as a "remarkable duel" is the product of Luther's exegesis of Galatians. He does not, however, consider this exegesis to have been original with him. Just as he took the term *mirabile duellum* from the language of the church's worship, so did his understanding of the duel come straight from Paul's own exegesis of the event of the cross. We already noted Luther's observation that "personification" of Christ's theological antagonists was Paul's way "to make the subject more joyful and clear."[22]

Such "personification" of the tyrants confronting the sinner and thus confronting Christ as the friend of sinners is not all that Luther appropriated from Paul's own exegetical practice. He tracks down and examines the substantive details of Paul's exegesis; today we'd say: "Paul's method." As we saw at the outset of this chapter, Luther acknowledges that Jerome is correct in noting that Paul doesn't use the passage in keeping with its original setting and intention in Deut. 21:22–23. Luther notes that Paul adds to the Deuteronomy text and subtracts from it. Any reader can clearly see that "Moses . . . here does not speak about Christ. . . . It is obvious enough that Moses is speaking about a criminal or a thief who has deserved the cross by his wicked deeds."[23]

Luther uses the word "apostolic" to describe the difference between Paul's free-wheeling and Jerome's seemingly more faithful exegesis. Obviously Paul was an apostle and Jerome was not. But that in itself is not what makes Paul's exegesis of Deuteronomy 21 "apostolic." The yardstick for what is "apostolic" exegesis is that it carries out "the proper task of the apostles: to illuminate the work and the glory of Christ and to strengthen and comfort troubled consciences."[24]

Jerome's pious attempts to keep the curse off of Christ failed this double yardstick. In both Gal. 3:13 and its following verse 14, Paul is taking two Old Testament passages—one about curse from Deuteronomy ("cursed is everyone that hangs on a tree") and one about blessing ("that the blessing of Abraham might come upon the Gentiles") from Gen. 22:18—and doing the apostles' "proper task" with each. "Paul treats this topic in a truly apostolic way. . . . Who would dare quote this passage from Moses, 'Cursed be everyone who hangs on a tree,' and apply it to Christ Himself?"[25]

For Luther, Paul's daring application is not apostolic whimsy. There

22. *LW*, 371.
23. *LW* 26:276.
24. *LW* 26:290.
25. *LW* 26:288.

is a "principle by which Paul applied this sentence . . . to Christ." And what is that principle? It is the principle that all the Old Testament (its laws of criticism and its promises of salvation, in short, its curses and its blessings) are factually and finally fulfilled in Christ.

So Paul is following a fundamental theological and exegetical principle when he bends Deuteronomy 21 with its curse to apply to Christ. Luther states that principle as:

> By the same principle . . . we can apply not only all of Deuteronomy 27 [the antiphonal curse liturgy from Mounts Ebal and Gerizim] but all collected curses of the Mosaic Law to Christ. For just as Christ for His own Person is innocent of this general Law, so He is of all others. And just as for us He violated this general Law and was hanged on the tree as a criminal, a blasphemer, a parricide, and a traitor, so He violated all other laws as well. For all the curses of the Law were gathered together in Him, and therefore He bore and sustained them in His own body for us. Consequently He was not only accursed; but He became a curse for us.[26]

> This is really the apostolic way to interpret the Scriptures. For without the Holy Spirit a man cannot speak this way; that is, he cannot include the entire Law in one word and gather it all at once in Christ, and, on the other hand, include all the promises of Scripture and say that these are fulfilled in Christ once and for all. Therefore this argument is apostolic and very powerful, based as it is, not on one passage in the Law but on all the laws; and Paul relies heavily on it.[27]

For both Paul and Luther, this is exegesis done with the Holy Spirit. But note that the Holy Spirit supplies no formal inspiration, but gives the Christ-connectedness for the Old Testament. The Holy Spirit offers, in effect, the content-insight that all the Old Testament bad news and all the Old Testament good news are to be funneled into the Christ.

That illumination does not happen, however, without serious work with the texts. Luther continues:

> You see here with what diligence Paul read the Scriptures and how carefully he weighed and considered the individual words of this passage [Gen. 22:18]: "In you shall all the nations be blessed." First he argues as follows from the term "bless": "If the blessing is to come upon all nations, then all nations are under the curse—even the Jews, who have the Law of Moses." And he quotes evidence from Scripture by which he proves that the Jews, who are under the Law, are under the curse: "Cursed be everyone who does not abide, etc."

> Next Paul diligently weighs the words "all nations," on the basis of which he argues as follows: "The blessing pertains not only to the Jews but also to all the nations of the entire world. But if it pertains to all nations, it is impossible for it to come through the Law of Moses, since no nations except the Jews

26. *LW* 26:288f.
27. *LW* 26:289.

had this." Moreover, although the Jews had the Law, still the blessing did not come to them through it; on the contrary, the more they tried to keep it, the more subject they became to the curse of the Law. Therefore there has to be another righteousness, one that far surpasses the righteousness of the Law; through it the blessing comes not only to the Jews but also to all nations in the world.[28]

We see Luther's examination of Paul's wrestling with the logic of the Old Testament texts as "diligently weighing the individual words of the passages." But this wrestling doesn't yet follow Paul's "principle" for apostolic exegesis. That comes in the next paragraph of Luther's analysis of Paul's exegesis.

> Finally Paul explains the phrase "in your offspring" as follows: "A certain man was to be born of the offspring of Abraham." I mean Christ, through whom the blessing was to come upon all nations. Since Christ was to bless all nations, whom He found to be accursed, He Himself had to remove the curse from them. But He could not remove it through the Law, because the curse is only increased by this. So what did He do? He attached Himself to those who were accursed, assuming their flesh and blood; and thus He interposed Himself as the Mediator between God and men. He said: "Although I am flesh and blood and live among those who are accursed, nevertheless I am the blessed One through whom all men are to be blessed." Thus He joined God and man in one Person. And being joined with us who were accursed, He became a curse for us; and He concealed His blessing in our sin, death, and curse, which condemned and killed Him. But because He was the Son of God, He could not be held by them. He conquered them and triumphed over them. He took along with Him whatever clung to the flesh that He had assumed for our sake. Therefore all who cling to this flesh are blessed and are delivered from the curse.[29]

Thus, in this reconstruction of Paul's own exegesis, Luther sees the two sides of "the proper task of the apostles: (1) to illuminate the work and the glory of Christ and (2) to strengthen and comfort troubled consciences."[30] Luther acknowledges that his own reconstruction of Paul's exegesis is a condensed one: "undoubtedly Paul treated these things at great length in the presence of the Galatians."[31] Yet compressed or expanded, such exegesis sounds like "nothing but riddles" to "those who know no other righteousness than that of the Law."[32] And even for believers this "is impossible to understand and to believe fully, because it is so contradictory to human reason."[33] The most incredible thing

28. *LW* 26:289f.
29. Ibid.
30. *LW* 26:290.
31. Ibid.
32. Ibid.
33. Ibid.

about the gospel is the gospel itself, that marvelous duel wherein Christ redeemed us from the curse of the law by becoming a curse for us.

To summarize: (1) the debate about exegesis—Luther's exegesis of Gal. 3:13 (contra Jerome) and Paul's exegesis of Deut. 21:22–23—is a debate about salvation. Hermeneutics and soteriology are corollaries. (2) Luther thinks he's following Paul's lead in "apostolic" exegesis. That means: (a) following the Holy Spirit's lead in linking Christ to both the entire Old Testament law and the entire Old Testament promise; (b) interpreting the law and promise material of the Old Testament in the way that Christ's crucifixion requires; (c) that may often come out as daring and audacious and not at all what the Old Testament author said.

For Luther, this exegesis of scripture is not arbitrary. Or rather it is no more arbitrary or bizarre than the cross is arbitrary and bizarre, which it is. The audacious cross becomes the norm for the audacity of apostolic exegesis. That means (d) that the achievement of Christ is brought to light as the work and glory it genuinely is, so that sinners thereby get the real help that they genuinely need, "strength and comfort for troubled consciences."

It was finally this pastoral failure to comfort troubled consciences that surfaces with monotonous regularity in Luther's critique of medieval theology. It failed to provide what sinners really need because it misread the diagnosis of their malady and thus mis-prescribed the needed remedy. Simply stated, the medieval misdiagnosis ignored the deep trouble that God's law inflicts upon sinners, namely, that it is God himself as critic, rightful critic, who constitutes the sinner's nemesis—willy-nilly and irrespective of the sinner's awareness thereof.

Ultimately, for Luther, the hermeneutical principle of distinguishing law and promise in biblical exegesis amounts to a pastoral and liturgical test for "apostolic" exegesis: Do sinners get the help they really need? Does Christ get "used" for what he's good for, which is the only way to give him glory?

Luther's Critique of Medieval Soteriology

We have seen that the debate about the meaning of the biblical texts related to Good Friday is interwoven with the entire texture of the plan of salvation that the interpreter of scripture has in mind. That same debate was evident in Luther and the Augsburg Confessors' rejection of the larger scheme of medieval theology.

Anselm of Canterbury was the architect for the major model of the plan of salvation that held sway during Luther's time. Four centuries before Luther's birth, at the very close of the eleventh century, Anselm had composed his *Why God Became Man* (1098). Reference to Anselm is infrequent in Luther's work, and perhaps he never read *Why God Became Man* firsthand. However, in his arguments with the papal representatives and scholastic theologians of his day, Luther addresses a central element of Anselm's bequest to the later Middle Ages, whether or not he's conscious of Anselm at the moment.

Luther's portrayal of the remarkable duel is a clear break with Anselm's model and a distinct alternative. It is strange that Luther does not name Anselm as the one he's criticizing with his own atonement theology. The key to the difference between Luther and Anselm lies in the depth diagnosis of the sinner's malady that frustrated his being at one with God. Anselm rightly diagnoses the human malady as man's being in trouble with God's law. In his model the law functions according to the pattern of civil law in a civil contract. Feudal patterns of liege lord and bonded peasants are in the background. Human beings owe God total fealty and honor, which they have failed to deliver. They are in default on their contract. Their rescue from the bad consequences of that default will come if they can somehow pay up or if some alternate can be found to make good on the contract.

For Anselm, humans cannot produce today the moral righteousness they owed God yesterday. Even if they lived twenty-four hours perfectly they would only make good today's contract commitment. Humans are incapable of covering their own default. Christ is God's own plan of salvation. He is the means for making good on the defaulted contract. Christ lives a contract-perfect moral life and dies with a perfect free conscience. *Why God Became Man* demonstrates why that alternate (substitute, vicarious) contract-deliverer needs to be both divine and human. Given all the sinners there are in default, an infinite amount of righteousness is needed. Thus the vicarious contract-deliverer must be divine, so that the product will be unlimited. But those who need to pay up are human, so the vicarious contract-deliverer must be human. That's why God became human.

Like Anselm, Luther understood that the human race was in trouble with God's law. And the trouble was serious. But for Luther it was *much worse* than Anselm envisioned. If, as scriptures say, the law puts sinners under God's curse, then civil law and civil contract won't serve as an accurate analogy. Civil law puts no one under a "curse." The trouble we are in with God's law is like that of a criminal's trouble in *criminal law*. The sinner's malady is not some contracted performance that we have failed to deliver. Rather, we are charged as rebels, as enemies and haters of God. We are wrong persons. Not our work, but *our person is under the law's judgment*. As in criminal law, God's law does not say to the sinner:

pay up or be punished. In criminal law, to pay up (for a rebellion, for treason) is to be punished. Not merely your works are defective, but your life is forfeit. To pay up you must lose your life.

Consequently "fulfilling" the law means something quite different in these two instances. In civil contracts, to follow Anselm's analogy, fulfilling the law means making good on the contract, or finding someone who can make good for you. And, if that doesn't happen, suffering the limited indemnity that the contract specifies for nonfulfillment. In *criminal law* the law is fulfilled when the rebel, the traitor, is executed. That is not making the contract "good" as occurs in the fulfilling of civil contracts. But it is making the implied contract "right" when the rebel's usurped life is forfeited for his rebellion. Of course, this is "bad" news for the rebel, but it is *justice*; it is right both for God and for the rebel.

According to the law of God, says Luther, *a dead sinner is a justified sinner*—one to whom justice was done. The law's "curse" expresses both the personal divine disfavor and the fair-and-square execution of justice. *Justi-ficare*, to "do justice" to a sinner under God's law, is to demand the sinner's life for satis-faction. Only the death of the sinner will make equal, make historically equitable, the historical truth of the relationship between the creator and the sinner.

Unpaid Debts or Rebellion? What's the Malady?

Anselm's model starts with the problem posed by the "paradox of justice and mercy," the Augustinian agenda bequeathed to the Middle Ages.[34] To be saved, of course, is humankind's problem. But for Anselm the paradox was basically God's problem since God was committed to be both merciful and just. That double commitment was taken as a matter of course. Scriptures were understood to obligate God to both. "The dilemma of the atonement lay in the need to face the contradiction between these two works, that is, to 'describe the mercy of God . . . as so great and so in keeping with (his justice)' that the paradox would be resolved."[35]

As Anselm says: "Clearly the man we are looking for must be such that he dies neither of necessity (since he will be almighty) nor by obligation (since he will never have been a sinner), one who can die of his own free will because it will be necessary."[36] This voluntary character of

34. Jaroslav J. Pelikan, *The Christian Tradition: History of the Development of Doctrine*, vol. 3, *The Growth of Medieval Theology (600–1300)* (Chicago and London: University of Chicago Press, 1978), 108ff.
35. Ibid., 109.
36. Ibid., 142.

Christ's suffering, dying not because he had to, but motivated only by the honor of the Father (injured and needing restoration) and the plight of mankind, is what made the suffering redemptive. "His 'obedience' in doing so was addressed to the justice of God, which could not prevail without his dying."[37] In Anselm's view, when the events of Good Friday are over, the equilibrium of the moral order of the universe is restored. God's in his heavens, all's right (legally right, moral *rectitudo*) with the world.

Significantly, in the Anselmic storyline, Easter plays no necessary role.

Luther disagrees with Anselm's atonement model, on the one hand, because of its unalterable legal texture and, on the other, because it is not legal enough. For Anselm, the law persists (is never really changed) but in Luther's view (and, Luther claims, in St. Paul's view), Anselm leaves the law short-changed. The law doesn't get what it is due. There is only substitutionary punishment for contract-in-default sinners, but not the execution of a one-for-all rebel-sinner, which is what the law demands. Anselm's Christ restores a world whose *rectitudo* (moral order) has been disrupted by sinners. In Anselm's view, Christ's crucifixion makes the disrupted moral order work again and returns it to equilibrium. Thus the law still persists. Christ did not bring about the "end of the law," small comfort for sinners.

Luther reads the scriptures as saying that the old model—the creation patterned originally according to *rectitude*—is not only disturbed by sinners; it is ruined. Rebellion doesn't merely disturb a citizen's relationship to his lord. It destroys that relationship. Restoring moral equilibrium to such a creation, if the malady is really that bad, would mean the moral order of a cemetery, a silent world populated with dead sinners. Tragic, but orderly, moral order restored—everything lawful once more. For Luther, the malady is not unpaid debts by otherwise good-hearted, or at least good-intending peasants to their liege lord. Rather, the malady is rebellion, hatred, distrust, enmity—a matter of human will and not just the human hand—against the creator Lord. Rectitude in such a system is justice for the criminals. But that is bad news for the criminals. It is nothing less than the death sentence.

The active nemesis in the Anselmic model is the Devil. But he is a modest nemesis since the moral order disallowed him any legitimate claim to sinners. Anselm operates with the standard medieval notion that, "Although the devil did exercise great *de facto* [in fact] power over men, he had no claim *de jure* [legally] over them."[38] Luther heard the scriptures giving the devil considerable *de jure* claim to humans. Rebels

---

37. Ibid., 143.
38. Ibid., 139. Italics added.

giving allegiance to God's opponent bestow *de jure* power to the lord to whom they entrust themselves. And in exercising his deadly tyranny over them, Satan is an executor of God's law, which *de jure* puts them under the power of death which Satan wields.

In contrast, Anselm's devil has no positive linkage to God's law, and by no means is he its executor. Throughout Anselm's model the malady diagnosis is mild. Anselm has no antenna for the law itself as humanity's nemesis, at least not a serious nemesis. Not serious enough that it could be called the "curse" as Paul does. Or if the "curse" is acknowledged, it is not as serious as Luther hears Paul portraying it. In this respect Anselm is law-shy. Together with most medieval theology, Anselm diagnoses the patient more optimistically than Luther hears the scriptures doing. Anselm doesn't do enough with the law; he short-changes it, not giving the law its due.

But on the other hand Anselm never exchanges the law for something better. Luther hears Paul saying the law needs to be replaced, abrogated, if sinners are to enjoy good news. Anselm seeks to make the law work beneficially for those who have come under its strictures when they default on their contracts. In Anselm's model God's mercy finds a marvelous way to resolve the paradox of justice and mercy. In Anselm's model God makes the law "work" for salvation without having to replace the moral order of the world. Anselm's Christ satisfies the law by performing perfect legal obedience that has infinite transferability. For Luther, though, Christ satisfies the law *and* abrogates it at the same time. Christ *satisfies* the law by dying the death penalty it rightly imposes. Christ *abrogates* the law on the cross since, while executing Jesus, the law was rebelling against its own liege Lord—the legal consequences of which the law knows only too well from its own long history of executing the death penalty on creatures who rebel against the creator! Anselm has no antenna for a discredited law. His legal loom cannot weave with thread like that.

New Creation, Not a Restored Moral Order

Anselm and Luther differ starkly in their reading of the daily life of sinners in God's legal world. Anselm's sinner needs the legal order restored to equilibrium and would shudder at the thought of the abrogation of God's law. For Luther the man or woman on the street is dogged by the inescapable deadly operation of that order. Ultimately, that order never fails to achieve "equilibrium" with sinners (i.e., through death), and so Luther shudders at the prospect that God's law will never be abrogated. The test case is in daily life "when the conscience struggles with the judgment of God," says Luther.[39] "This is the most difficult thing there is." The parallel negative thesis to being "justified and saved through Christ" is the "abrogation of the law." Thus, for Luther, continuing under any alleged "moral order" of God's universe for one who continues to be a sinner is the exact opposite of salvation.

And so abrogation of the law is central to the good news that Christ brings to sinners. "The knowledge that the law has been abrogated is of great value for confirming our teaching about faith and for providing a sure comfort for consciences, especially in their deep anxiety. . . . This is a thing that cannot be emphasized enough."[40]

"Therefore we say that the Law of the Decalog has no right to accuse and terrify the conscience in which Christ reigns through grace, for Christ has made this right obsolete. . . . Therefore the entire Law has been abrogated for believers in Christ."[41]

Instead of leaving the moral order of the universe intact by restoring its defaulted contracts to paid-up contracts—Anselm's model of salvation—the atonement Luther sees in the New Testament is one that replaces that legal order with a new one, new at the center of the "order," a new loom on which to weave the new creation. Grace and forgiveness in Christ are replacement for the moral order of God's law. Anselm's new creation in Christ is a new way to make the old creation work harmoniously. For Luther, Christ's forgiving sinners is the abrogating (via cross-fulfillment) of the moral order of the law. The "new" of the new creation is "brand new." Its "principle" of operation is Christ. Christ-forgiven sinners do not live in the legal order with civil contracts paid up. They live "in the forgiveness order" with their criminal penalty, the death penalty, already behind them. Life beyond an executed death penalty is a genuinely new creation.

The cost for Christ to do that is the law's taking his life. That is *not* because God is unwilling to forgive sinners without getting a pound of flesh. Not at all. The facts are that for Christ to forgive sinners, he must undergo the "tyrant" that objects to sinners being forgiven at all. That tyrant is the law, with its rightful claim on the sinner's life. What gives the law its clout is its own divine authorization to object to the forgiveness of sinners. An accounting-office scheme, a bookkeeping model (like Anselm's) whereby legal justice and divine mercy can both operate without conflict—with no remarkable duel—is unknown to Luther and, he thinks, unknown to the scriptures of both testaments.

39. *LW* 26:445.
40. *LW* 26:445.
41. *LW* 26:447.

Legal justice and divine mercy come to a "settlement" in Anselm's theology and both persist after Good Friday.

Luther's "breakthrough," as he called it, in reading the Bible was that God's law and God's gospel and their respective righteousnesses (performance and mercy) cannot be coordinated in a settlement. They *contradict* each other. Thus for Luther, legal justice and divine mercy clash on Good Friday. On Easter Sunday we see which one is dead. In some theoretical speculative principle, justice and mercy might be coordinated. But on Good Friday—in actual human history—they were not. Not coordination, but conquest is the upshot of Christ's being made a curse for us.

The Joyful Exchange

How does Christ's being made a curse for us and his victory in the amazing duel become the victory of the sinner for whom it was intended? Luther's answer is "by faith." One of his favored expressions for portraying how faith works is *"der fröhliche Wechsel"*—the happy tradeoff, the fortunate transfer, the joyful (even "jumping-for-joy") exchange. "By this fortunate exchange with us He took upon Himself our sinful person and granted us His innocent and victorious Person. Clothed and dressed in this, we are freed from the curse of the Law." And how do we get so clothed and dressed? The exchange happens "by faith alone, because faith alone grasps this victory of Christ. To the extent that you believe this, to that extent you have it."[42] If you believe it, you have it. If you do not believe it, you do not have it.

For Luther, then, saving faith is the action of trust or confidence (*fiducia*). What gives faith such power (so that a sinner can claim justification by faith, even faith alone!) is *faith's object*: the promises of God in this crucified Messiah. But here in the language of the fortunate exchange another accent surfaces about faith. Faith is possession, having something you previously did not have. Faith is "having Christ and all his benefits."

Trusting Christ gives the sinner new ownership. In the mechanics of the exchange, faith is actually an exchange of ownership, a bilateral exchange. Christ takes ownership of my sinful personal property and I become owner of his. Note the personal *possessive* pronouns in the following:

> Therefore the one and only way to avoid the curse is to believe and to say with sure confidence: "Thou, O Christ, art my sin and my curse," or rather:

42. *LW* 26:284.

"I am Thy sin, Thy curse, Thy death, Thy wrath of God, Thy hell. But Thou art my Righteousness, Blessing, Life, Grace of God, and Heaven. . . ." So long as sin, death, and the curse remain in us, sin damns us, death kills us, and the curse curses us; but when these things are transferred to Christ, what is ours becomes His and what is His becomes ours. Let us learn, therefore, in every temptation to transfer sin, death, the curse, and all the evils that oppress us from ourselves to Christ, and on the other hand, to transfer righteousness, life, and blessing from Him to us.[43]

Earlier, Luther writes, "For you do not yet *have Christ*, even though you know that He is God and man. You *truly have Him* only *when you believe* that this altogether pure and innocent person has been granted to you by the Father as *your* High Priest and Redeemer, yes, as *your* Slave."[44]

In preaching on the resurrection texts of 1 Corinthians 15, Luther also uses the language of happy tradeoff:

As He died and lay under the sod as you and I must die and be buried, thus He also rose again for our sakes and made an exchange (*Wechsel*) with us; as He was brought to death through us, we shall be restored from death to life through Him. For by His death He has devoured our death, so that we all will also rise and live as He arose and lives. Therefore He is rightly called *primitiae*, "the first fruits of those who have fallen asleep," since He takes the lead and draws the whole throng after Him.[45]

Making the Most of Easter and the Resurrection

As we have seen, Luther's theology of the cross is not at all antithetical to the theology of resurrection. The contrast between glory and cross theologies is not that one celebrates victory and the other defeat. It is not that one concentrates on Easter Sunday and the other on Good Friday. It is not that one is positive, optimistic, upbeat—while the other is negative, pessimistic, doleful.

Something of that antithetical perception, though, pervades Douglas Hall's powerful apologia for the theology of the cross. His book, *Lighten Our Darkness*,[46] is a full-scale criticism of the triumphalist, optimistic, success-oriented, de facto establishment theology of North American Christianity.

For Hall, both the liberal and conservative manifestations of this triumphalist theology are genuinely part of the problem, rather than resource for solution. They have no substantial "good news" for people amidst the genuine and vast "darkness," the growing experience of

43. *LW* 26:291, 292.
44. *LW* 26:288. Italics added for emphasis.
45. *LW* 28:109.
46. Douglas John Hall, *Lighten Our Darkness: Toward an Indigenous Theology of the Cross* (Philadelphia: Westminster, 1976).

negativity in the micro- and macrocosm of daily life in the Western world. The glory theologies prevalent everywhere promote illusion—"calling evil good and good evil."

Hall asserts that a theology of the cross spotlights our darkness and "calls the thing what it actually is." Hall doesn't want to ignore the resurrection, but he is hesitant about getting there too quickly, too cheaply, lest the light that shines from the cross of the resurrected one too quickly blind us to the darkness. Hall wants to confront the real life-threatening destruction in which we continue to live, in which we continue to have to live, and in which we willingly and alas often gladly participate to produce even more of the same.

For Hall, these negativities are the end product of our world mucked up by human sinfulness, wherein the blight of that human wickedness sheds darkness everywhere. Hall's theology of the cross then proclaims that God is with us in the midst of the darkness to lighten our darkness. That does not mean that God changes our darkness into his light. Rather, God makes it possible for us to see that our world, especially after millennia of human management, is real darkness. The "light" of the cross opens our eyes to our own darkness, to see how dark our darkness really is.

For Hall, Christ's resurrection does not mean that the darkness is conquered. It proclaims, rather, the hope that with God-in-Christ with us in the darkness—suffering the dark night of our sin and death on the cross and thus enabling us to see it as our darkness—there may yet be a way out of it. That is the promise of Easter. But it is still touch-and-go. For Hall, any anticipatory celebration of that victory needs to be very circumspect. The triumphalist, optimistic trap is so ineluctable. It is not at all obvious anywhere that the darkness has been overcome. Lightened? Yes. Overcome? That is our hope. Easter encourages us to encourage one another to keep on fighting the darkness. But it hardly gives us grounds for relaxing our clenched teeth. Good Friday norms Easter, and we have cross over glory and open-eyed suffering realism (and, at most, *sober* joy) over illusory optimism and empty euphoria about cross-less Easters.

Luther's theology of the cross makes more of Easter than does Hall. On what grounds? Because Luther makes more of the cross. Hardly anywhere does Hall take account of the major antagonist Luther sees in the Good Friday duel, namely the law of God. In Hall's scenario, God is only on one side of the conflict of Good Friday. All the anti-God forces of darkness (both human and demonic) are on the other side.

Luther sees powerful nemeses on the scene. But Luther ups the ante on the negativities of daily life experience. In, with, and under our darkness is the incriminating clockwork of the law of God. As in Genesis 3 and ever since, God himself is walking in the garden (now populated with sinners). Our self-chosen darkness is compounded by God's refusal to just let us stew in our juice. No, God *adds to the misery* by laying his judgment and curse upon the race in addition.

For Luther the duel is decisive. As we saw above, the "rightful" powers of darkness, while exercising their legal rights against the Christ, were simultaneously guilty themselves of rebelling against their creator. The upshot of that duel was *genuine and real defeat* of the powers of darkness. The resurrection of Jesus is not a second "happy" message alongside the "sad" message of Good Friday. His resurrection is the report of *what was actually happening* in the marvelous duel. The resurrection is the first reported event in the history of the law-free, death-proof new creation. Christ, raised from the dead, is the "first fruits" to come from the "grain of wheat falling into the earth and dying." And that particular grain of wheat—given what all it was "in His person"—"if it dies, it bears much fruit." This "much fruit" added to the "first fruits" constitutes the here-and-now participation of those who believe in Christ. Since faith equals transfer—their lives for his—those who believe in Christ do already now have ownership of the Easter victory.

Luther preached a series of sermons on Sunday afternoons from August 1532 to April 1533. He went verse-by-verse through St. Paul's great resurrection chapter, 1 Corinthians 15. Luther is hardly unrealistic about the continuing "darkness" in the world at large and the particular forms of it that vex Christians. But over and over again he sets forth the irreversible logic that our own resurrection is integral to our being able to have faith in God. Even more, the resurrection is integral to God being God. "If you were to stay under the ground, God would first have to become a liar and not be God." Of course, even the Christ-truster will not escape death's grasp, but when that occurs God carries through on his *fait accompli* in Christ: "Death, I will be your death," and says to death: "I will devour you and will revive him whom you devoured, or I will no longer be God."[47] To be shy about resurrection is to be shy about God being God.

More Than Halfway Out of Death

And not merely the final resurrection on the last day is our possession, but even now on this side of our own graves, we are "more than half" way out of death in Christ. In several successive sermons Luther rings

47. *LW* 28:98.

the changes on the Christian being "more than half" resurrected already. Our resurrection is

> . . . more than half finished. . . . For the main and best part of this has already come to pass, namely, that Christ, our Head, has arisen. But now that the Head is seated on high and lives, there is no longer any reason for concern. We who cling to Him must follow after Him as His body and His members. . . . As in the birth of man and of all animals, the head naturally appears first, and after this is born, the whole body follows easily. Now since Christ has passed over and reigns above in heaven over sin, death, devil, and everything, and since He did this for our sake to draw us after Him, we need no longer worry about our resurrection and life.[48]

If that still sounds too general, as though applying to the Christian church as Christ's body, Luther makes it individually and anatomically specific. "Now He takes the Christian by the hand and pulls him more than halfway out of the grave; only the left foot remains in it."[49] And that left foot itself may be more than halfway out: "All the hold death still has on us is by a small toe. This, too, will extricate itself soon. Therefore we who have now reached the end of the world have the defiant comfort that it will be but a little while, that we are on our last lap, and before we are aware of it, we shall all stand at Christ's side and live with Him eternally."[50]

The images of body parts already out of the grave are homiletical. They proclaim the "defiant comfort" that Christ-connected believers *have already now*. Luther's theology of the cross announces the light "already now" replacing our darkness. The mechanics for the operation are the marvelous duel and the terrific tradeoff of the exquisite exchange. In contrast, Hall's theology of the cross does not yet see darkness replaced. There is illumination, but the powers of darkness have vacated blessed little space for the light to create something palpably new.

Admittedly the power of darkness has not disappeared. Both Luther and Hall agree on that. But Luther finds the darkness more powerful than Hall does. Divine law runs the network. Hall reads the power of darkness to be "only" human and demonic wickedness. But even for this "reduced" power on the side of darkness, Hall finds that the Light from God has not yet brought an exchange of light *for* (in the place of) darkness. Why? Because the darkness is so powerful. Is that the same as Hall saying: Because the Light is so weak? If so, then Luther also has a more potent Light. Luther sees darkness present and powerful, but

48. *LW* 28:110.
49. *LW* 28:133.
50. *LW* 28:120.

conquered at the center of its theological dynamo (law) for those who believe in Christ, but only for those, of course.

Here once more we come back to the debate previously encountered in Luther and Anselm. Just how bad is the bad news? Just how good is the good news? Does the good news work in fact to trump the bad news? The "debate" between Anselm and Luther as well as between Hall and Luther is simultaneously pastoral, soteriological (genuine salvation, not phony theologies of glory), and exegetical (for example, the Johannine texts on the light of the world that "shines into the darkness, and the darkness has not overcome it").

Luther's diagnosis claims to expose a deeper malady. Because the apostolic exegesis proclaims Christ's full conquest of that malady, the prognosis for the patient already now is palpably promising. The common denominator of being "law-shy" is one we noted both in Hall and in Anselm, although each in a unique way.

Luther's theology of the cross—in its radical reformation format—could improve and assist us by clearing our vision of the law-shyness that is prevalent in contemporary theology and church life. Facing the full grimness of theological diagnosis is probably not possible, at least not tolerable, without correspondingly greater exposure to the goodness of the good news. Only the theology of the cross supplies the courage that enables us to go down to the rock-bottom depths one step at a time. After each deeper level of diagnostic analysis, we need to look back over our shoulder to see how the good news can and does lighten even this cellar of our darkness. Then having emboldened our hearts, cross theology nudges us on to ask once more "and is it even worse than that?" If we do indeed find that it is still worse—that there is even one step farther down yet—the same cross theology once more calls us to look back again to the cross and resurrection of Christ and trust that "already now" this "still worse than that" has been and is being met and conquered.

Articulating the Hub

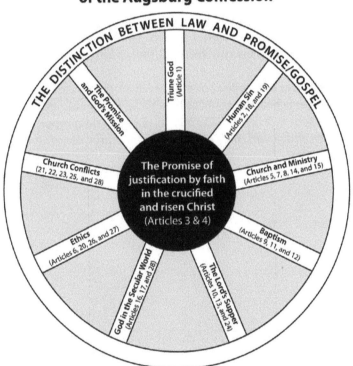

Gift and Promise: the Theology of the Augsburg Confession

THE DISTINCTION BETWEEN LAW AND PROMISE/GOSPEL

The Promise and God's Mission

Triune God (Article 1)

Human Sin (Articles 2, 18, and 19)

Church Conflicts (21, 22, 23, 25, and 28)

The Promise of justification by faith in the crucified and risen Christ (Articles 3 & 4)

Church and Ministry (Articles 5, 7, 8, 14, and 15)

Ethics (Articles 6, 20, 26, and 27)

Baptism (Articles 9, 11, and 12)

God in the Secular World (Articles 16, 17, and 28)

The Lord's Supper (Articles 10, 13, and 24)

The Spokes: Articulations of the Promise, the one and only doctrine of the Gospel.

The preceding three chapters have described the hub of the Augsburg wheel, "the most important topic of Christian teaching," according to the Apology of the Augsburg Confession. This central teaching is made explicit in article 4 of the Augsburg Confession and its Apology. It is the teaching that sinners are justified by faith in Christ, and by that faith alone.

All the other articles of faith *articulate* this hub. In these articles, the Confessors show how what they believe and teach is an expression of this central message of the scriptures. That is, they articulate the most important topic of Christian teaching: how God gets sinners un-sinned. These articles of faith are the spokes of our wheel. As such, they articulate what the Confessors believe and teach with regard to the Trinity, sin, the Son of God—and all the other topics covered in the other articles of the Augsburg Confession.

The rim in our Augsburg Wheel diagram is the proper distinction between law and gospel about which Dr. Schroeder wrote in the preceding chapters. This rim keeps all the articles firmly connected to the hub.

In the chapters that follow, one for each of the spokes in the wheel, students of Dr. Schroeder show us how those articles of faith connect to the hub, and how, when held firmly in place by the proper distinction between law and gospel, they bring the gift and promise of God into our lives today.

4

The Trinity as Gospel

Arthur (Chris) Repp

When the sixteenth-century reformers confessed the triune nature of God, they were not only asserting their orthodoxy; they were confessing the gospel itself. To confess God as Father, Son, and Holy Spirit is to confess God as saving, not only as great or awesome—and that is good news. Dr. Repp shows how the Confessors wanted to make that clear in their day and how the Holy Trinity is still good news for us as well.

> *"The triune nature of God can be comprehended only as an unfolding of the pure gospel."*
>
> — Oswald Bayer[1]

The title of this chapter has already given away its main point: the church's teaching about God as Trinity is deeply entwined with the central Christian affirmation, the gospel—the Good News about Jesus Christ. It may be said to be a corollary of the gospel. That is to say that the understanding of God as Trinity, Father, Son, and Holy Spirit, flows inevitably and necessarily from the gospel's message of salvation.

That may be news to some. There is an aphorism well known to seminarians, which states that the Trinity has three persons, two natures, one essence, and no explanation. Behind the humor lies an uneasiness about this doctrine. We Christians know the Trinity is a foundational

---

1. Oswald Bayer, *Martin Luther's Theology: A Contemporary Interpretation* (Grand Rapids: Eerdmans, 2008), 335.

tenet of Christianity, an ancient hallmark of the faith, but we often don't really know what to do with it beyond that. Sadly, this may be true even of some of our clergy, who presumably should know better. I have heard more than one sermon on Trinity Sunday, the sole point of which was to stress the incomprehensibility of God's triune nature. "The Trinity is not something we can understand," a preacher of recent memory opined. "It is a mystery that we must simply believe." Without further elaboration, such an approach makes the Trinity into a "shibboleth,"[2] a mere password for Christian insiders that does little more than identify us as belonging to the right club.

Making Sense of the Jesus Event in the Early Church

And yet the Trinity is not simply a mystery to be acknowledged but not understood. Rather, the Trinity is an understanding developed by Christians over the course of their first four centuries as they sought to make sense of the Jesus Event and the salvation it proclaimed. From its earliest days, the church confessed that Jesus of Nazareth, particularly in his crucifixion and resurrection, was the focal point of God's activity in the world for the sake of the world. Early Christians even identified God by reference to his having raised Jesus from the dead.[3] In the Gospel according to Luke, Jesus leads his disciples through the Hebrew scriptures and reinterprets them as being about himself.[4] Philip does something similar for the Ethiopian eunuch.[5]

Moreover, already in the earliest days of the church Jesus was confessed as "Lord" and sometimes "God."[6] The latter was most obvious in the Gospel according to John, not only in the famous prologue, which essentially reinterprets the creation account of Genesis 1 with Jesus the *Logos* at its center, but also in Jesus' farewell discourse.[7] What could it mean for Jesus to be the *Logos* through whom all things were made, or the son whom the Father loved before the foundation of the world? What could it mean for Jesus to be confessed as Lord, a title also used for God throughout the Hebrew scriptures?[8] What did it mean for Jesus to be savior?[9] How could one affirm all of this without also positing the

---

2. See Judg. 12:6.
3. See, for example, Rom. 4:24, Acts 3:13–15.
4. Luke 24:27, 44–45.
5. Acts 8:35.
6. See, for example, 1 Cor. 8:6: "yet for us there is one God, the Father, from whom are all things and for whom we exist, and one Lord, Jesus Christ, through whom are all things and through whom we exist," and Rom. 10:9: "because if you confess with your lips that Jesus is Lord and believe in your heart that God raised him from the dead, you will be saved." See also John 20:28: "Thomas answered him, 'My Lord and my God!'"
7. See John 14:8–11; 17:20–24.
8. The Greek word for Lord (κύριος) is used to translate the Hebrew אֲדֹנָי (Lord), which is also used in place of the name of God, יהוה.
9. See, for example, 1 John 4:14.

existence of multiple gods? It was in the working out of these questions that the church's teaching on the Trinity emerged.

Development of Trinitarian Theology in the Patristic Period

While there were no immediate or obvious answers to these questions, it was clear from the church's earliest days that monotheism, deeply embedded in the religious context out of which Christianity grew, was never up for debate. There could only be one God. Precisely because of this commitment, early attempts at making sense of Jesus and his work pulled in one of two directions. Either they emphasized Jesus' divinity at the expense both of his humanity and of his distinction from God the Father, or they asserted his humanity at the expense both of his divinity and of his unity with the Father. In other words, either Jesus was God (the only God!) in human form[10] or he was in some way a part of God's creation: a prophet like Moses,[11] an angel, or a man whom God had granted elevated status.[12]

Efforts that emphasized Jesus' divinity identified him with God but understood his presence on earth as a theophany—God making an appearance clothed in a form that humans could comprehend—but shied away from asserting his transformation into a real human being. Those who emphasized Jesus' humanity saw Jesus as God's agent. They acknowledged that, as God's emissary, Jesus was perhaps above mere mortals in the order of creation, divine to one degree or another, but they were reluctant to identify him as God per se.

The mainstream of the Christian movement early on identified the extremes of these tendencies as heretical, that is to say, as endangering the doctrine of salvation, a judgment later shared by the Lutheran reformers.[13] To stress Jesus' divinity at the expense of his humanity, exemplified by Christian Gnostics and other Docetists, was to make a sham of his incarnation, and more importantly, of his crucifixion and resurrection. The cross and resurrection had been central to Christian proclamation from the start (see, for example, Acts 3:13–16). Rendering these key events as mere illusion seemed to call into question the salvation they were said to accomplish.

To stress Jesus' humanity at the expense of his divinity was to raise doubt about scriptural witness like that of the Gospel of John. And it

---

10. See Acts 14:11; Phil. 2:7.
11. See Acts 3:22.
12. Jaroslav Pelikan, *The Christian Tradition: A History of the Development of Doctrine*, vol. 1, *The Emergence of the Catholic Tradition (100–600)* (Chicago and London: University of Chicago Press), 175.
13. *BoC*, 36.

undermined the language of early Christian worship, which called upon Jesus as Lord and God.

Trinitarian theology developed slowly and unsystematically (occasionally) in reaction to these extremes. It was not fully developed until the Arian controversy of the fourth century, played out in the context of a new relationship between church and state, forced the issue. The theology of those who came to be called Arians recognized both the importance of maintaining the unity of God in the monotheistic tradition as well as the unique, elevated status of Jesus, the Son of God, as God's agent of salvation. Their solution was to hold that the pre-incarnate Son of God was as close to being God as one could get without actually being God. Jesus was the first creation of God, they claimed, who then became an agent of the rest of creation. While they acknowledged that he was intimately involved in every activity of God, they insisted that he was not to be confused with God as such. The Son of God had at some point come into being, while God had not. There was a time when the Son of God had not existed, even if that "time" was before the creation of time itself.[14]

For the Arians' opponents, who may be called the Nicene party after the creed that epitomizes their theology, making the Son of God anything less than God endangered human salvation. This conviction was at least partially rooted in Neoplatonism, the philosophical milieu in which the theological discourse of the day was conducted. A key construct of Neoplatonism was understanding God's activity in the world as procession and return.[15] God's activity in Jesus was seen as a procession into the world of which humans are a part in order to return to God with a redeemed humanity in tow, as it were. The only way this could work, reasoned the Nicene theologians, was if the agent of our salvation was fully divine, was God himself. If he were not, he could not fully return us to be united with the Godhead, the ultimate goal of our salvation. Their solution was to hold that the Son was "of the same being"[16] with the Father, a definition that made its way into the Nicene Creed in 325 CE and was reaffirmed after a lengthy struggle at the second Council of Nicea in 381 CE.

However, in the wake of the Arian controversy, toward the end of the fourth century, it became apparent that a corrective was also needed

---

14. This refers to the Arian slogan, "there was when he was not." See the discussion of Arianism in Pelikan, *The Christian Tradition*, 192–200.

15. Procession and return may be understood as its own struggle to reconcile the Greek notion of the impassible, immovable, absolute, unchanging God with God's activity in the world, which necessitates change. See the discussion in Paul Rorem, *Biblical and Liturgical Symbols within the Pseudo-Dionysian Synthesis* (Volume 71 in Pontifical Institute of Medieval Studies, 1984), 58–65.

16. *Homoousios* (ὁμοούσιος) in Greek.

in the opposite direction. The opposition to Arianism had sometimes emphasized Jesus' divinity and identity with the Father to such an extent that his full humanity was compromised. This was also found to be problematic, and was addressed by the Cappadocian Father Gregory of Nazianzus, who famously asserted, "that which He has not assumed He has not healed."[17] In other words, if Jesus did not become fully human, he could not fully save us.

It was also over the middle years of the fourth century that the Holy Spirit's divinity and co-equality with the Father and the Son was affirmed, thanks largely to the Nicene party's chief representative, Athanasius of Alexandria. By the same logic previously applied to the relationship of the Father and the Son, the Holy Spirit could only be understood as God as well. The Holy Spirit was an agent of creation, present from the beginning with the Father and the Son. And it is through the Holy Spirit that we are incorporated into Christ in baptism and partake of God. This activity can be none other than God's own doing.[18] The classic formulation of the doctrine of the Trinity as one being in three persons was thus established, and it was further solidified in the christological debates of subsequent centuries. At every step, the underlying issue was maintaining the integrity of human salvation. Never was the doctrine a matter of mere speculation.

The Trinity and the Lutheran Reformation

Just as the doctrine of the Trinity was developed to safeguard the gospel of salvation in the ancient church, so the Lutheran reformers appealed to the Trinity as historical support for the central article of faith, the doctrine of justification.[19] In the first article of the Augsburg Confession, the doctrine of the Trinity appears as though it is the foundation and prerequisite of what is to follow ("the decree of the Council of Nicea . . . is to be believed without any doubt"[20]). However, it is more consistent with the trajectory of the Confession to understand the Trinity as the gospel itself. Martin Luther used the Apostles' Creed devotionally, as a reminder of what God has done and continues to do for us. "The historical indicative becomes a promise by being announced to me," writes Werner Elert. "When it turns to me, I hear the 'for me' which makes of the 'historical faith' a 'saving faith,' faith which itself is God's doing, God's gift."[21]

17. Gregory of Nazianzus, Epistle 101.
18. See Athanasius, *Letters Concerning the Holy Spirit*, Letter 1.
19. Werner Elert, *The Structure of Lutheranism* (St. Louis: Concordia, 1962), 208.
20. *BoC*, 37 (article 1, Latin Text).
21. Elert, *The Structure of Lutheranism*, 204–5.

Moreover, as the Lutheran Confessors at Augsburg in 1530 were making the case for the orthodoxy of their teaching, it was important for them to distinguish themselves from other Reformation theologians who were calling into question the doctrine of the Trinity. In some cases these theologians were advocating what seemed more an Arian than orthodox understanding of Jesus vis-à-vis God the Father. One of these was particularly close to home: Johannes Campanus, a former student at Wittenberg and a member of the delegation to Marburg in 1529.[22]

For Luther, the revelation of God in the Trinity was never a comprehensive revelation of everything that is to be known about God. The fullness of God is ultimately beyond all human knowing. But what is given for us to know—the revelation of God as Father, Son, and Holy Spirit, working on our behalf to save us from sin, death, and the power of the devil—is good news precisely *in contrast with the God we do not know*, but which (see quote below) we experience apart from this revelation. This God Luther called the hidden God (*deus absconditus*). While Luther understood God to be omnipresent in creation, he insisted that God must not be sought everywhere because God does not wish to be found there. It is precisely because God is everywhere that God must hide where God does not wish to be found. The hidden God is not the God we call upon nor even speak about objectively. The hidden God is rather experienced subjectively in the hostility of the world as *a force that is against us*. This force we do *not* experience as a person, as Oswald Bayer notes:

> It is anything but self-evident that this neuter "It" [the *deus absconditus*] can become a personal "You." Theology cannot start without further ado by speaking about God as "You"—and Luther does not start this way either. The almighty "You" brings comfort only after it is contrasted with the almighty "It."[23]

Luther's familiarity with the Old Testament and his concern to avoid dualism led him to conclude that this "It" is indeed God, and not some other. And although this idea hardly seems clear or consistent throughout the corpus of his writings, Luther in some places explicitly identifies the devil as a manifestation of the hidden God. "To seek God apart from Christ—that is the Devil," he wrote in a commentary on Psalm 130.[24]

But Luther is consistent in asserting that where God wishes to be found and known is in the revelation of Christ crucified. And this is done

---

22. See Carolyn M. Schneider, *I Am a Christian: The Nun, the Devil, and Martin Luther* (Minneapolis: Fortress Press, 2010), 41–42.
23. Bayer, *Martin Luther's Theology*, 204.
24. Ibid., 205.

through means, through the gospel proclaimed and embodied in Word and Sacrament. As Luther noted in the defense of Christ's presence in the sacrament, "He is present everywhere, but he does not wish that you grope for him everywhere."[25] Where God wishes to be "groped for" and found is in the Word, the gospel of Christ crucified and risen, where God is revealed as "for us" (cf. Rom. 8:31). This Word—together with water, wine, and bread—is also delivered to us sacramentally in Baptism and the Lord's Supper. It is by this Word that we know God as Trinity, by whose name—Father, Son, and Holy Spirit—we are incorporated into the church, the body of Christ, and to whom we pray.

Thus the triune nature of God is not merely incidental or nominal for Luther. It is also more than simply inherited, traditional language. The Trinity is central to our salvation, for it is *within the Trinity itself* that our salvation is played out when the Son turns the Father's heart toward us even before the foundation of the world.[26] It is to this revealed Trinitarian God and this God's promises that we appeal against the threatening, oppressive experience of death and damnation at the hands of the hidden God.

The Trinity and the World as We Know It

This insight of Luther regarding the hidden and revealed God seems particularly useful in light of our contemporary scientific understanding of the universe, which for many calls into question God's very existence. As astronomers have observed, the universe is trying to kill us.[27] Almost all of the universe is hostile to life as we know it. We're only alive because we have a relatively stable sun small enough to not burn itself out too quickly before life could come into existence. We're in the sun's "Goldilocks zone," far enough away not to have our water evaporated and not so far away that everything is in a deep freeze.

We're alive because our planet is massive enough that there is enough gravity to hold onto our atmosphere. It is also big enough that it still has a molten iron core that generates a magnetic field, which protects us from the sun's deadly radiation while still allowing it to give us the warmth and light we need. Another factor in our survival to date is the gravity of massive Jupiter, which has intercepted countless deadly asteroids and comets capable of ending human life on earth.

This fundamental hostility of the universe to human life is the hidden

25. *The Sacrament of the Body and Blood of Christ—Against the Fanatics, LW* 36:342.
26. See Bayer's discussion of Luther's hymn, "Dear Christians, One and All, Rejoice," in *Martin Luther's Theology*, 214–25.
27. See, for example, Philip Plait, *Death from the Skies!: The Science Behind the End of the World* (New York: Viking Penguin, 2008), 1.

God, writ large. And yet what we experience as hostile is also—at the same time—what makes life possible. It is an intrinsic part of the creative process. The component bits of matter from which we are made have been forged in the furnaces of dying stars.

At a fundamental level, however, the modern scientific understanding of the universe has not revealed to us anything that we did not already know about the world's hostility toward us. The people of Luther's day were well acquainted with mortal threats of all kinds, whether from earthquakes, floods, disease, famine, or war. Moreover, above all these was the threat of eternal separation from God and damnation in hell, a fate far worse than mere death. Against the background of these threats, Luther developed his central theological insights.[28]

Luther would have been awed at what we know now, but not surprised that the creation is so menacing. And he would surely remind us of the part we play in aiding and abetting the hostility of the creation by our own hostility toward one another, toward the rest of creation, and even toward God. But in the face of such hostility, he would no doubt nevertheless direct our attention to the God revealed in Christ and his promises against all that the hostile creation can throw at us—a creation that in the fullness of time God's creative and redeeming work will make new and hospitable.

This, ultimately, is the crux of the Christian proposition, and the point of the doctrine of the Trinity. It is precisely as Trinity, focused in the person of Jesus Christ, that God goes about this saving work. In the incarnation, God becomes one with the creation while nevertheless remaining distinct from creation as the uncreated one.

The Trinity is good news because it embodies the reconciliation that God is at work to bring about with the world. The triune God is both source and sourced, subsuming in God's very self—in the Father and the Son—both sides of the dependent relationship implicit in the creation. This is a radical claim.

As Robert Bertram has noted, we are naturally comfortable with the image of God as the Father, as the source of creation, the one in control. We are profoundly uncomfortable, however, with God as the child, God as dependent. That is *our* place, we object, not God's. And yet in the Trinity this is also who we know God to be.[29] Joined by faith to Christ, who by his incarnation has bridged the creator/creation divide, we are

28. This is the central thesis of Heiko Oberman's *Luther: Man between God and the Devil* (New Haven: Yale University Press, 1990).
29. See Robert Bertram, "Putting the Nature of God into Language: Naming the Trinity," in *Our Naming of God: Problems and Prospects of God-Talk Today*, ed. Carl E. Braaten (Minneapolis: Augsburg Fortress, 1989), 91–110.

thereby brought into this reconciled, dependent relationship, which is the life that God intended for us all along.

The Trinity and the Holy Spirit

Little has been said in this chapter about the Holy Spirit, the third person of the Trinity. While this might strike some readers as a significant oversight, it reflects the emphasis both of the early church's development of Trinitarian doctrine as well as of the Lutheran Confessions. It is well known that in the original redaction of the Nicene Creed from 325 CE the third article read, in its entirety, "And in the Holy Spirit." This brief phrase was expanded in the Nicene-Constantinopolitan Creed of 381 CE (our present-day Nicene Creed) to speak of the Spirit as the Lord and giver of life, proceeding from the Father (as distinct from the Son who is *begotten* of the Father), and who is properly worshipped just as the Father and the Son are. Perhaps because by this time the co-equality of the Father with the Son was no longer at issue, the church did not find it necessary to say here that the Holy Spirit is also "Light from Light, true God from true God, of one substance with the Father" (or the Son), though the writings of the Cappadocian Fathers show that this was understood to be the case.[30]

The Nicene Creed goes on to associate the Holy Spirit with the work of the church, and here the Lutheran reformers were in full agreement. In article 5 of the Augsburg Confession they assert that when the church is doing its job of communicating the gospel through Word and Sacrament (see also article 8), the Holy Spirit is able to do the Spirit's job of creating faith in those to whom the gospel is communicated. That faith, of course, is the crucial link for us to the salvation accomplished in Jesus. Faith is what connects the branches to the vine (John 15:1–8). The Trinity is good news because this saving faith, which lies at the heart of the Lutheran Reformation proposal, is *God's own work*, the work of God the Spirit.

The Holy Spirit, given to us in Baptism, joins us to Christ through faith—joins us to his death and also to his resurrection. Raised with him to new life, his Father becomes our Father, and we become children of God together with Christ our brother. This is no mere revelation. Through this means of grace God acts and *we are changed*.

---

30. See, for example, Basil of Caesarea. St. Basil the Great: *On the Holy Spirit* (Crestwood, NY: St. Vladimir's Seminary Press, 1997).

But as we have seen above, the Jesus Event has also *changed God*. The transcendent God is now tied to immanence and particularity, embedded in our reality, committed to our salvation. The triune God is thus forever connected to the Jesus Event, and to the particular promises that arise from it—the Spirit Event in which we as Christ's church are now engaged.

Rise, shine, you people! Christ the Lord has entered
our human story; God in him is centered.
He comes to us, by death and sin surrounded, with grace unbounded.[31]

---

31. Ronald A. Klug, "Rise, Shine, You People!" *Evangelical Lutheran Worship* (Minneapolis: Augsburg Fortress, 2006), Hymn 665.

5

Sin

Kathryn A. Kleinhans

The Confessors at Augsburg do not minimize the problem of sin. Rather, as Dr. Kathryn Kleinhans reminds us, they speak of sin as nothing less than rebellion against God, the desire we all have to trade places with God and to put ourselves rather than God at the center. This desire, in us by default, can result only in death for us. Kleinhans claims that it is the "hub" and its promise of forgiveness that allows the Confessors to acknowledge (in article 2) the full extent of our sinful state. It is only because of the death and resurrection of the very Son of God that we can acknowledge the nature of our sinfulness and its implications. Indeed, to minimize our sin would be to minimize the benefits we have from Christ.

Default Setting, or, "I Never Met a Sinner Who Was That Original"

In 1973, psychiatrist Karl Menninger's book *Whatever Became of Sin?* chronicled the redefinition and marginalization of the concept of sin in modern society. He concluded by challenging clergy to reassert their moral leadership by revitalizing this important but neglected doctrine. Alas, Menninger's plea has not been heeded. Even some clergy have joined with psychologists and biologists in explaining away "sin" as a characteristic of finitude and therefore not really as sin. In 1999, a debate within the pages of the Lutheran journal *dialog* focused on the question,

"Is sin an abusive doctrine?" The lead article by pastoral theologian Gary Pence provided a clear example of Menninger's lament. Pence proposed to replace the confession that "we are by nature sinful and unclean" with the statement that humans are "by nature limited and unfinished."[1]

But Menninger's experience as a psychiatrist led him to reject the human tendency to minimize the problem of sin. Doing away with the language of sin hardly results in the elimination of the feelings of guilt so common to Menninger's patients and to the human experience. And of course those engaged in the work of the criminal justice system know that guilt itself can be quite real even when feelings of guilt are absent.

In the fifth century, there was also an important theological debate about sin. The British monk Pelagius argued that humans have the ability to choose not to sin, although they do not exercise this ability. Augustine, Bishop of Hippo in North Africa, argued that humans were born sinful and did not have such an ability. Put simply, Pelagius thought it was (at least in theory) possible not to sin. Augustine countered that it was *not* possible not to sin. If it's not possible for us not to sin, sin is part of who we are; it is a dimension of our fallen human nature. For Pelagius, the possibility of not sinning was only a theoretical one; he did not believe that any human other than Jesus had actually never sinned. But against Augustine's understanding that humans are born sinful, Pelagius believed that human sin was a result of the sin-ridden environment humans are raised in and the fact that all our human role models (except for Jesus Christ) are sinners. In short, the debate between Augustine and Pelagius was a form of the age-old "nature vs. nurture" debate.

Augustine's view was approved by church leaders, and Pelagius's view was condemned. Augustine's view that sin is part of fallen human nature is known as the doctrine of original sin. The phrase "original sin" points back to the very first sin committed in the Garden of Eden (Genesis 3). Because original sin affects all human beings (except for Jesus Christ), it is sometimes referred to as "the hereditary sin of Adam." Unfortunately, Augustine's particular understanding of the mechanism by which original sin affects the rest of humanity is unsophisticated. In his view, original sin was transmitted through the act of sexual intercourse leading to conception.

This view of original sin as a biological inheritance has long been criticized because it focuses on sex as the primary mechanism of sin. The theory of evolution also posed a challenge to the claim that original sin is transmitted through sexual reproduction. Evolutionary science

1. Gary Pence, "Sin: An Abusive Doctrine?" and "Response to My Responders," *dialog* 38, no. 4 (Fall 1999): 294, 303.

calls into question and undermines the claim that all humans are the biological descendants of one first couple. However, these critiques are best understood as criticisms of a particular explanation of original sin. The concept of original sin itself does not depend on biological transmission or on being the result of a historical event; the claim is descriptive rather than explanatory. To the extent that it is helpful to use language like "hereditary sin of Adam," it may be more appropriate to think of this as a legal inheritance rather than a genetic inheritance.

Later theologians made a distinction between original sin and actual sins. As the name suggests, actual sins are actions, the sinful deeds a person does. Medieval Catholic theology described original sin as the loss of the original righteousness with which Adam and Eve were created and which their descendants were intended to share. Because this lack was thought to be remedied by baptism, much of the focus of Christian life in the Middle Ages was placed on actual sins. The penitential system of confession followed by prescribed deeds of penance was developed as a remedy for the consequences of actual sins.

When we talk about sin (if we do), the focus is often on particular deeds, actual sins. Is this a sin? Is that a sin? Is this a bigger sin than that? Are some sins worse than others? Those are not unimportant questions, particularly with regard to the effects our sins have on our relationships with others. (For example, Jesus says in Matt. 5:28 that "everyone who looks at a woman with lust has already committed adultery with her in his heart"; but despite Jesus' raising the bar on our sinful attitudes, most married couples would consider the physical act of adultery to be a worse offense than a lustful look.) Questions about the relative severity of actual sins, however, can distract us from the more fundamental point. The root problem for Martin Luther and the Lutheran Confessions is sin, singular, not sins, plural.

The word "original" in the phrase original sin has two meanings for us, even apart from its association with the biblical stories of creation and fall. "Original" sin does not mean a sin that's particularly creative. The first sense in which original sin is original is that it is there already *at my origin*, from my very beginning. As the psalmist says, "Indeed, I was born guilty, a sinner when my mother conceived me" (Ps. 51:5). The second sense is causal: original sin is *the origin of my sinful deeds*. In other words (and despite popular opinion to the contrary), I'm not a sinner because I do sinful things. I do sinful things because I'm a sinner. With apologies to Shakespeare, "To sin or not to sin: that is not the question!" We do not start out as morally and religiously neutral, able to avoid sin if we so choose.

In the language of the liturgy, "I confess that I am captive to sin and cannot free myself." This is not religious hyperbole. In Twelve Step programs for recovery from addiction, the first step is to admit one's fundamental powerlessness over one's addiction. The addict recognizes that his or her problem is not just a problem of behavior; it is a problem of identity, of who one is. One often hears, "I'm not an alcoholic because I drink; I drink because I'm an alcoholic." That is why it is customary for introductions at Twelve Step meetings to take the form, "Hi, my name is ____, and I'm an alcoholic (or other type of addict)." Not to acknowledge one's identity as an addict is to keep the behavior at arm's length from one's inmost self and to project a measure of control that is simply not the case.

The way I explain the doctrine of original sin to my students is to talk about the default settings on a computer. Whatever version of whatever program you're using, it comes with certain features already set in place. Those default settings are there at its origin. And because those default settings are in place, the computer behaves in certain ways. The user, who sits outside the system, can change some of those default settings, but the computer cannot change itself. In the case of original sin, alas, we are more like the computer than the user. Original sin is our default setting, which we do not have the ability to change from within.

Let's move from the singular to the plural: "We confess that we are captive to sin and cannot free ourselves." We original sinners, with our default settings, are *networked, part of a system of sinners*. The system reinforces itself. In that sense, Pelagius was on to something. Our social environment and our human role models do have the effect of compounding human sin, in ourselves and others. Sinful nurture reinforces sinful nature. But the networking is not the cause of the sin, which is already a part of the component units (us!). Regardless of whether one thinks of the Fall as a historical event, the doctrine of original sin points to a givenness of sin in human experience; humans simply do not have access to a pure, sinless state of existence.

Martin Luther's explanation of the first article of the Apostles' Creed in the Small Catechism provides additional insight into the problem that afflicts us. Luther explains the confession that God is creator by personalizing it: "I believe that God has created me together with all that exists. God has given me and still preserves my body and soul: eyes, ears, and all limbs and senses; reason and all mental faculties. In addition, God daily and abundantly provides . . . all the necessities and nourishment for this body and life. . . . For all of this I owe it to God to thank and praise, serve and obey him."[2]

2. *BoC*, 354–55.

The verb "owe" (*Schuldig sein* in Luther's German) clearly implies a debt. I am indebted to God. Everything I am and have is from God. My obligation as a human creature is to thank and praise, serve and obey my Creator, with my whole self, for my whole life. But it is impossible for me to pay off this debt. From the moment I draw my first breath, I am always already behind on my obligation. The debt language helpfully reminds us that the guilt of sin is real, legal obligation, independent of whether or not we feel guilty.

Luther's explanation to the Ten Commandments furthers this understanding. The "shalts" and the "shalt nots" are not simply a ten-item task list. It is customary to divide the commandments into two "tables," the first table consisting of those commandments concerning our relationship with God and the second table consisting of those commandments concerning our relationship with others. This may be useful, but is not entirely accurate. Luther's explanation to each of the commandments is grounded in our relationship with God: "we are to fear, love, and trust God so that" we act in accordance with God's commandments. Even those debts that we owe to others (not to steal, not to kill, etc.) are grounded in the primary debt we owe to God as Creator—Creator of us and Creator of all the others with whom we are related.

Deadly Diagnosis, or, "We're Not Getting Out of Here Alive!"

For Luther, as we have seen, keeping the Ten Commandments is grounded in the fear, love, and trust of God. But this is the problem. The Lutheran Confessions insist that we are unable by nature to fear, love, and trust God. Article 2 of the Augsburg Confession defines original sin as being without fear of God, without trust in God, and with concupiscence. Concupiscence is a technical term often defined as lust, particularly sexual lust, but that is too limited an understanding. "Concupiscence" literally means "with desire," and there are many possible objects of our desire. The Confessions use the term to describe an innate human tendency to sin. Particular objects of desire and particular sinful actions are overshadowed by the inescapable fact of the self's desire, regardless of what it is that we desire. Just as water's natural tendency is to run down an inclined slope because of gravity, so our natural tendency is to follow our own inclinations because of original sin.

It is commonly said that nature abhors a vacuum. In the absence of the fear, love, and trust in God for which we are intended, our own desires fill the gap, displacing God as our rightful center. In the words of the

Apology of the Augsburg Confession, "For our weak nature, because it cannot fear, love, or believe in God, seeks and loves carnal things."[3] We are created for right relationship with God. In the absence of that right relationship, we attempt to satisfy our longings with lesser things. We attempt to fill—or become—the center.

The 1967 film *Bedazzled* offers a vivid image of original sin as the temptation to replace God with something else, namely, "ourselves." Dudley Moore's character asks Lucifer (played by Peter Cook) how it was that he fell from heaven, having been one of God's angels. Peter Cook illustrates by sitting atop a postal collection box pretending to be God. He invites Dudley Moore to dance around his makeshift throne singing his praises. After a short time, Moore says, "I'm getting a bit bored with this. Can't we change places?" Lucifer replies, "That's exactly how I felt! I only wanted to be like him." Bingo. The desire to trade places with God, to put ourselves rather than God at the center, is the textbook illustration of original sin. It is how Genesis 3 describes the "original" original sin, the sin of Adam and Eve. Their fundamental disobedience was not simply eating the fruit from the tree of the knowledge of good and evil, but giving in to the temptation to become like God.

Feminist theologians have criticized this image of self-centeredness as the primal human sin. For many women, it is argued, the problem is not pride but self-denial. Women in many cultures are socialized to put their own needs aside, putting their husbands and/or children at the center of their lives. For women, then, self-effacement and self-deprecation, rather than self-centeredness, may be the most typical form of sin.

An insight from Augustine's theology offers a way of encompassing both of these forms of sin. Starting from the premise that God is to be loved above all things, Augustine describes sin as disordered love. We are created to love God wholly. We are to relate to everything else in a derivative way, in light of God. From an Augustinian perspective, while the form of the problem as it is construed by traditionalist theologians and feminist theologians may differ, the root problem is still disordered love. Whether I put myself at the center of my universe, or whether I put someone else at the center of my universe, God is still displaced. This is a double problem. When our loves are disordered, we fail to love God as God should be loved, and we also fail to love ourselves and our neighbors appropriately, whether too much or too little.

Whether I am too self-centered or too self-effacing, this is a double-bind from which I cannot escape. Once out of order, I cannot straighten myself out any more than an out-of-order machine can fix itself. I am in

---

3. *BoC*, 115:24.

bondage to sin, and the more I struggle against these bonds, the tighter they become. The Confessions refer to this bondage as both "an abiding deficiency in an unregenerate nature" and "a disease."[4] To continue with this medical metaphor, we might say that our sinful actions are only symptoms of the deeper disease that is original sin. Treating the symptoms may provide short-term relief but doesn't touch the root cause of the problem. An accurate diagnosis is necessary.

Alas, in the case of sin, the disease is terminal.

In the Large Catechism, Luther begins his explanation to the first commandment by describing what it means to have a god. It is not our religious words but our hearts that reveal who or what we worship. What we rely on as the ultimate source of good in our lives is, functionally speaking, our god. Luther names money, possessions, power, fame, and even family as things to which we pay god-like attention and which we give god-like power over us. For Luther, the difference between the true God and these false gods is that only the true God will never fail us. The true God created us and provides for us, and it is this God who promises mercy to sinners. When we confuse penultimate things with the Creator, we are entrusting our lives into the wrong hands. Our problem is not only that our idols cannot save us, but also that our trust in them puts us under indictment for our failure to keep the first commandment.

As we noted earlier in the chapter, this disordered idolatry has both individual and corporate dimensions. Original sin is a description of the fallen human condition, not just of an individual. We are born into and live our entire lives within dysfunctional systems. These systems are disordered by putting our fear, love, and trust in penultimate things. We worship all kinds of ideologies and -isms, not just as independent individuals but as members of groups. Whether a society stakes its future on capitalism or communism, an economic system still replaces God as the focus of our trust. Whether we put our faith in scientific progress or in military power, neither of these things can save us. They certainly cannot save us from ourselves.

A Wartburg College senior once began a chapel message by commenting on the symbolism found within the chapel. He walked through the chancel, pointing out the cross, the candles, the missal-stand in the shape of two stone tablets. Finally he arrived in the balcony under a red "Exit" sign, where he pointed out something that none of the rest of us had noticed: there is no exit by that sign! "What could it mean?" he asked, as he pounded the walls around the sign, listening for hollow spaces and feeling for secret openings, all to no avail. His conclusion: the

4. *BoC*, 116:31 and 113:6.

"Exit" sign where there is no exit is also a symbol—a symbol of sin—a symbol of all the things that seem to promise us a way out but in reality offer nothing but a dead end. The problem of sin is not simply that there is no exit. No, the problem of sin is the relentless human tendency to fling ourselves, time and again, into that solid wall, stubbornly believing we can find, or make, a way out for ourselves. But there is no exit. Trying to find, or make, our own way out, for Luther, leads only in one of two possible directions: pride or despair. In either case, the road leads to the death of the sinner.

Congruence, or "I've Got Some Bad News and Some Good News"

Martin Franzmann's hymn, "O God, O Lord of Heaven and Earth," provides a powerful image of sin as a God-sized problem that requires a God-sized solution:

> We walled us in this house of doom, where death had royal scope and room,
> Until your servant, Prince of Peace, broke down its walls for our release.

> You came into our hall of death, O Christ, to breathe our poisoned air,
> To drink for us the deep despair that strangled our reluctant breath.[5]

A deadly situation, like a deadly disease, requires a total all-out response. The size and scope of the problem and the size and scope of the solution must be congruent, to use a mathematical term. The term "congruent" refers to figures that are the same in size and shape: same lengths, same angles, etc. In other words, the problem and the solution must match.

The discussion of sin in the second article of the Apology of the Augsburg Confession makes clear and repeated use of comparative terms. The Apology criticizes those who "minimize" (in the Tappert translation) or "trivialize" (in the Kolb and Wengert translation) the problem of sin. The Confessors' concern is that those who minimize the problem of sin also minimize the benefits we have from Christ: "Knowledge of original sin is a necessity. For we cannot know the magnitude of Christ's glory unless we recognize our sin."[6] The terms "minimize" and "magnify" connote congruence between the doctrines of sin and redemption. If sin is only a small problem, we only need a small Savior. If, however, we receive salvation only through the death and resurrection of the very Son of God, sin must be a big problem indeed.

The Exultet sung at the Easter Vigil—a liturgy highlighting baptism

---

5. Martin Franzmann, "O God, O Lord, of Heaven and Earth," *Lutheran Book of Worship* (Minneapolis: Augsburg, 1978), Hymn 396.
6. *BoC*, 117:33.

into the death and resurrection of Christ—expresses the magnitude of both problem and solution well:

O happy fault, O necessary sin of Adam,
which gained for us so great a Redeemer!

The point is not that we rejoice in our sinfulness as such. The point, rather, is that we can't admit the full extent of our sinful state until we have first heard the promise of forgiveness, of God's all-encompassing grace. The Exultet looks back from the perspective of faith. Without the promise of grace and new life, the deadly diagnosis would be too much to bear.

In *The Freedom of a Christian*, Luther describes this congruence as a "happy exchange" between Christ and the believer.

Because faith unites the believer with Christ as intimately as bride and groom are joined in marriage, . . . it follows that everything they have they hold in common, the good as well as the evil. Accordingly the believing soul can boast of and glory in whatever Christ has as though it were its own, and whatever the soul has Christ claims as his own. Let us compare these and we shall see inestimable benefits. Christ is full of grace, life, and salvation. The soul is full of sins, death, and damnation. Now let faith come between them and sins, death, and damnation will be Christ's, while grace, life, and salvation will be the soul's; for if Christ is a bridegroom, he must take upon himself the things which are his bride's and bestow upon her the things that are his. If he gives her his body and very self, how shall he not give her all that is his? And if he takes the body of the bride, how shall he not take all that is hers?[7]

The problem—ours—is congruent with the solution—the grace, life, and salvation that we receive through faith in Christ.

Christ's death and resurrection for our sake is the definitive evidence of the scope of the problem of human sin. If our sinful condition were not deadly, if the diagnosis were not terminal, if the main problem were simply dealing with the consequences of our sinful actions, then the death of Christ would be quite literally overkill. Indeed, some theologians have criticized the cross as a theology of divine child abuse: the Father is only satisfied by inflicting punishment and death on the Son. But the cross is no sadistic whim. If our redemption could have been accomplished another way, if sin could have been cured by any other treatment plan, would not a wise and loving physician have done so?! Read backwards, from the perspective of faith, the death and resurrection of Christ witness that no other solution to the problem of human sin was possible.

7. *LW* 31:351.

We see this in the Synoptic Gospels in the accounts of Jesus' passion predictions. When Jesus talks about his impending suffering and death, the disciples don't understand. Peter rejects the path that Jesus lays out. But Jesus insists, three times in each of the Synoptic Gospels, that it is necessary for him to suffer, be killed, and be raised from the dead; no other understanding of Messiah or Savior will do. Jesus' language of necessity underscores the extent and the deadly seriousness of the problem of human sin, which he freely chooses to take on for our sake.

Simul Iustus et Peccator, or, "There Are Two Kinds of People in the World"

Christ's taking our sin and death upon himself does not offer an immediate fix, however. *Simul iustus et peccator* is a Latin phrase that means "simultaneously righteous and sinner." This is how Luther describes the condition of Christians. Some theologians have mistakenly said that *simul iustus et peccator* is how Luther describes the human condition, but this is a misunderstanding. For Luther this is a description of *Christian persons*, not of all persons. In and of ourselves, by nature, we remain sinners. Only when we are joined to Christ in faith, by grace, are we declared righteous and made righteous through the work of the Holy Spirit.

For Luther, there are two kinds of people in the world, but the line he draws is not between sinners and saints. All are sinners. All remain sinners until their death. For Luther, the two kinds of people in the world are all sinners; but those without faith are sinners under divine judgment (the default setting) while those with faith are *forgiven sinners* (for whom God in Christ overrides the default setting). Forgiven sinners have a dual, simultaneous identity: in themselves, they remain sinners; in Christ, they are considered righteous. It's not that original sin has been eradicated but rather that the sinner is now clothed with the righteousness of Christ. To use the language of addiction therapy, in which recovery is understood not in terms of cure but of living with and in spite of the diagnosis, the Christian is never a "former sinner" but always a "recovering sinner," and the recovery period is lifelong.

There is a powerful realism here. The cancer that is sin has metastasized and cannot be surgically removed without killing the patient. The patient, while he or she lives, remains on permanent life support, with the life-giving blood of Christ being constantly pumped through his or her system. Forgiveness is a gift, but the gift is inseparable from the giver. Grace is not a transaction applied piecemeal to our account. I do not become "less sinner" and "more saint" in some quantifiable sense. In and of myself, I am entirely sinful. Joined with Christ, I am entirely made right with God. My sinful self, which the Lutheran Confessions refer to as the Old Adam, dies only when I die; but joined with Christ, I receive new resurrected life.

Many people are critical of the church because it's "full of hypocrites." The church is certainly full of sinners, but not necessarily hypocrites. Hypocrites are people who pretend to be something they're not. When we admit our sinfulness, we cease to be hypocrites. Confessing that we are captive to sin and cannot free ourselves is congruent with our confession of faith that God in Christ is the one who frees us from our captivity.

To confess is to acknowledge or admit. In Greek, the word is *homologein*, which literally means "to say the same thing as." In Christian usage, confession has two regular forms: we confess our sins, and we confess our faith. In both cases, we are saying of ourselves what God has first said. We confess that we are captive to sin and cannot free ourselves, not because we are masochistic or depressed but because we acknowledge God's word of judgment. When we confess our faith, we are also acknowledging God's word, the word of promised mercy.

Interestingly enough, Luther himself recommends the practice of individual confession, although it is not much practiced by Lutherans today. He values confession for the sake of absolution: hearing the words of forgiveness. In the Catholic Church of Luther's day, confession was mandatory: a complete oral confession of all one's sins must be made to a priest at least once a year. Luther made the practice voluntary; said that it could be made to any Christian; and encouraged Christians to confess the sins they felt most burdened by. Of course God forgives sin, and one can confess privately in one's own heart. The purpose of oral confession to another person, for Luther, is that one might hear the words of mercy spoken audibly. It is for this reason that Luther's recommended liturgy for individual confession asks the penitent, "Do you believe that the words of forgiveness I speak to you are from God?" The point of this question is not to affirm the authority of the confessor[8] as an individual, but rather to recognize that the confessor serves as God's vehicle for speaking God's word of mercy.

---

8. Editor's note: "Confessor" here refers to the one to whom confession is made.

Sin Boldly!

In 1521, Martin Luther wrote these words in a letter to his colleague Philip Melanchthon:

> If you are a preacher of grace, then preach a true and not a fictitious grace; if grace is true, you must bear a true and not a fictitious sin. God does not save people who are only fictitious sinners. Be a sinner and sin boldly, but believe and rejoice in Christ even more boldly, for he is victorious over sin, death, and the world. . . . Do you think that the purchase price that was paid for the redemption of our sins by so great a Lamb is too small? Pray boldly—you, too, are a mighty sinner.[9]

Sometimes when people hear the phrase "Sin boldly" attributed to Luther, they assume that it is sarcasm or a joke. On the surface, it sounds like a clear contradiction of St. Paul, who wrote, "Should we continue in sin in order that grace may abound? By no means!" (Rom. 6:1–2). But Luther clearly meant something else. He was aware that sometimes we can be paralyzed by the fear of making a bad choice or taking the wrong step. An old Far Side cartoon illustrates the dilemma perfectly. A man stands in hell, surrounded by flames, looking at two doors. One door is labeled "Damned if you do." The other door is labeled "Damned if you don't." A devil stands behind the man with a pitchfork at his back, saying, "C'mon, c'mon, choose!"

In such a context, Luther's advice—"sin boldly, but believe and rejoice in Christ even more boldly, for he is victorious over sin, death, and the world"—offers reassurance. It's okay to choose. Even when no available option is without sin, "there is therefore now no condemnation for those who are in Christ Jesus" (Rom. 8:1). We are not "Damned if you do, damned if you don't" sinners. We are forgiven sinners.

Twentieth-century German Lutheran theologian Dietrich Bonhoeffer also knew this to be true. In his *Ethics*, Bonhoeffer argues that acting responsibly involves the "willingness to become guilty." Like Luther, Bonhoeffer does not assume a position of innocence or even a position of neutrality from which one chooses innocence or guilt. Bonhoeffer's point, rather, is that trying to avoid guilt can be a form of self-justification that distances us from divine grace. According to Bonhoeffer, "Those who, in acting responsibly, seek to avoid becoming guilty divorce themselves from the ultimate reality of human existence; but in so doing they also divorce themselves from the redeeming mystery of the sinless bearing of guilt by Jesus Christ, and have no part in the divine justification that attends this event."[10] As Luther framed it

---

9. *LW* 48:281.

centuries earlier, Christ died for real sinners, not for fictitious sinners. As Jesus himself put it even earlier, "Those who are well have no need of a physician, but those who are sick; I have come to call not the righteous but sinners."[11]

This is no cheap grace. Bonhoeffer's "willingness to become guilty," like Luther's "Sin boldly," is not an excuse for sinning. What we do matters. It matters to God, and it matters to others. But it does not matter ultimately. God in Christ is in the business of saving sinners.

10. Dietrich Bonhoeffer, *Ethics*, Dietrich Bonhoeffer Works, Volume 6 (Minneapolis: Fortress Press, 2005), 276.
11. Mark 2:17.

6

Church, Ministry, and the Main Thing

Marcus Felde

Pastor Marcus Felde discusses the Augsburg Confession's claim that the ministry of the church is the ministry of the gospel—and nothing else. Using examples from parish ministry, with regard to marriage in particular, Felde illustrates the Confessors' point in articles 5 and 7. God instituted the office of preaching, giving the gospel and sacraments so that we could receive the promise God makes to us in Jesus the Christ. What a gift from God! What a gift that the Confessors articulate the connection between the promise, the office of preaching, and the ministry of the church!

"In combat, the main thing is to keep the main thing the main thing. Otherwise, you die."

At least, so I hear. I have never been a soldier. But I would like to borrow the maxim and apply it to church and ministry. In church and ministry, the main thing is to keep the main thing the main thing. Otherwise, people do not receive life. At least, not what Jesus called "life."

Chapter 1 of this volume is titled "Preach One Thing: The Wisdom of the Cross." This chapter will expand on that advice by commenting on what the Augsburg Confessions teach about the nature of church and ministry in articles 5 and 7.

Article 5 of the Augsburg Confession ("Concerning the Office of Preaching") flows seamlessly from article 4 ("Concerning Justification").[1]

Melanchthon had just finished defining the faith-instilling work of the gospel when he wrote:

> To obtain such faith God instituted the office of preaching, giving the gospel and the sacraments. Through these, as through means, he gives the Holy Spirit who produces faith, where and when he wills, in those who hear the gospel. It teaches that we have a gracious God, not through our merit but through Christ's merit, when we so believe.[2]

By gospel he meant what he had been talking about in article 4—that

> . . . we receive forgiveness of sin and become righteous before God out of grace for Christ's sake through faith when we believe that Christ has suffered for us and that for his sake our sin is forgiven and righteousness and eternal life are given to us.[3]

Going ahead to article 7 ("Concerning the Church"), we ought to be clear what the AC means when it declares that "[the holy, Christian church] is the assembly of all believers among whom the gospel is purely preached and the holy sacraments are administered according to the gospel."[4]

What I want to argue and illustrate (with reference to doing weddings) is that those quotes from the Augsburg Confession are as true and crucial as ever. They are not just sentimental old shibboleths of a debilitated denominational or ethnic tradition. They express a focused and empowering view of what it means to be *church*, and to be *ministers* of the church for the sake of the world. Articles 5 and 7 set forth the gospel—in clear contradistinction from the law of God—as that which the church has been given so that it might give life to the world.

Those brief articles from the Augsburg Confession are not stating the obvious. It is not easy for the church and her ministers to live according to their teaching. But when the church and its ministers *seem* to be doing *much more* than preaching the gospel, the truth might just be that we are accomplishing less than we are meant to do. When we talk a lot about other topics, the *main thing* easily gets lost, to the detriment of God's life-giving work in Christ. We become those who say "Peace, peace," when there is no peace.

Simply to distinguish law and gospel from one another—that elementary art that the confessions hold up as foundational to theology—is not enough. For those of us who have been trained to distinguish one word of God from the other, the easiest mistake might

---

1. Subsequent editors, meaning to be helpful, divided the Augsburg Confession into numbered articles, which had the unfortunate consequence of concealing this vital segue.
2. *BoC*, 40.
3. *BoC*, 38f.
4. *BoC*, 42.

be to act as though the church has similar authority to speak both of those words from God. As though we separate the two words just to divide our task into two parts. But article 5 does *not* say

> to make the world better God instituted the office of preaching, giving the *law and* gospel and the sacraments through which the minister can comfort the afflicted *and afflict the comfortable*, and present a vision of how society *ought to be, coaxing and wheedling and guilting and inspiring people into better participation in God's clear will.*

Furthermore, article 7 does *not* say

> The holy, Christian church is the assembly of all willing listeners among whom the *law and* the gospel are preached and the holy sacraments are administered according to the *law and* the gospel, i.e., the word of God.

Nor does it read like this:

> The holy, Christian church is the assembly of all willing listeners among whom, *among other things*, the gospel is preached. . . .

No, the church is the church *of the gospel, pure and simple.* Ministers of the church are ministers *of the gospel.* The law of God is not one half of our responsibility and charge. The law of God is (*let there be no mistake*—for I anticipate that I shall be accused of denying this!)—the law of God is indeed God's characterization of the hopeless situation into the midst of which is plunked this "other" Word, the gospel.

Sadly, our society understands "to preach" as "to tell people what to do." That is not gospel but law. But as Dr. Frederick Danker tirelessly pointed out, both of the Greek words in the New Testament that get translated "preach" actually denote speaking the gospel. One of those words is *euangelizomai*, "to evangelize"; the other is *kerysso*, "to herald or proclaim."

Yes, we often repeat that God's word is both law and gospel, and we are careful to distinguish them from each other and give each its due. And we clearly state that the law is indeed from God. However, there should be no doubt in the world's mind or in the congregation's mind—when it receives our preaching and other ministry—that pride of place belongs to the gospel, which is always about what *God* has done and given, never about what *we* do. Without this clarity, we "get killed," you might even say. Even having a denominational slogan like "God's Work. Our Hands," can be misleading, since it seems to blur the distinction between the saving work of God (which according to the gospel is what God does in Christ) and the things we do as a result of that work being accomplished in us.

I am a minister of the gospel. I am not a minister "of *the law and* the gospel." I am a minister "of the gospel." The congregation in which I have the joy to be ministering with the Word and sacraments is a community that belongs to the gospel. Our building is home to the gospel. Which does not mean the law has no place among us. But law is used in this place to bring people to the gospel which brings us to faith. We do not use the law to improve people's behavior, no matter how bad that behavior is. Because the church does not exist to bring people up to snuff, but to bring us up to God.

I am a minister of the gospel. Which is why I regularly stand in front of my congregation and say:

> In the mercy of almighty God, Jesus Christ was given to die for us, and for his sake God forgives us all our sins. *As a called and ordained minister of the church of Christ*, and by his authority, I therefore declare to you the entire forgiveness of all your sins, in the name of the Father, and of the Son, and of the Holy Spirit. Amen.

I never announce a corresponding word of law—although I know God's law, and stand in fear of it. I do not say:

> As a called and ordained minister of the Word of God, and by the authority of Christ [or of God], I declare to you the sinfulness of your actions, and I call you to account for them. I warn you in his name, *because of the office I hold and because you have called me to tell you the whole truth about God*, that you had better shape up in this or that way.

Nor do I even say something more "positive" but still in the nature of law, like this:

> By virtue of my calling and ordination, I lift up before you the following inspiring vision of how much better the world will be, and how much better you will feel, if you will conform your lives to the Golden Rule and live out the law of love.

No, my calling is singular. Singularly evangelical.

Some may dismiss what I have said so far, thinking that my view reflects mission shrinkage. "Are we not also called to be prophetic?" some will ask. Yes, I would answer, except that if our prophesying detaches itself from and no longer serves our gospel ministry, it loses the specific authority the church has because it bears the name of Jesus. The world is in desperate need of reforms of every sort—as I write, the Middle East is in violent turmoil. But we must not allow our impatience to make everything better in concrete, specific ways that obscure the peculiar way in which God's forgiveness makes things right by instilling hope and faith and love. If we doubt the value or effectiveness of God's grace in

Jesus Christ, of course, we will find something else to do to make the institutional church useful. We will give people things to do. Set out hurdles. Establish guidelines for conduct. Any substitute mission will do. But my experience has convinced me that our true mission is more likely to shrink than expand, when we offer palliative care to the world instead of the gospel itself.

What We Talk about When We Talk about Gospel

What should we talk about in church, to be faithful to our task as defined in the Augsburg Confession? Let me give a couple negative examples.

Several years ago I was in a workshop led by a church leader who was teaching about the difference between law and gospel. The gospel, he said, is *that we should love one another*. The gospel, he said, is not a bunch of rules. Christians live under the gospel, under the law of love, not under that other law. (I am sure I am not doing justice to the entire presentation, but that was the gist of it.)

More recently, I read an open letter from a bishop who suggestively asked, "Is the earth-born reality of daily life a means of grace? Is it possible that God offers healing and forgiveness, hope, and promise in the world as energetically as God offers these gifts in Baptism and Holy Communion? Do you think of your life as a sacrament—a means of grace—for others?"

Well, no, I don't. I remember a mentor many years ago saying that we are called "to accept the atonement, not to repeat it." While I am happy to share the good news about Christ with others, I don't think my life quite rises to the level of a sacrament. And without dismissing the idea of helping others, I think it is unwise to think we can just look around and, wherever we see good things happening, say "There is the gospel!"

But confusion on this order of magnitude is nothing new. Francis of Assisi is supposed to have said (but did not say), "Preach the gospel every day. If necessary, use words." (He did not actually say that—sorry, google it.) Many people cite this aphorism to substantiate their opinion that the good we do for others equates to the gospel. But it does not. Rather, it is the fruit of the gospel working in our lives.

What we mean by "the gospel" is made fairly clear, I think, in the first few chapters of this book. My task here is not to explain that over again but to propose that, in the course of our ministry and in the course of the church's life, it is essential to be clear what we mean by "the gospel" if it is to be the main thing in both church and ministry.

We do that first of all by distinguishing the gospel from the law. How? The simplest rule of thumb is probably to ask whether we are pointing to ourselves or to Christ. When we are pointing to ourselves—what we must do, what we shouldn't have done, what we must not touch, how we are to feel, what we ought to think—we are talking about the law. When we proclaim the gospel, on the other hand, we will be talking about what God has done in Christ—his life, death, resurrection, and the giving of his Spirit.

When a minister is always talking to people about what *they have done* or what *they should do*, or what *they are called to do*, and when a church (for example, in its house organ) constantly trumpets the good some people do or deplores the evil deeds of others, then the minister and the church will be seen as ministers of law. Perhaps law that is from God (for example, not to kill), but sometimes just the agenda of the minister or of the church (for example, to support a bill in Congress).

When the law is discussed, taught, promulgated, or encouraged in such a way that it is meant to provide people with the means to be good people who live good lives, then a righteousness is being promoted that is other than the righteousness promoted by the gospel. For, as Luther said in the quote Edward Schroeder cites in the first chapter, the law's righteousness is a different thing from the gospel's righteousness.

A Case in Point: Marriage Preparation

Let me tell you how this distinction has made a difference in one area of my ministry as a called and ordained servant of the Word.

Like most ministers, I often have the opportunity to officiate at weddings. When I returned from seven years as a missionary in Papua New Guinea to serve for the first time in an American parish, I sought to pick up the best practices I could. Among other things, I took a workshop on how to prepare a couple for marriage. I learned how to administer an instrument ("Not a test!") to a couple so that I could help guide them through the important transition to life as a married couple.

I required such preparation by every couple seeking to be married in my church. I set up times to administer the instrument, administered it, and sent it off to be processed by a computer. Then I guided the couple through the resulting (very helpful!) printouts in a series of meetings.

It was always interesting. Many of the people I worked with in this way found our time together very helpful, even important. I don't remember anyone getting angry with me or resenting the process, at least that I could tell. And I really think it is a great idea, in and of itself! Young people make a lot of mistakes at that crucial point in their lives, and it would be wonderful if we could head off some of those problems by getting people to talk, and to examine themselves and each other through a wisdom-lens. No problem there.

After a few years in the parish, I went to graduate school and then spent another seven years in Papua New Guinea. I returned to the parish and resumed my earlier practice of firmly insisting that "premarital counseling" was a prerequisite to a wedding in church.

But I became less sure about whether that was the right thing to do. It came to a head for me when it was reported to me that a wonderful young person was heard telling someone that they had "flunked" the "test" I had given them.

I had taken care not to call it a test; in fact, I had insisted it was not. I had assured them that the results would simply show up areas in which they could "grow." Despite my interpretation of what we were doing, from their perspective the areas of growth amounted to criticisms, no matter how I tried to finesse it.

And they were right. But they were wrong. Or, rather, I was wrong. Probably for the rest of their lives, they would remember my (unintentionally) stigmatizing their relationship, at the very moment when they were hoping for a blessing from the church and from God. I had conveyed to them that they were not as compatible as some couples, or not as ready as they should be, or in need of improvement. Perhaps their marriage was not "made in heaven"?

No other minister of the gospel would ever again have the same opportunity I had enjoyed to sit with a couple at this key moment in their life and talk about God. Church. Gospel. Life. Joy. But instead of my leaving them with a clear impression that the church was about the gospel—and the minister was a minister of the gospel—I had given them the impression that my job was to protect society by preventing, if possible, all those sad things that can happen if a marriage is not just right.

I do not doubt that they, *and every single couple ever to marry*, stood and stand in the need of greater wisdom than they already have. "Get wisdom," Proverbs tells us. "Get insight." Absolutely. We need more. Read *Family Circle*. Talk to your mom and dad. Ask friends who are already married. Watch movies. Read good fiction! Even, go to a counselor if you feel up to it. Get wisdom.

But at church?

When the people asked of Jesus, "Where did this man get this wisdom?" (Matt. 15:34; compare Mark 6:2), I seriously doubt he had been sharing wisdom the way James Dobson does in his popular book *Life on the Edge*.[5] Or like Ellen Fein in *The Rules*, or her other books on dating.[6] The peculiar "wisdom" of Jesus always disturbed the best people by giving hope to the worst. That wisdom was, in form and content, different from the rules of nation and temple. It bestowed the blessings of peace, not upon achievers but upon those who believed.

So, who was I to "sit in judgment" upon those young people? I was a minister *of the gospel*, for crying out loud. I had tried to bring some gospel into our meetings, but I had been talking with my mouth full of other topics like how to reconcile differing holiday traditions and whether to share a checkbook.

I am familiar with the common rationale for clergy involvement in marriage preparation. Hey! What a unique opportunity! You can catch them and hold them, because you can hold over them the (implicit) threat that they might not be able to have their wedding at your lovely church!

But what place does threat have in church?

Plus, studies show that marriages preceded by such preparation are statistically more likely to succeed!

Succeed? What is success in marriage? Didn't Jesus, by saying that "Whoever looks at a woman to lust after has committed adultery with her in his heart,"[7] indict universally all husbands as failures?

A pastor who was my classmate in seminary once boasted to me that none of the people he had prepared for marriage had yet been divorced. Of course, that was over thirty years ago. I should check how that's going.

As much as any pastor, I wanted to be a successful minister. But, rationalize as I might, I felt that the insistence on such premarital sessions as standard operating procedure amounted to a breach of covenant. People were coming to church and leaving with the wrong takeaway. As I have matured, I am even more convinced of this. I think that too close an identification of the church's mission with setting a certain standard or "high bar" for personal life or family life risks losing both the gospel and the law.

We can lose the law, because moralism always employs a watered-down version of the law. We become insufficiently critical, like all hypocrites. And we lose the gospel, because it is not necessary when people are convinced, as a side effect of our moralism, that they can be good enough without it.

What is the truth about marriage? The high-bar truth about marriage, when we look into God's law, has to do with faith. Luther's Small Catechism shows us that all Ten Commandments—and, by extension,

5. James Dobson, *Life on the Edge: The Next Generation's Guide to a Meaningful Future* (Nashville: W Publishing Group, 1995).
6. Ellen Fein and Sherry Schneider, *The Rules: Time Tested Secrets for Capturing the Heart of Mr. Right* (New York: Warner Books, 1995).
7. Matt. 5:28.

all the commands of God—are elaborations of one law: that we should fear, love, and trust in God above all things; and that we should love our neighbor as ourselves. That is also the law about marriage—that husband and wife should love and serve one another totally and freely, out of love for God. That "high bar" is one none of us measures up to. Don't tell me being married for fifty years means people have satisfied the commandment about adultery. That is no equivalent to loving God—and letting that love of God work itself out in your courtship and marriage, every day. God asks so much of us married people, that none of us should be proud of our marriage.

When, in discussing marriage, we talk about how to show respect, what kind of habits help love grow, "best practices," and such—we dumb down the law of God. Which is not to say such things are not necessary and good—only that they are not the fullness of what God has to tell us about marriage. So when we settle for sharing relationship maxims, we are giving up the opportunity to bring the gospel into the picture.

Again, what is the truth about marriages? I am lucky enough to be a part of a wonderful marriage, but I can be a quarrelsome person, and no one knows this better than my longsuffering wife. (Not that I'm all *that* bad.) I learn much about marriage from reading not marriage manuals, but secular short fiction and novels. To the degree that I have been privy to the underside of people's lives, I think there is much truth in them. Consult Martin Luther, Small Catechism, "Lord's Prayer": ". . . for we daily sin much and indeed deserve only punishment. So, on the other hand, we, too, truly want to forgive heartily and to do good gladly to those who sin against us."[8]

When I told a widow (not a member of any congregation of mine) that I was "sorry about the death of her husband," she replied, "I'm not. Finally, I don't have to ask someone if I can go out or anything." I'm not saying that all marriages are always horrible, only that the lifting up of a standard for public approval—for example, staying married a long time and never getting divorced—can lead to the hypocrisy (as Schroeder calls it, "hypo-crisy") of shallow judgments, which does not allow us to get true peace.

I have struggled with how best to recover some congruence between my divine call and the ministry I perform with people getting married. I am a long ways from writing a book on the topic, but these are some steps I have taken in that direction.

- I share with people who are going to be married at my church a sort of diffidence about "being married in church." No peculiar blessing

8. *BoC*, 358.

attaches to this rite. It is not a sacrament among us Lutherans. We do not despise the marriage of people in other venues, nor even common law marriage. (Curiously, the Lutheran hymnal [*Lotu Buk*] in Papua New Guinea has a rite "for blessing those who have already been married the way people do," "*Liturgi bilong givim blessing long ol I marit pinis long pasin bilong ol man.*" It does not pretend they have not been married.)

- I tell the couple that the only blessing the church really has to offer, the coin of our realm, is actually the one they receive anyway at church, which has to do with Christ. We can't promise more successful marriages or more progeny or God's approval of certain acts, and we certainly can't provide a manual.

- I talk about marriage in terms I borrow from Luther's *Freedom of the Christian*. Paradoxically, the Christian is at the same time "perfectly free lord of all, subject to none"; and "perfectly dutiful servant, subject to all." This is not as catchy as fifty-fifty or its clever variants. This is a call to discover, within the vocation of marriage, the peculiar mixing of freedom and caring for others. We are able to respond to this call because our hope and joy and peace are not expressed contingently but as a gift from God. That is to say, they can know themselves to be holy and righteous and acceptable to God, forgiven of their sins, even as they can know themselves to be ever falling short of the high calling of mutual, free love for each other. This righteousness through forgiveness is not a hypothetical they need to work themselves up to, but a gift given verbally and sacramentally through the promise made known to them through Jesus Christ their Lord. Christian righteousness, even within marriage, is not an endpoint but a starting point, a gift given us in our baptism.

I hope that by discussing marriage in such terms I help them avoid some of the terrifying judgments to which they will find themselves subject as married people, which actually began the moment they met and will continue to the day they die. Are they succeeding? Are they in love? Will they always feel the way they do today—or the day they agreed to marry? Is their marriage as good as those of their siblings? Why don't they have kids? Are they having too many children? Why don't they control their kids better? Why do you keep doing that thing you do? Or, to quote from a Liza Donnelly cartoon in *The New Yorker*, "When, exactly, did all the stuff you love about me become all the stuff you hate about me?"[9]

9. *The New Yorker*, August 5, 2013, 40.

Actually, I should not say that I help them "avoid" those terrifying judgments, but rather that I show them how, with the gospel, they can "face" them and overcome them.

Back when I was dating my future wife Christine, I was a fan of Thomas Hardy. (I know. *Bleak*.) Anyhow, I was struck by the pessimism of his conclusion to the account of the wedding of Jude (the obscure one) and Arabella. My memory is imperfect, so I won't put this in quotes, but when Jude and Arabella stand up at the altar, according to Thomas Hardy, they *promised to do what nobody in the history of the world had ever succeeded in doing—love one another forever.* The story didn't get better after that, only more tragic.

It is indeed a frightening thing people do, getting married. Truth be told, no one has ever "succeeded" unless by using standards a lot lower than those of Jesus Christ. It is necessary therefore that the church of Jesus Christ, and the ministers of that church, bring to bear at wedding-time the grace of God which offers hope, hopefulness, and a way to joy *even* for those who are married.

It is tempting for the church, involved as it has been for centuries in this aspect of people's lives, to try to use its substantial clout to protect society against evils that present themselves in the arena of love and marriage. But if the institutional church is co-opted by those who wish to prevent abortions or premarital or extramarital sex or divorce or homosexual marriage—or by those who simply wish to invest society's rules about marriage with the authority of Christ's church—then the gospel will get lost. Christ will not be made much of, and people will not receive the consolations of the gospel.

I have tried in this chapter to illustrate the significance for church and ministry of what Edward Schroeder (in chapter 2) enumerates as the "fourth" contemporary application of Luther's hermeneutic which is on display in the Augsburg Confession. (This is the application that occurs, not in the realms of academe, but in the preaching and teaching of a Christian congregation and wherever two or three gather together in the Name.) As Schroeder admits, this application is most important. Here in the church we must keep the main thing the main thing, or people will not receive the life Jesus died to confer.

In church and in ministry, the main thing is to keep the main thing the main thing. Nothing competes so effectively to become the "main thing" in church and ministry as that other word from God, the law. The Augsburg Confession, in its day, stood not just against misconstruing, trivializing, or overlooking the law of God, but against *using* it in a way that confuses it with the gospel. In order for gospel to work, it must not be confused either in substance or in form with the law.

Whenever gospel and law are conflated or confused, the church will need to re-form along the lines of its chief article, so that people are delivered not merely from bad behavior (personal or societal) but from sin and death. When the gospel of Jesus Christ is front and center and is confessed to be the church's essential mission, both joy and peace will be delivered to God's people here and now, without conditions.

7

The Promise of Baptism for the Church Today

Steven E. Albertin

God offers grace through baptism, the Confessors said, and God offers it to all, regardless of age. Furthermore, since the benefits of baptism depend only on God's promise, we can return to our baptism again and again throughout our lives and make use of God's promise of grace. When we trust it we have it. Pastor Steven Albertin demonstrates his own pastoral concern as well as that of the Confessors as he highlights the Augsburg Confession's theology of the cross with regard to baptism, the understanding of baptism as a gift, and the joyful connection between baptism and repentance.

As the Lutheran Church struggles with its identity and mission in the pluralistic culture of the twenty-first century, the sacrament of baptism promises to be a powerful resource that can bring clarity to its identity and vigor to its mission. The doctrine and practice of baptism are neglected resources in the life of the church. It is time to recover the prominence of the sacrament of baptism. Such a recovery will help the church speak to this pluralistic world in a way that powerfully proclaims the gospel. Baptism properly understood and practiced will be an effective resource for such a recovery because it so explicitly clarifies "the most important topic of Christian teaching," that people "are justified by faith in Christ."[1] In so doing, it "magnifies the honor of Christ and brings the abundant consolation that devout consciences need."[2]

This understanding of baptism passes what Edward Schroeder has memorably described as "the double-dipstick test." This "test" clarifies whether a teaching or practice in the church is properly "grounded" in this "main doctrine of Christianity." There is the theological test: (1) Does it make the crucified and risen Christ necessary? There is the pastoral test: (2) Does it offer the conscience comfort? Such theological clarity concerning the centrality of Christ will have significant pastoral and missional consequences for the church. Clarity about the meaning of baptism that is properly grounded in "the main doctrine of Christianity" promises to strengthen a church that is often confused about what it has to say to the world and, as a result, is often unable to offer that world the good news that only Christ can give.

Confusion about Baptism . . . and the Gospel

The Apology of the Augsburg Confession describes justification by grace through faith for the sake of Christ (the hub of the wheel) as "the main doctrine of Christianity." When this doctrine is properly understood and used, (1) it "magnifies the honor of Christ," and (2) it "brings to pious consciences the abundant consolation that [they] need."[3] This twofold test ("the double-dipstick test") can be applied to any Christian teaching or practice. When baptism (1) illumines and magnifies Christ and (2) brings to pious consciences the abundant consolation that they need, it is connected to the "hub" and does what God intended it to do.

When there is confusion about the value of baptism, and when its value is not connected to the "hub," it is because there is confusion about the need for Christ and his benefits. When there is confusion about the gospel and the very "hub" of the Christian faith, the vitality and mission of the church suffers.

The reasons for the decline of mainline Christianity and Lutheranism in particular in North America in the twenty-first century are complex. However, at its core is a confusion about the gospel. When there is confusion about the gospel, it is not surprising that there is confusion about the value of baptism. Properly connecting the spoke of baptism to the hub of the gospel can be a powerful means by which to recover the gospel and "main doctrine of Christianity" and revitalize the mission of the church.

---

1. *BoC*, 120.
2. *BoC*, 121.
3. *BoC*, 121.

Baptism Is Justification

When the Lutheran Reformation emerged in the sixteenth century, baptism was not a major issue of contention with Rome. In the Augsburg Confession and its Apology, there is only one short article (article 9) on baptism. There the confessors defend the necessity of baptism and the traditional practice of infant baptism, which had been rejected by the Anabaptist wing of the protestant reformation.

On the surface this simply seems to be a dispute about a sacramental practice. However, the issue goes much deeper. Luther's Small and Large Catechisms address baptism in much greater detail than either the Augsburg Confession or the Apology. In the Large Catechism, Luther relates baptism to Penance:

> These two parts, being dipped under the water and emerging from it, point to the power and effect of baptism, which is nothing else than the slaying of the old Adam and the resurrection of the new creature, both of which must continue in us our whole life long. Thus the Christian life is nothing else than a daily baptism . . .[4]

Luther's linking of baptism to Penance is significant. Even though articles 11 and 12 in the Augsburg Confession and its Apology do not explicitly connect baptism to Penance, the theological connection is clear. Such a connection implies much more is at stake in article 9 than a dispute about infant baptism. If "the Christian life is nothing else than daily baptism," and the Christian life is grounded in Christ and his benefits (the doctrine of justification), then a dispute about baptism is a dispute about justification.

Article 9 of the Augsburg Confession and Apology argues for (1) the necessity of baptism and (2) the validity of infant baptism.[5] At first glance, both matters seem to be non-issues. From the earliest days of the church, baptism of believers has been assumed. Likewise, the New Testament argues neither for nor against infant baptism. From its earliest days the church in both East and West baptized infants. Infant baptism was simply not contested.

From the outset of the church's mission, Christ's command to baptize is coordinated with the command to proclaim the gospel. Baptism and Christ go hand in hand. You do not do one without the other. They are both "necessary." The church could not imagine proclaiming Christ and his promise without baptizing. Likewise, the church could not imagine

---

4. *BoC*, 465.
5. "Concerning Baptism it is taught that it is necessary, that grace is offered through it, and that one should also baptize children, who through such baptism are entrusted to God and become pleasing to him." *BoC*, 42.

baptizing without proclaiming Christ and his promise. They both are at the heart of the church's mission.

The Necessity of Baptism

The Confessors' insistence that baptism is "necessary for salvation"[6] is not argument for the independent significance of baptism as if it were some sort of "magical rite" that saved by the mere doing of it.[7] What makes baptism "necessary" is that it "necessitates Christ." It announces to the baptismal candidate and all those gathered for this communal event that it necessarily took the life, death, and resurrection of Christ to forgive sins, destroy death and the devil, and end God's judgment of the ungodly. Apart from Christ there is no hope. Apart from Christ there is no salvation. Only through Christ do sinners receive the unconditional promise of the forgiveness of sins and eternal life. Only through Christ do sinners receive the unconditional affirmation of their worth in a world where that worth is continually called into question and under attack. That kind of promise is offered only where Christ's name is proclaimed and his story is told.

Therefore, the Confessors insist that baptism is "necessary for salvation." Baptism is necessary because Christ is necessary. If baptism is "necessary for salvation," then it must be taught and practiced in a way that proclaims justification by faith. It must offer Christ and his benefits in such a way that comforts its recipients. Then it will be connected to the "hub" of the wheel. It will proclaim justification by faith.

The Confessors' insistence on the necessity of baptism is rooted in their joyful realization that baptism does what it says. Just as Christ is actually present in the proclamation of the gospel and in the Sacrament of Holy Communion—actually justifying the hearer of the Word and the recipient of the sacrament—Christ is actually present and acting in the sacrament of baptism. When baptism washes the baptismal candidate, the candidate actually dies and rises with Christ. The candidate is actually justified.

In the Large Catechism, Luther marvels at what God accomplishes in baptism:

> In baptism, therefore, every Christian has enough to study and practice all his or her life. Christians always have enough to do to believe firmly what baptism promises and brings—victory over death and the devil, forgiveness of sin, God's grace, the entire Christ, and the Holy Spirit with his gifts. In short, the blessings of baptism are so boundless that if our timid nature

---

6. *BoC*, 43.
7. "*ex opera operato*" (Latin).

considers them, it may well doubt whether they could all be true. Suppose there were a physician who had so much skill that people would not die, or even though they died would afterward live eternally. Just think how the world would snow and rain money upon such a person! Because of the throng of rich people crowding around, no one else would be able to get near. Now, here in baptism there is brought, free of charge, to every person's door just such a treasure and medicine that swallows up death and keeps all people alive.[8]

Baptism is not just a demonstration of what already is. It is not a symbol of a universal truth. The truth is that human life is under the powers of sin, death, and the judgment of God. The popular mantra heard in many American churches—"God is good all the time. All the time God is good!"—ignores this truth. It reflects the soft deism that afflicts so much of American Christianity where churches are often embarrassed to make claims for the necessity of Christ. That Christ is necessary for salvation is too exclusive and particular. In this popular view, the goodness of God permeates the world. Christ is "necessary" only because Christ is the clearest revelation of God's universal goodness. The goodness of God is not necessarily connected to Christ.

From such a theological perspective, it is not very surprising that parents, who do not see Christ's promise in baptism as important or necessary, ignore baptism. There is no urgency to baptize since God's love is present everywhere. ("God is good all the time. All the time God is good.") It can be postponed and put off since God's saving presence is available in so many other ways in the world. Since Christ is not necessary, neither is baptism.

In the Confessors' teaching, though, Christ's command to baptize is linked with his command to proclaim the gospel to the ends of the earth. Christ commands both baptism and proclamation because they are important. There is a sense of urgency with the command to proclaim the gospel and to baptize. Both connect the world to Christ. Apart from Christ and his name there is no life and no salvation.

However, this command is a not a "legal" command. It is not part of life under the reality of the law. It is not some *quid pro quo*, "this for that" contract. It is not "let's make a deal" or a conditional offer that is dependent upon the candidate's "decision," "commitment," or ability to meet the conditions of the offer. This command is the "command" of the gospel. The gift of baptism is the gift of the gospel. Its power is not dependent upon the response of the receiver. It is "valid" regardless of the response of the recipient. It is unqualified, categorical, and absolute because God's saving work in Christ is unqualified, categorical, and

8. *BoC*, 461–62.

absolute. Nothing more needs to be done—by God or humans—to make it complete.

The unrepeatable nature of baptism also reinforces the necessity of baptism. Once a person has been baptized, it is not repeated. It is once-and-for-all. As such it mimics the once-and-for-all and unrepeatable nature of Christ's death and resurrection. Christ's saving action did it all. It does not need to be improved upon or added to. Baptisms do not need to be redone as if they didn't "take" the first time. Baptism is not repeated until it "works."

However, a "response" is called for. A reaction is expected. A gift begs to be opened. A suitor is thrilled when his courtship concludes in winning the heart of his beloved. A promise is "fulfilled" when the recipient "trusts" it. The "main doctrine of Christianity" recognizes that reality. The "main doctrine" is justification by grace *through faith* for the sake of Christ. That is the goal of baptism. That is the proper use of baptism: to offer the promise of Christ so that faith is created and sustained.

The promise of baptism may be neglected, ignored, or even disbelieved during the course of life. Humans remain free to disbelieve the gospel. For sinners, such a struggle is inevitable. However, the cause for such a struggle is in the mystery of human freedom and fallenness; it is not in any weakness or inadequacy of baptism. The promise of baptism remains permanent and effective. It begs to be remembered. It provides the foundation to which Christians can return daily for assurance and strength to continue the journey of Christian discipleship.

The Necessity of Infant Baptism

Because faith sometimes fails to emerge in the life of the baptized, some have questioned the value of "infant baptism." That certainly was the basis of the Anabaptist rejection of infant baptism at the time of the Reformation. The Anabaptists[9] were dissatisfied with the medieval church's practice of infant baptism. In the world of medieval Christendom, baptism was a rite of citizenship and a plank of civil religion. There was no commitment from parents to nurture the baptized child in the faith.

The Anabaptists were not all that unlike many today who question the value and necessity of infant baptism. They reason that, if infant baptism is no more than a social custom or a family rite that demands

---

9. Anabaptists were Christians of the sixteenth-century "Radical Reformation" who taught that infant baptism was unscriptural and, therefore, null and void. Anabaptists required that baptismal candidates be able to make their own confession of faith.

no serious commitment by parents and sponsors to raise the baptized in the Christian faith and life, infant baptism should not be performed. In many churches that practice infant baptism, the commitment to raising children in the faith has been superficial. Thus the church has been unable to withstand the corrosive effects of a post-Christian world. Many Lutheran congregations are familiar with the post-confirmation drift of youth and young adults into indifference and sometimes rejection of organized religion. The critics of infant baptism argue that in such a world infant baptism should be delayed, if not abandoned. Unless parents and sponsors show sufficient commitment to raise the child in the faith, baptism should be postponed at least until the family is committed or until the candidates are old enough to decide for themselves and appreciate the difference that Christ can make in their lives.

However, contrary to the critics of infant baptism, the practice of infant baptism is not the problem. The problem is that the teaching and practice of baptism have not been sufficiently grounded in the "hub." Baptismal teaching and practice that has not been sufficiently connected to the necessity of Christ and his comforting promise create a church in which infant baptism is not valued and nurturing the faith is neglected. In the midst of such spiritual indifference, not only is infant baptism not valued; participation in the faith community is also not valued. If Christ and his benefits are not valued, neither will baptism be valued.

If Christian faith is all about one's ability to feel the presence of God or to be conscious of one's belief, then why baptize infants who can show no evidence of such feelings or consciousness? However, when do people give sufficient evidence? How much is enough? Attempts to establish an age of discretion or accountability seem arbitrary and subjective. Then the focus on baptism moves the objective reality of Christ and his benefits to human subjectivity and work. Christ and his work are undermined. The promise is qualified. Grace becomes conditional on feeling God's presence. Most of all, the comfort of Christ is put in question. The assurance of baptism is compromised. The main doctrine of Christianity is contradicted. The double-dipstick test is flunked.

For Lutherans there is probably nothing in our communal church life that so dramatizes our state as sinful human beings, utterly dependent upon the grace of God, as infant baptism. Despite our adult attempts to point to our "growth in Christ," our "maturing discipleship," and our "increasing sanctification," we continue to remain sinners who daily need to return to our baptisms (cf. Luther's fourth question on baptism in his Small Catechism: "What does baptism mean for daily living?") and remember its promise. Regardless of our foolish attempts to convince ourselves that we have actually gotten better, become more "grown-up" and become less dependent on the grace of God, every day we remain as helpless as infants at the font dependent upon the gracious promise of God in Christ. Every day we need to be delivered from our childish and foolish ways. Every day we "die through daily contrition and repentance, and . . . a new person is to come forth and rise up to live before God in righteousness and purity forever."[10]

To say that Lutherans practice infant baptism does not mean they regard baptism to be for infants only. A better way to refer to the reformers' attempts to describe the meaning and scope of baptism is to call it "baptism without age restrictions." Everyone of every age, predicament, and station in life is in need of the grace of God in Christ.

As the Lutheran Church moves to a less and less privileged place in society and as fewer parents bring their infants and children to the church for baptism simply because it is "the thing to do," baptisms will happen less often but to a much larger variety of ages. "Adult" baptisms will become more frequent in a society where church participation is much more countercultural and less socially expected. In such a cultural situation, it will be tempting to downplay the value of infant baptism. However, continuing to insist on the church's right and duty to baptize infants will be an important way to publicly proclaim that baptism and the promise of Christ are for *all* ages, abilities, and stations in life.

Baptism and Confession: Remembering the Promise

As stated earlier, it is noteworthy that in both the Small and Large Catechisms, Luther connects baptism to the sacrament of Penance. Making such a connection moves baptism from being merely an event of the past to an event of the past that continues to have vital meaning and significance for the present. Such a connection reminds us that "remembering the promise" of baptism can be a vital resource for living the Christian life.

In the Large Catechism, Luther criticizes St. Jerome for making repentance the "second plank on which we must swim ashore after the ship founders." Such an interpretation leaves baptism in the past. In the present moment, it is up to the penitent to swim to shore. Luther instead argues that baptism is the ship to which the penitent can return for safety and comfort in the rough seas of daily life. Returning to baptism and its promise gives the penitents the comfort they are seeking:

---

10. *BoC*, 360:12.

Therefore let all Christians regard their baptism as the daily garment that they are to wear all the time. Every day they should be found in faith and with its fruits, suppressing the old creature and growing up in the new. If we want to be Christians, we must practice the work that makes us Christians, and let those who fall away return to it. As Christ, the mercy seat, does not withdraw from us or forbid us to return to him even though we sin, so all his treasures and gifts remain. As we have once obtained forgiveness of sins in baptism, so forgiveness remains day by day as long as we live, that is, as long as we carry the old creature around our necks.[11]

The reformers were critical of the medieval church's practice of Penance because it undermined the promise of baptism. Undermining the promise of baptism undermines Christ and his benefits. The medieval practice emphasized the penitent's enumeration of sins and one's commitment to rectifying one's wrongs through satisfactions. The offer of forgiveness was dependent upon the penitent's ability to fulfill these commitments. The benefits of Christ in baptism were dependent upon what the penitent was able to do. As a result, both baptism and Penance were disconnected from the "hub." Both flunked the "double-dipstick test." (1) Christ was no longer necessary; the commitment of the penitent is what counted. (2) Christ's comfort was lost; the assurance of forgiveness was qualified. The promise of baptism was dependent not upon what God had done in Christ but was dependent on what the penitent could do. When the promise of the gospel is "up to us" and not "up to God," then the good news of the gospel is lost. Guilt ensnares consciences. Doubt challenges faith. Fear undermines trust in God. Terror sabotages the peace that only Christ can give.

For Luther, contrition and repentance are the joyous fruits of a faith grounded in the irrevocable promise of baptism. Since baptism is "once and for all," there is no sin that can undo its promise. Therefore, Christians need not fear confessing even the most grievous and terrifying of sins. Sins "get to" be confessed because the penitents can trust they will receive the forgiveness they crave. Baptism becomes the foundation from which the Christian can engage in the lifelong struggle against sin, death, and the power of the devil. Baptism becomes the foundation from which Christians can live out their faith in service to their neighbor and care of the world.

The twenty-first-century critics of infant baptism challenge such a robust understanding of baptism and its continuing value in the daily life of the Christian. The critics claim that an event from infancy that one cannot recall is of dubious value. How can something of which there is no recollection be a meaningful resource for living the Christian

---

11. *BoC*, 466, 467:83–86.

life? Would not an experience that can be vividly recalled, remembered, and relived be a much more meaningful resource for faith and life? Therefore, say the critics, baptism ought to be postponed until an age when the recipient can appreciate the event and remember the experience.

There is no doubt that experiences that can be remembered have a significant and enduring effect on how one lives one's life. However, such experiences are subject to the vagaries and changes of passing time. Memories can fade. However, the practice of infant baptism reminds us that what matters is the "fact" of baptism and what baptism promises rather than our ability to recall the details of the original experience. The "fact" of baptism has current value because the value of baptism is based on the "fact" of Christ's once-and-for-all sacrifice—and not my ability to recall the day when I was splashed in the font or dunked in the river. My inability to recall the day of my baptism is not a liability but an asset. It reminds me that baptism has value not because of anything I can do but because of everything God did.

Remembering the promise of baptism can be an important tool in revitalizing the mission of the Lutheran Church in the twenty-first century. Remembering the promise of baptism is no different from remembering the promise of Christ and the difference Christ makes for life. When the church connects baptism to the "hub" of justification by faith—when justification by faith is proclaimed in such a way that magnifies Christ and the comfort Christ brings to troubled lives—baptism will be an essential tool for its mission. The church will seek to give to all, regardless of their age or stage in life, the blessings of baptism because those blessings are the blessings of Christ.

Parents will want their children not only to be baptized but to value the "fact" of their baptism just as they value the "fact" of Christ's death and resurrection for their lives. Daily remembering baptism will enable them to die to their old selves and be raised again with Christ. Christians at every stage in life will value the "necessity of baptism" just as they value the "necessity of Christ" for meaning and hope in their lives. Baptism will be the foundation for a mission that loves the world with the gracious, once-and-for-all love of God in Christ.

Remembering the Promise in the Present

How might remembering the promise of baptism be put to use in the twenty-first-century mission of the church? I have been seeking to do that in my ministry for over thirty-five years. A central part of that ministry has been my weekly preaching to the congregations I have served. Below is a sermon I offer as a practical example of how one might connect baptism to the "hub" of justification by faith. The sermon makes use of the "double-dipstick" test: (1) magnifying Christ in such a way that (2) sinners are comforted and set free for service in God's world.

"THE LAST CHAPTER FIRST"
Mark 1:4–11
The Baptism of Our Lord

Are you familiar with the "whodunit?" style of murder mystery? Agatha Christie is famous for using this formula in her murder mysteries. Novels, film, and such popular crime-solving TV shows as "CSI" use the same formula. It begins with a crime. A murder is committed, but we don't know "whodunit." As the plot unfolds, one suspect after another parades before the viewer. Finally, in the last chapter, the last scene, the last five minutes, the brilliant detective, Inspector Poirot or Sherlock Holmes or someone like them, exposes the culprit: "The butler did it!"—Crime solved. Mystery ended. Questions answered. Story concluded.

However, suppose we went to the library to check out an Agatha Christie murder mystery we had never read. Suppose that instead of starting at the beginning of the book, we cheated. We read the last chapter first and then went back and read the story from the beginning.

Or suppose we recorded an episode of "CSI" on our DVR. However, when it came time to watch it, we cheated. We watched the last five minutes first, and then went back and watched the entire episode from the beginning. In both cases, we would literally have changed the story. It would no longer be a "whodunit?" because now we would know from the beginning who was the murderer and how the story would end. You would experience the story in a new way. We would have a new story.

That is the gospel. That is the Christian life. That is what happens in every Christian baptism. That is what happened at the baptism of Jesus. The last chapter happened *first!*

We live our lives always wondering where our story might lead us. Where will the plot go? What will be the last chapter of our lives? What will they say about us when our story has ended, the book is closed, and we are gone?

We spend our lives scrambling to answer these questions. A youth trembles because, if he does not make the soccer team or get invited to sit at the right lunchroom table by the right kids, his life does not matter. A young adult frets because graduation is coming, and she is going to have to decide what to do with her life. Colleagues nervously confer with each other at the local coffee shop because they must decide between career and family. The unexpected death of an old friend compounds a man's worry about the shortness of breath that has plagued him for weeks. Daily there are reminders of the "last chapter." We cannot avoid them, postpone them, or pretend they do not exist.

Into this world comes John the Baptist warning everyone to get ready for the "last chapter." No one can escape. Repent of your sins. Clean up your act. Get back on "the straight and narrow." God is coming. The Messiah is near. Soon the curtain will fall, the screen will flash "The End," and the last chapter will begin. The question is whether there will be a happy ending or not.

We may not have John the Baptist breathing down our neck, but there is no shortage of those like him cluttering our world with their warnings and predictions. They promise us delightful endings and blissful last chapters *if* we only do our part to follow their program, keep their rules, and do our duty. Don't let any of them ever tell you that they are "spiritual" but not "religious." Don't let any of them tell you that they don't believe in god. Everyone has a "last chapter" for which they dream, a "last chapter" for which they hope, a "last chapter" for which they try to write a happy ending. Everyone has a god.

However, just when we think that we have written our "last chapter" with a happy ending, life comes crashing down upon us. Or, shall I say, "God comes crashing down upon us"?

Today's first reading from the Book of Genesis[12] reminds us that God not only created the world once upon a time, long ago, in the distant past, but also that God continues to be involved in the ongoing development of creation. God did not walk away and leave us on our own.

That is the scary part, is it not? Regardless of how hard we work at writing our own "last chapter," the scriptures still insist that God has the last word. God decides when the show has ended and the curtain will fall. God finally writes the "last chapter" on life and history. That is hardly good news for sinners who have secrets hiding in their closets. I have yet to see anyone escape the cemetery. As our Ash Wednesday liturgy reminds us every year: "From dust we came and to dust we shall return."

It is our fear of that fate and our dread of that God that make us shudder and drive us to monstrous deeds of foolishness. Steven Spielberg's film *War Horse* and its darkly realistic picture of World War I portrays the brutal insanity of war and how desperate people will become to write a "last chapter" that will make their lives matter.

Into that world comes Jesus, offering himself to John the Baptist, the

---

12. Gen. 1:1–5, the first reading appointed for the Baptism of Our Lord, Year B.

ultimate doomsday prophet, willing to become a part of our story. By submitting to John's baptism, Jesus offers to join our story and suffer with us the "last chapter" from which no human can ever hope to escape. However, as Jesus plunges into those deadly waters, something happened that had never happened at any of John's baptisms. The heavens were "torn apart." The Holy Spirit like a dove descends upon Jesus. A voice from heaven, from the creator of heaven and earth, declares that this Jesus is like no other. This Jesus is God's beloved Son. No dreadful "last chapter" will ever let his life crumble into dust that will be trampled and forgotten. God will treasure Jesus always and forever, no matter what.

There is only one other time in the Gospel of Mark when something is "torn apart" like this. That happens precisely at the moment Jesus dies on the cross. This time it is not the heavens that are "torn apart," but the curtain in the temple dividing the Holy of Holies from the rest of the temple.

The Gospel of Mark deliberately connects these two events by describing each event in a similar way. As the Gospel of Mark begins and Jesus is baptized, it is as if we are reading *the last chapter first*. When the heavens are "torn apart" at Jesus' baptism, we are already catching a glimpse of the next time something will be "torn apart," at Jesus' death. At Jesus' baptism the heavens are "torn apart" and God declares that Jesus is His Son. At Jesus' death it is the curtain in the temple that is "torn apart." This time it is not a voice from heaven but the centurion at the foot of the cross who declares that Jesus is the Son of God. It is at the cross that someone finally figures out who Jesus is. Jesus' baptism already pointed ahead to this dramatic conclusion.

On the one hand Jesus' death was no different from the "last chapter" all of us must suffer. On the other hand, Jesus' death was like no other. Because Jesus is the beloved Son of God, God will not abandon him to the dustbin of history. Even though Jesus willingly became the "friend of sinners" and deserved a "last chapter" no different from ours, God would not let it end there.

God kept the promise made to Jesus at his baptism. Because of that promise, Jesus' "last chapter" would be different. God raises Jesus from the dead—and promises that same "last chapter" to all of us who are afraid that our "last chapter" will end in the cemetery.

Do you see what good news this means for us? Jesus' baptism is our baptism. When we are baptized, God gives to us Jesus' "last chapter." God offers us Jesus' fate and destiny. In our baptism we get *the last chapter first*.

At the beginning of every Christian life, whether as an infant held in her parent's arms, as a child holding the hands of his godparents, or as an adult weathered by years of living, God invites us to join Jesus in the Jordan River. God gives us the gift of Holy Baptism. God gives us Jesus' *last chapter first* so we can be confident of where the plot of our life is headed.

Trusting that promise, we can create a new "storyline." We no longer have to live in the dark, in suspense and unsure of "whodunit?" We no longer have to scramble to write our own "last chapters," afraid that we will disappear into the dustbin of forgotten yesterdays. We are free to live our lives in the peace that the world will never understand.

In the waters of baptism we have received the risen Christ. His "last chapter" has become ours. Our "storyline" changes as we live our lives differently from what they would have been. Confident of our "last chapter," we no longer need to live in fear, always having to look out for ourselves because no one else will. We belong to a new community and a new family, where God is our Father and Jesus is our brother. We live hand in hand, loving and supporting one another, fearlessly unafraid, utterly selfless, because we have received *the last chapter first.*

8

Christology at the Table

Marcus C. Lohrmann

The sixteenth-century Confessors wanted everyone to know that they had not abolished the Mass, but used it for its intended purpose: to comfort terrified consciences. So they confessed that, in the Lord's Supper, the risen Christ comes to sinners offering the forgiveness of sins made possible by his death and resurrection. The Confessors emphasized that the Lord's Supper is God's action (not ours) on our behalf; and that in the Lord's Supper we receive the body and blood of Christ, nothing less. They confessed that forgiveness is received simply by trusting the promise that Christ makes in the meal: "My body given . . . my blood shed . . . for you . . . for the forgiveness of sins." In this chapter Bishop Marcus Lohrmann, following the law-promise distinction described in Chapter 2, interprets the treatment of the Lord's Supper in Matthew's Gospel. Encountering once again the theology of the cross, the meal with its promise passes the "double-dipstick" test: making full use of Christ's benefits to provide full comfort to troubled consciences.

Lutheran Christians insist that at the heart of the Christian faith is the understanding that we are justified by God's grace through faith in the crucified and risen Christ. Concerning such justification, the Lutheran confessors declared in the Augsburg Confession:

> Furthermore it is taught that we cannot obtain forgiveness of sins and righteousness before God through our own merit, work, or satisfactions, but that we receive forgiveness of sin and become righteous before God out of

grace for Christ's sake through faith when we believe that Christ has suffered for us and that for his sake our sin is forgiven and righteousness and eternal life are given to us. For God will regard and reckon this faith as righteousness in his sight, as St. Paul says in Romans 3.[1]

How does God work to create such faith? The Augsburg Confessors continue:

So that we may obtain this faith, the ministry of teaching the gospel and administering the sacraments was instituted. For through the Word and the sacraments as through instruments the Holy Spirit is given, who effects faith where and when it pleases God in those who hear the gospel, that is to say, in those who hear that God, not on account of our merits but on account of Christ justifies those who believe that they are received into grace on account of Christ.[2]

The purpose of this chapter is to give particular attention to "the Table" as an instrument of the Holy Spirit.

By "the Table" we mean the sacrament that the Lutheran confessions refer to as the Lord's Supper, the Eucharist, Holy Communion, and the Breaking of the Bread (each with its specific accents). We give it special attention in order: (1) to clarify the nature of the Host at this Table; (2) to inquire concerning the gifts that this particular Host would bestow; and (3) to ask concerning what the reception of these gifts might mean for those who gather at this Table. This attention will take place with an acknowledgment of the current context for this conversation and with the recognition of the way in which the current context shapes the discussion.

The Contemporary Context

It is a cliché to say that the era of Christendom is past, at least in most areas of the United States. The number of active participants in the Lutheran Christian tradition, along with those in other mainline traditions, has experienced significant erosion. Significant demographic changes, the increasing secularization of the culture, and church conflict are among the factors contributing to that reality. Complicating this situation is the fact that most Lutheran Christians have not been adept at heeding the holy writer's counsel to "Always be ready to make your defense to anyone who demands from you an accounting for the hope that is in you; yet do it with gentleness and reverence."[3] All of these realities are not good signs for a specific tradition that, prior to the 1960s,

1. *BoC*, 40.
2. *BoC*, 41.
3. 1 Pet. 3:15.

primarily relied upon birth rates and immigrants from Europe to swell the ranks.

Part of the challenge is the failure of Lutheran Christians to have the skills, desire, or capacity to share the "hope" that is in them. But it also seems the world does not appear to have much interest in what the church has to say. Indifference is fostered by the ongoing suspicion of institutions beyond which one is an immediate participant and the common perception that the church is "harsh and judgmental" at best and irrelevant at worst.

The problem is not limited to the failure of the Lutheran Christian tradition in the United States to connect with those unfamiliar to this tradition. It is also the case that this tradition has increasingly failed to connect with those who are born and baptized into it. A troubled pastor of a once-growing congregation recently inquired of me, "Where is everybody? Where are all the children?" A Sunday-morning drive through many of our communities soon reveals that, among other things, they are working, at the ball parks or other places of recreation, or at the shopping malls. The failure to forge connections with those "born and baptized" into the Lutheran tradition is accelerated by those instances when people experience personal pain or perceive a lack of responsiveness from the church. Congregational conflict, whatever the source, tends to drive many away and to underscore the sense that "the church is not for me."

Making the Connection between the Context and the Table

Many Lutherans who were born in the late twentieth century were born and baptized into a tradition that had a very specific understanding of the Table. That tradition accented the holiness of the Lord's Supper. Participation was limited to those who were baptized members of the church and who had passed a rigorous program of instruction often linked with the rite of confirmation. A "worthy" participation in this meal was linked directly to both theological understanding and the sufficiency of the participants' faith. In many congregations those invited to the Table were limited to those within one's own theological/ denominational tradition. Within this tradition one easily could sense the "serious" nature of the Lord's Supper. Much within this tradition was commendable.

But this tradition is not without its risks. While the accent on theological understanding is critical, often that understanding failed to mature beyond confirmation. With a limited, narrow understanding that some had "passed" the requirements necessary for "worthy participation," this specific practice can contribute to the sense that some are "in" while others are left "out"—including children who might wonder how long they must endure this "boring" prolongation of the service. Because of the "serious" nature of this Table, worship often lacked a sense of joy.

Given the current cultural context, Lutheran Christian leadership has been reexamining the traditions related to the Table. As a result, congregations have developed varying policies with regard to First Communion and "requirements" related to preparation. In preparing to write this chapter I invited a small number of Christian leaders for several conversations. Prior to the conversations, participants were asked to read the core biblical texts related to the Table, the Augsburg Confession, the Apology to the Augsburg Confession, Martin Luther's Small and Large Catechisms, and the statement of the Evangelical Lutheran Church called *The Use of the Means of Grace*.[4] Participants were asked to reflect upon their own faith, their positions and responsibilities of leadership in the church, the mission of the church, and other key questions related to the Lord's Supper.

The conversations were rich. What are some of the key issues related to the Table? Participants responded that they include such matters as (1) the unity of the church; (2) who is invited/admitted to the Table (i.e., only baptized Christians who have been instructed in the meaning of the Table or all who are gathered in worship or some variant?); (3) what is the responsibility of the presider and worshipper in determining who should be "admitted"?; (4) is confession necessary prior to participation in the meal?; (5) what is the relationship between participation in this Table and God's mission through the church (e.g., Matthew 25 and 28)?; (6) how much does the contemporary church's need to be loved and to be perceived as welcoming and inclusive shape pastoral practice?; (7) in what manner does the worship service shape the understanding/ practice of the Table and vice versa?; (8) what is the relationship between Baptism and the Eucharist?; (9) in what way does this Table shape all gatherings at the Table?

Each question is worthy of an essay, a seminar, or a book. But given the understanding that this Table is one of those "instruments of the Spirit" through which God creates faith, the prior question that informs all other questions is: "Who *is* the Host of this meal?" What does it mean for this Host to be the Christ? What are the gifts/benefits the Host intends to give to those who are at the Table? Finally, how do these

---

4. *The Use of the Means of Grace* (Minneapolis: Augsburg Fortress, 1997). Adopted for guidance and practice by the Fifth Biennial Churchwide Assembly of the Evangelical Lutheran Church in America, August 19, 1997.

gifts make a difference in the lives of the recipients and in the church's mission to the world, particularly given our historical context? These are questions raised in the sixteenth century by the Augsburg Confessors as they sought to "make use" of the crucified and risen Lord and offer the gifts of God's grace in Christ to troubled sinners. Hence, we have the title for this chapter, "Christology at the Table."

Many a presiding minister will use the Eucharistic prayer to create the context for the Table. Others may offer a simple word of introduction. For example, she may say, "Our Lord Jesus is the Host at this Table. . . ." The words are intended to remind the gathered assembly that this meal is not the possession of a particular congregation or denomination. *The one who presides is, in fact, Jesus Christ.* Those who come to the Table need to know something about the one who is the Host. The story needs to be told.

Accounts of the "institution of the Lord's Supper" are present in the Gospels of Matthew, Mark, and Luke. While John's Gospel has no account of that Passover meal, a very robust Eucharistic theology informs the entire Gospel, particularly the "Bread of Life" discourse in John 6. St. Paul provides an intriguing account of the Lord's Supper within the context of a lively discussion about whether or not the Corinthian church is, in fact, celebrating the Lord's Supper. To explore the questions raised above, this chapter will examine the Gospel according to Matthew.

Christology at the Table and the Gospel of Matthew

Who is the Host at this Table? The Gospel of Matthew begins, "An account of the genealogy of Jesus the Messiah (Christ), the son of David and the son of Abraham."[5] With that modest beginning, Matthew asserts that the story he unfolds has to do with the promises God has made to God's people throughout the ages and how those promises will unfold in Jesus the Christ. If the first words ground Jesus in the long story of the people of God, then Matthew establishes the link between God's purposes and this child. The angel of the Lord declares that Mary and Joseph should ". . . name him Jesus, for he will save his people from their sins."[6] Quoting Isaiah, Matthew observes that this is in fulfillment of God's promises through Isaiah: "'Look, the virgin shall conceive and bear a son, and they shall call him Emmanuel' which means, 'God is with us.'" No matter what is about to unfold, that is the truth of what God will accomplish in Jesus.

This Christ, this anointed one, is good news for the world. So "wise

5. Matt. 1:1.
6. Matt. 1:21.

men from the East" come to worship him. But not all will embrace this birth announcement. In an ominous sign that points to Jesus' future, Herod, the presumed "King of the Jews," plots to kill this infant. For the moment, as he and his parents find refuge in Egypt, Jesus is spared the treachery, though other infants are not.

At his baptism Jesus is identified as "the one who will fulfill all righteousness" while a "voice from heaven" declares that this one is "my Son, the Beloved, with whom I am well pleased."[7] In the same baptismal action Jesus is linked both to the fate of humanity and to God's purposes. Such a linkage ensures the truth that Jesus, like every human being, will be tempted to be something other than he is. In the presence of such temptation, Jesus is sustained by the word of God and the angels who "came and waited upon him."[8]

Jesus' ministry begins with the proclamation, "Repent, for the kingdom of heaven has come near."[9] He is, after all, about the work of calling humanity to turn away from eyes that are on themselves to eyes that look to what God is now doing. He goes about, "teaching . . . proclaiming the good news of the kingdom and curing every disease and every sickness among the people."[10]

As Jesus teaches the law, he makes it clear that the "righteousness of God" is something more than perfunctory obedience. It has to do with one's heart. "You have heard that it was said, 'You shall love your neighbor and hate your enemy.' But I say to you, love your enemies and pray for those who persecute you so that you may be children of your Father in heaven."[11] The manner in which Jesus "raises the stakes" in the consideration of the law leaves everyone found "wanting."

Evidence of Jesus' divine authority is present everywhere. The sick are healed, the storm is calmed,[12] and demons are cast out.[13] Most approve, but some "beg him to leave their neighborhood."[14]

Who is the Host, the Christ? Look at the company he keeps. That is, after all, how one is known. Scandalously, and evidently with some frequency, Jesus positions himself with those who are "tax collectors and sinners." To those who protest such behavior, he says, "Go and learn what this means, 'I desire mercy, not sacrifice.' For I have come to call not the righteous but sinners."[15] Here is already a clue to a divine diagnosis. Those who may miss out on the "goodness" of the good news are those

7. Matt. 3:13–17.
8. Matt. 4:1–11.
9. Matt. 4:17.
10. Matt. 4:23.
11. Matt. 5:43.
12. Matt. 8:23–27.
13. Matt. 8:28–34.
14. Matt. 8:34.
15. Matt. 9:10–13.

who do not perceive their own sin or need for mercy. Jesus, the Christ, is one who calls his hearers to a discipleship that leads to a dying: "whoever does not take up the cross and follow me is not worthy of me." Jesus continues with the stunning observation that "those who find their life will lose it and those who lose their life for my sake will find it."[16]

This Host who tenderly welcomes children[17] is clear that he himself will not always be welcomed. He acknowledges that he will be the source of offense and points to his own ultimate rejection: "For just as Jonah was three days and three nights in the belly of the sea monster, so for three days and three nights the Son of Man will be in the heart of the earth."[18] When many are mystified by his words, Jesus will confirm the extent of the blindness as he quotes the prophet Isaiah, "You will indeed listen, but never understand, and you will indeed look, but never perceive."[19] Incredibly, his hometown "took offense at him" and his divine power is stymied "because of their unbelief."[20] Yet Jesus' hospitality knows no end. In the presence of a great crowd, this Host "has compassion" and "after giving thanks," breaks the loaves of bread, and "gave them to the disciples, and the disciples gave them to the crowds."[21] Do we have an early suggestion with respect to how the benefits of this Host transform receivers into givers?

As Matthew tells the story, the identity of the Host moves front and center. In a pivotal moment Jesus inquires of his disciples concerning what people are saying about him. More poignantly for them (and for us!) he asks their opinion. Peter responds, "You are the Messiah (Christ), the Son of the living God." Jesus affirms such a profound understanding but now rejects the assumed definition of Christ. He insists, ". . . he must go to Jerusalem and undergo great suffering at the hands of the chief priests and scribes, and be killed and on the third day be raised." Peter cannot get beyond the words related to suffering and death and protests vigorously in a manner that mirrors the original temptation. But Jesus indicates that his vocation also is the vocation of those who "want to become my followers." Once again, Jesus states, "For those who want to save their life will lose it, and those who lose their life for my sake will find it."[22]

As Matthew unfolds the story, the identity of the Host is revealed further. When Jesus enters Jerusalem, the crowds welcome him with the ancient hymn with which a king was welcomed, "Hosanna to the son

---

16. Matt. 10:38–39.
17. Matt. 10:40.
18. Matt. 12:38–42.
19. Matt. 13:14.
20. Matt. 13:54–58.
21. Matt. 15:32–39.
22. Matt. 16:15–26.

of David! Blessed is the one who comes in the name of the Lord."[23] In many contexts today, the hymn is still sung as the community gathers to receive both Host and gift at the Table. However, the hopeful welcome spills over into chaos. Jesus enters the temple, turns over these tables, and declares, quoting the prophet, "My house shall be called a house of prayer; but you are making it a den of thieves."[24]

The tension escalates as Jesus grieves over Jerusalem and exclaims, "Jerusalem, Jerusalem, the city that kills the prophets and stones those who are sent to it! How often have I desired to gather your children together as a hen gathers her brood under her wings and you were not willing!" With that comes the word of judgment: "See, your house is left to you desolate." Will the next words be received finally with fear or joy? "For I tell you, you will not see me again until you say, 'Blessed is the one who comes in the name of the Lord.'"[25]

The trajectory now is unmistakable. The disciple, Judas Iscariot, will gain infamy for his betrayal. Although they will protest otherwise, all shrink back from Jesus. The Host will pray that "the cup" of suffering and death "pass from me." But, in words that echo the prayer he taught his disciples, Jesus cries to the Father, "yet not what I want but what you want."[26]

It is not enough for Jesus as Christ to be a great teacher, miracle worker, and source of compassion. Given the nature of humanity and his vocation to be "fulfiller of all righteousness," he cannot be the Christ without the necessity of experiencing temptation, anguish, betrayal, rejection ("You will all become deserters . . ."[27]), and, ultimately, crucifixion.

In the presence of deadly opposition to Jesus, and perceived opposition to themselves, Jesus' friends will determine that he is not "Christ enough" for them. His opponents will deem Jesus as guilty of blasphemy, misrepresenting God. The religious and political community will combine to mock this "pretender," sentence him to death, and continue the scorn until he is dead: "He saved others; he cannot save himself. He is the King of Israel; let him come down from the cross now and we will believe in him. He trusts in God; let God deliver him now, if he wants to; for he said, 'I am God's Son.'"[28]

For this Host, at this critical time, deliverance does not come. The judgment of his friends ("this Christ is not sufficient") and of his enemies ("he is

23. Matt. 21:9.
24. Matt. 21:12–13.
25. Matt. 23:37–39.
26. Matt. 26:36–39.
27. Matt. 26:31.
28. Matt. 27:42–43.

an imposter deserving of death and under the judgment of God") is confirmed. Jesus' words from the cross (and the only words he speaks from the cross in Matthew and Mark!) seem to acknowledge that judgment, "My God, my God, why have you forsaken me?"[29] The critical question now is, if this verdict is true—if it is confirmed—then is it not bad news not only for this Christ but for the whole of humanity? Matthew now offers a clue that something else might be happening, some good news might be possible. In this terrifying moment the Roman officer and those with him concur, "Truly this man was God's Son."

The deadly silence continues until the break of dawn several days later. The women who at the crucifixion had "looked on at a distance" now draw near to a grave, the apparent destiny not only for all humanity but also for this one who is "God with us." In a great surprise, they receive the greeting from "an angel of the Lord": "Do not be afraid; I know that you are looking for Jesus who was crucified. He is not here; for he has been raised as he said."[30]

As Matthew tells the story, the risen Christ Jesus encounters his worshipful and fearful disciples. He announces the divine verdict: "All authority in heaven and on earth has been given to me." In a manner that indicates that this divine verdict is good news also for them and for all humanity, Jesus gives the authority to them: "Go therefore and make disciples of all nations, baptizing them in the name of the Father, and of the Son, and of the Holy Spirit, and teaching them to obey everything that I have commanded." The one who is "Emmanuel, God with us" now declares that God is with them too: "And remember, I am with you always, to the end of the age."[31]

What is the divine word about this Christ, this Host of the Table? One can now revisit Jesus' response to the question concerning which of the disciples will be granted positions of particular honor in the kingdom: "You know that the rulers of the Gentiles lord it over them and their great ones are tyrants over them. It will not be so among you; but whoever wishes to be great among you must be your servant. . . . Just as the Son of Man came not to be served but to serve and to give his life as a ransom for many."[32] Jesus' resurrection signals the divine "Yes" to this vocation which also will be the vocation of those who are at the Table, who will "drink the cup that I am about to drink."[33]

29. Matt. 27:45.
30. Matt. 28:5.
31. Matt. 28:16–20.
32. Matt. 20:25–28.
33. Matt. 20:22.

Taking Another Look at the Christ at the Table

Jesus' resurrection imparts renewed clarity concerning the significance of that moment when Jesus gathered to eat the Passover meal with his disciples. That meal celebrates the fulfillment of God's promises to a people now enslaved in Egypt. It is Israel's definitive story. To participate in this meal is to know that this story also is yours. But, as Matthew tells the story, the mood for this particular Passover is not celebrative. The opposition against Jesus clearly is growing. The disciples are "greatly distressed."[34] One of them is preparing to make his way out the door in an act of ultimate betrayal. But when the day is done, despite their protests otherwise, all will take flight.

In the midst of this ominous situation, the Host points to a promise-filled future which will not take place apart from a body that is broken and blood that will be "poured out." It is essential to hear the story again.

> While they were eating, Jesus took a loaf of bread, and after blessing it he broke it, gave it to the disciples, and said, "Take eat, this is my body." Then he took a cup, and after giving thanks, he gave it to them saying, "Drink from it, all of you; for this is my blood of the covenant which is poured out for many for the forgiveness of sins. I tell you, I will never again drink of this fruit of the vine until that day when I drink it new with you in my Father's kingdom."[35]

Placed within the whole of Matthew's story, these words are fulfilled—filled full. The one who has "all authority" gives it all up. He is "servant of all" who offers the gift of himself so that the ultimate divine verdict may be "forgiveness of sins." Yet, it must be said, even as Jesus gathers his dearest at the Table, they have no idea about the gift he is giving them. In the precise moment of their betrayal, Jesus makes clear that his life will be "poured out for many for the forgiveness of sins." The "many" will begin with those who are gathered at this Table. By their participation in his body and blood, his dying will be forever linked to their dying. His resurrection will signal the Father's approval of the beloved Son as well as forgiveness of sins and resurrection for those who are incorporated into Christ in this meal. At this moment, however, the disciples perceive none of this. Yet they receive Christ into their very bodies with the promise that this Christ "will drink it new with you in my Father's kingdom."

---

34. Matt. 26:22.
35. Matt. 26:26–29.

Considering the Questions Again from Matthew's Perspective

The chapter began with the intent (1) to clarify the nature of the Host at this Table; (2) to inquire concerning the gifts this particular Host would bestow; and (3) to ask concerning what the reception of these gifts might mean for those who gather at this Table. From the perspective of Matthew, the Host at this Table is Jesus, the Christ, the fulfiller of "all righteousness" and of God's promises. God's deliverance of Israel from slavery to freedom is fulfilled in this Christ who gives his body and blood that the ultimate freedom, namely, forgiveness of sins, might be a reality for all. In Jesus, we come to know the God who is with us and for us.

What are the gifts this Host would share? What does the reception of these gifts mean for those who gather at this Table? In the first instance, the very invitation to the Table constitutes the good news that the Host who has "all authority in heaven and on earth" chooses to exercise that authority by forgiving the sins of those at Table. In addition, the Host has declared that, because one receives Christ, one can know God is with her and for her in any and all circumstances. Faith gets to trust that promise no matter what. The invitation to the Table is an invitation that offers ongoing consolation "for the weary": "Come to me, all you that are weary and are carrying heavy burdens, and I will give you rest. Take my yoke upon you, and learn from me; for I am gentle and humble in heart and you will find rest for your souls."[36]

Considered from the perspective of the crucified and risen Lord, one could harvest many other texts from Matthew that offer the benefits of the Host. For example, as one comes fretful to the Table, the command of Jesus becomes the promise of the Host: "Strive first for the kingdom of God and his righteousness, and all these things will be given to you as well."[37] The promise of the risen Lord to his disciples is one of great comfort to disciples of every age: "And remember, I am with you always, to the end of the age."[38]

What does the reception of the Host's gifts and benefits mean for those who go from the Table into the world, that is, their daily lives? Perhaps the most obvious is that Christ is within them with the promise that "where two or three are gathered in my name, I am there among them." Those who have received God's forgiveness in Christ have the joy of getting others in on that forgiveness.[39] Again, one can reap a harvest of stories from Matthew. To "receive Christ" in bread and wine is to be empowered to "be Christ" in the world. That includes the freeing

36. Matt. 11:28–29.
37. Matt. 6:34.
38. Matt. 28:20.
39. Matt. 18.

possibility of denying oneself to discover life in its fullness. That involves welcoming children and seeing in them the signs of the in-breaking kingdom. It involves the vocation of being "light" in the world so that others may "give glory to your Father in heaven."[40] To "receive Christ" is to have eyes and hearts open to welcome Christ in the most vulnerable, "the least of these."[41]

The beginning and the end of a story deserve particular attention, and this is especially true for Matthew's story. Matthew begins by introducing us to Jesus the Christ. He concludes with the risen Christ exercising his authority by sharing it with the disciples and sending them out: "Go therefore and make disciples of all nations, baptizing them in the name of the Father and of the Son and of the Holy Spirit, and teaching them to obey everything that I have commanded you."[42] Those who leave the Table, together with those first disciples and those of every generation, have the blessed responsibility and authority to get others in on the gifts of this Host. Our participation in Christ's church at this moment signals that the disciples put that authority to good use. Such is our privilege as we still gather at the Table and are sent from the Table into the world.

Some Implications for Ministry in This Context

This chapter began with a review of that central Lutheran accent that we are justified by God's grace through faith in the crucified and risen Christ. The Augsburg Confession asserts: "So that we may obtain this faith, the ministry of teaching the gospel and administering the sacraments was instituted. For through the Word and the sacraments as through instruments the Holy Spirit is given, who effects faith where and when it pleases God in those who hear the gospel."[43] The chapter briefly described the (always) challenging context for the Lutheran Christian tradition, raised some contemporary questions, and then explored Matthew's "christology at the Table." Can this christology at the Table shape a response to the challenges faced by the church today?

We learn from a survey of the Gospel of Matthew that any discussion of christology at the Table must be linked to the telling of the story of Jesus the Christ. But it will not do simply to tell stories about Jesus as a great teacher, a confronter of the status quo, a miracle worker, a pursuer of justice, or even as one who conquered death. Rather, in the telling of the story, attention must be given to Matthew's understanding of the

40. Matt. 5:16.
41. Matt. 25.
42. Matt. 28:19–20.
43. *BoC*, 40.

identity of this Jesus as Christ, who he is and what he is about, what that has to do with God, how God is *for us* in Christ Jesus, and how that makes a difference for us and for God's mission in Christ for the world. Apart from the telling and hearing of this story, the eating and drinking at the Table are merely another eating and drinking. But with the telling of this story, the Holy Spirit is at work creating faith. With the particular telling of this story around the Table, Jesus the Christ is still Host and Feast, forgiving sins, promising his presence, and sending those fed to be signs of and participants in his in-breaking kingdom.

The challenges to God's mission through the church, including that part of the church that reflects the Lutheran Christian tradition, are significant. In the presence of these challenges it is tempting to "go light," that is, to speak of a universal grace of God's love apart from the crucified and risen Lord. Or we may choose to make that story merely an "example of God's love" as opposed to the instrument through whom God would move us from death to life. It may be tempting to craft worship services designed to "attract" with minimal attention to the (de facto) story that is being told, perhaps even absent the presence of the crucified and risen Lord. The Table can be presented in such a way as to minimize both our Lord's invitation and his empowerment to "take up the cross and follow" in favor of making it a "love feast where all are welcomed."

Others are inclined to assume that by practicing long-held traditions they are being faithful to "the tradition" (the tradition that according to Paul, "I received from the Lord what I also handed on to you"). But those customs become meaningless performance of ritual when they do not connect the proclaimed word of the crucified and risen Lord to the Host and the Table. It is a betrayal of "the tradition" when those gathered at the Table presume that because they have followed the rules or kept certain customs or taken classes they are insiders. And it is a betrayal of "the tradition" as well when it is forgotten that this Table has something to do with what happens after one leaves. When such is the case, the stranger can easily feel condemned, out of place, and not welcomed either in the gathered community or at the Table. Ironically, though, those who believe that the Table is exclusively for them may in the process miss out on the gifts of the Host.

Not surprisingly, in both instances the church may be inclined to forget that the church is God's mission to the world, particularly when "the world" seems hostile or indifferent to the Word that shapes our lives. When yielding to such temptations, we forget that God sends us into all the world. That may include going to places where we get to welcome children when others are sending them way. Or it may lead to eating with "the tax collectors and sinners" of our day or meeting Christ in those places where those who are gathered are considered "the least" valued in society. With such forgetfulness, we indicate that we have forgotten how God in Christ acted first for us while we were (and still are) plotting our own betrayals.

Given those temptations and the inclination to forget that the church is God's mission to the world, what would it mean for Christian leadership to consider what it means to be invited to the Table with Christ as Host and Feast? What then would be "at stake" in terms of what takes place in worship or in the church's life in the world? As indicated in the opening paragraphs of this chapter, the Augsburg Confession insists that we make use of Jesus' death and resurrection in order that "for his sake our sin is forgiven and righteousness and eternal life are given to us." We have reviewed how Matthew makes use of the story of the crucified and risen Lord, particularly as we have reexamined the gospel through Matthew's account of the Lord's Supper.

Who is the Host at this Table? What are the gifts and benefits that this Host would bestow to those gathered at the Table? What difference does the reception of these gifts and benefits make for those who are fed at this Table and for their life in the world? These are questions addressed by the Augsburg Confessors. By God's grace, Matthew already has provided some direction.

9

On the Other Hand: God's Care for the Creation and Its Dilemmas

Marie A. Failinger

The church's only authority is the authority of the gospel, says the Augsburg Confession. It is the authority to forgive sins. The church does not have authority from God to exert worldly power. But God also operates outside the church, exerting power through civil authorities too. It is the power to promote justice. Professor Marie Failinger, an attorney and professor of law, borrows the language of the Reformers to speak of how God operates in two kingdoms (or "governances"), one for the care of creation, the other for the redemption of creation. She advocates for recognition of our "creative creatureliness" to pursue social justice without claiming that, as Christians, we have divinely authorized answers to difficult and complex problems.[1]

Luther was a strong advocate for the Christian vocation of citizenship, but Lutheran doctrine really complicates the question of how Christians should engage lawmakers on difficult questions of public policy, or even be good lawmakers themselves. Most Christians today live in constitutional democracies, or nations that at least purport to reflect

---

1. Edward Schroeder was first my freshman theology teacher at Valparaiso University, and then a counselor about how one lives a Lutheran life. But he has been even more my teacher as I have turned back to Lutheran theology to provide useful insights to my fellow lawyers and law professors about the demands of justice upon secular law.

values such as the rule of law, the duty to govern fairly, and basic human rights like life, liberty, and equality. To ensure that the secular law of their nation reflect critical values, Christians must convince citizens and lawmakers of widely divergent religious, social, and cultural backgrounds—who hold a spectrum of political views—to support the passage and enforcement of laws they believe are just.

When no political consensus emerges on difficult moral and social issues, which is most often the case, Christians have to decide whether a proposed law is so important to the common good that they are willing to essentially coerce others who disagree into obeying the law. Or, they may have to decide how much they are willing to compromise on some values in order to protect others.

Lutheran teaching complicates reflection on what laws are just. In particular, Lutheran teaching, on the two kingdoms or two governances (or, in Edward Schroeder's words, the two regimes[2]) and on the orders of creation (or, as Schroeder calls them, "the Creator's ordainings"), suggests a more nuanced understanding of what constitutes just laws. Through these doctrines, Lutherans have tried to articulate carefully how God shapes both individual human callings and institutional structures to serve the needs of the world.

To describe God's work in our world, Luther spoke about the distinctive work of God's two "hands," a firm recognition that God is actively involved in the world in every age. With the "left hand," God continues to care for the bountiful beauty founded in the beginning and crafted anew every moment, in the world inhabited by God's creatures, God's created ones. Indeed, we describe God's left-hand work as that of a loving father or mother to capture our closest human ideal of a protective, creating, disciplining, and encouraging companion on the journey we make from birth to death. Werner Elert's *Law and Gospel* describes God's "left-hand" work in these words:

> *Nomos* ("law") is a concept of order, denoting a particular relationship of man to God, as well as to the entire creaturely world. By means of creation, man

2. See AC 28:10–13, 18: "Therefore, since this power of the church bestows eternal things and is exercised only through the ministry of the Word, it interferes with civil government as little as the art of singing interferes with it. For civil government is concerned with things other than the gospel. For the magistrate protects not minds but bodies and goods from manifest harm and constrains people with the sword and physical penalties. The gospel protects minds from ungodly ideas, the devil, and eternal death. Consequently, the powers of church and civil government must not be mixed. The power of the church possesses its own command to preach the gospel and administer the sacraments. It should not usurp the other's duty, transfer earthly kingdoms, abrogate the laws of magistrates, abolish lawful obedience, interfere with judgments concerning any civil ordinances or contracts, prescribe to magistrates laws concerning the form of government that should be established. . . . In this way our people distinguish the duties of the two powers, and they command that both be held in honor and acknowledged as a gift and blessing of God." *BoC*, 93.

is placed into the world; by means of *nomos*, he is held secure in it. . . . Nomological existence . . . consequently also means that we are not at the mercy of an arbitrary authority, a blind fate, a chaos of accidental hit or miss; rather, with all other creatures, we too are subject to the lawfully ordered reign of God.[3]

Lutherans have described God's "left-hand" ordering of our world by speaking of what we lawyers would call the distinct "jurisdictions" of state, church, and household. Lutherans would also include "orders of creation" newly formed as the creation comes anew from age to age.

But in Edward Schroeder's own words,

[c]aring for creation, as good and necessary as it is, does not yet redeem creation. . . . Christ's work of redemption brings sinners back [from alien ownership] under God's ownership and management, specifically God's "mercy management. . . ." The secular world, at its best, operates on God's law for caring (equity, fairness, and care for others), not at all on God's gospel of redemption. . . . This "left-hand/right-hand" picture of God's two-fold work in this one world is what Lutherans have in mind when we "dedicate ourselves to the care and redemption of all that you, God, have made."[4]

The work of the secular law, which is the subject of this chapter, is the work of God's left hand. Luther's view that human reason—everyone's reason—is a good gift from God in the service of protecting and revitalizing this earthly life for us all seems to afford Christians a firm starting place for considering whether that law orders the creation as God intends.

In the Augsburg Confession, we recognize that secular law, as a product of human reason, is a good gift when kept in its proper place of governing human beings in this space and time; and that Christians, with all others, bear the responsibility of making and enforcing it.[5] However, determining what those particular laws should be is complicated, especially for those Lutherans reluctant to sign on to a "third use" of the law. We recognize that all persons have access to what Christians have called "natural law," God's creative activity and intentions that Paul says are "written on [our] hearts" (Rom. 2:15). But

3. Werner Elert, *Law and Gospel*, trans. Edward H. Schroeder (Philadelphia: Fortress Press, 1967), 14. This is an essay taken from *Zwischen Gnade und Ungnade: Abwandlungen des Themas Gesetz und Evangelium* (Munich: Evangelischer Presseverband für Bayern, 1948).
4. Edward H. Schroeder, "The Care and Redemption of God's Creation, or God's Two Projects in the One World: Care and Redemption Capitalizing on the Image of God as Ambidextrous, a Proposal for Using Luther's Two Kingdoms Theology in Daily Life," Lutheran Professional Church Workers Conference, St. Louis, Missouri, March 11, 1999, http://www.crossings.org/library/schroeder2/God.pdf.
5. AC 16:1, 2 holds, "Concerning civic affairs they teach that lawful civil ordinances are good works of God and that Christians are permitted to hold civil office, to work in law courts, to decide matters by imperial and other existing laws, to impose just punishments, to wage just war, to serve as soldiers, to make legal contracts, to hold property, to take an oath when required by magistrates, to take a wife, to be given in marriage." *BoC*, 49.

even Christians do not agree on the specifics of natural law on, for example, marriage and the family. And, because non-Christians will disobey even what all agree is the natural law, such as the duty not to murder others, the secular law serves an important "civil use" in restraining such evil and contributing to just, peaceful, and productive communities.

Christians are another story. Luther concluded that out of the freedom Christians experienced as saved persons, they would respond in joyful service to their neighbors, willingly pouring out their lives in ways that might not be seen in the lives of non-Christians. Thus, the secular law might seem almost irrelevant to Christians, because the secular law's behavioral demands are exceedingly modest compared to the neighbor-love one might expect from a Christian. Yet, it was Luther who reminded us that we Christians are *simul justus et peccator*—at once free and yet enslaved to sin. Of course, logically, when and as they are sinners, in what we lawyers might call "their sinful capacity," the secular law would also apply to restrain and penalize Christians. And, there is the Augsburg Confession's acknowledgment that it is Christians' duty to keep the secular law in recognition of its place in the created order and for the benefit of their non-Christian neighbors.[6]

Thus, paradoxically, while non-Christians live under the secular law (in its civil use), Christians seem to be freed from following the secular law on this earth, and yet encouraged to follow it, as sinners and as obedient respondents to God's preserving work in the world. Indeed, it gets worse: because of the twofold governance of God in the world, Luther and the Augsburg Confession seem to require that Christians obey the secular law as a good governance of God *even when they profoundly disagree with it*, and at the same time require them to *stand against their rulers* if the law commands them to sin.[7] When Christians

---

6. AC 16:5, 6a provides, "In the meantime the gospel does not undermine government or family but completely requires both their preservation as ordinances of God and the exercise of love in these ordinances. Consequently, Christians owe obedience to their magistrates . . ." *BoC*, 49, 51. For a fuller discussion of why Christians, who are no longer under the secular law, should still obey it, see Johannes Heckel, *Lex Charitatis: A Juristic Disquisition on Law in the Theology of Martin Luther*, ed. and trans. Gottfried Krodel (Grand Rapids: Eerdmans, 2010).

7. AC 16:6, 7 provides, "Consequently, Christians owe obedience to their magistrates and laws except when commanded to sin. For then they owe greater obedience to God than to human beings (Acts 5[:29])." *BoC*, 51. This raises an interesting complexity: How do Christians decide when the secular law "commands them to sin" and when they should "obey God rather than men"? At some points, Luther appears to offer a bright-line distinction for when we should obey (i.e., distinguishing secular commands to surrender on theological issues from commands about temporal action) and other times not. See Martin Luther, "Temporal Authority: To What Extent It Must be Obeyed?" in *Martin Luther's Basic Theological Writings*, ed. Timothy Lull (Minneapolis: Augsburg Fortress Press, 1989), 668–74. See also Heckel, supra note 6, at 107–14 for another account of the Christian duties of obedience and disobedience to the ruler.

should respect the calling of their governors, and when they should stand against those governors, is hard to figure out.

We might contrast the Lutheran approach with two other ways of imagining how God works in the development of secular law. One approach, sometimes portraying God as the watchmaker who sets the world ticking but then stops being involved, suggests that what happens on this earth is up to us humans alone, so we can pretty much decide for ourselves what the secular law should be and not worry about "what God thinks" of our efforts. A second, contrasting view suggests that God has given us fairly comprehensive commands about how we should live in this world in sacred scriptures or historical interventions, and we human beings only fill in the details.

Lutherans have largely rejected both of these approaches in favor of the more complicated view that God and human beings are co-creating and co-preserving this world throughout history. In this view, people don't simply depend on their own brainpower to figure out how to shape secular law. Rather, they must be open to hearing, seeing, and interpreting the action of God in the world in constructing institutions designed to protect human life and its flourishing. The problem, of course, is that God is always absconding from our efforts to contain and understand God; the evidence of God's work in this world is only available through God's masks, who include other people pursuing their own vocations. We can never be sure we have fully captured or understood God's will, particularly given our penchant for reshaping that understanding according to our own self-justifying wills.

Even if this is the complicated truth of human existence, it does not seem to help a Lutheran citizen very much in deciding what, say, the law in Minnesota—where I live and teach—should declare on socially contested issues. Yet, secular law requires us to make concrete decisions in writing and adjudicating law. So a Lutheran citizen must be able to make a case to others who do not share his or her theology about whether a woman should be legally permitted to have an abortion, whether a tax system is unjust and must be reformed, who should be able to legally marry whom, and what legal constraints the state should put on people's pollution on their own property. That case must be strong enough to gain voluntary compliance with the law from most citizens, which often means putting aside explicitly theological arguments (i.e., "God said, so therefore we should not do X") in favor of political arguments that can be accepted by people from a wide range of religious and nonreligious viewpoints.

Affirmative Action and Lutheran Theology

Because practical problems put moral arguments to the best test of whether Christians have anything unique to say about the political conversations about just law, we might consider one of the many dilemmas of our time to see what Lutheran doctrine *can* contribute to the political conversation about secular law. The so-called "affirmative action" debate has roiled American society for decades, and affected governments as different as Brazil and the European Union. In essence, this debate asks whether governments or businesses legally may (or must) provide racial and ethnic minorities with better treatment in awarding admission to elite universities, government contracts, jobs, and other opportunities because of past discrimination against them or their forebears.

Around the world, but particularly in the United States, courts are being asked to decide whether national constitutions prohibit these programs or not. Indeed, the United States Supreme Court recently decided yet another affirmative action case in June 2013—the question of whether the University of Texas undergraduate admission system could consider the race of applicants as a factor in admissions, or whether this consideration would be a violation of the equal protection clause of the Fourteenth Amendment to the Constitution.[8] Beyond the constitutional question, scholars and ordinary citizens must frame secular principles of justice and equality to decide whether to urge lawmakers to require, permit, or prohibit affirmative action programs.

Lutherans themselves have not been of one mind about affirmative action. On one hand, social statements of the American churches have advocated acknowledgment of the sin of racism and the recognition of a civil right to equal opportunity, and some church institutions have instituted equal opportunity practices that recognize affirmative action as a social good.[9] On the other, prominent Lutherans such as Justice

8. In the case, *Fisher v. University of Texas at Austin*, 631 F.3d 213 (5th Cir. 2011), the Fifth Circuit Court of Appeals held that the Texas program, which considered applicants' race as one factor in the admissions process, had in good faith made the determination that such consideration was necessary to fulfill its compelling interest in a diverse student body. The United States Supreme Court dodged the question of whether any affirmative action program that included a consideration of race would be held constitutional by remanding the case for the Fifth Circuit to decide whether the University had considered all reasonable race-neutral alternatives first.

9. For example, the American Lutheran Church issued a social statement in 1966 that claimed that "to deny equality of opportunity to any person is to deny the revelation of Scripture, the counsel of reason, and the laws of our nation," and yet recognized that Lutherans would differ "as to which measures or which laws can best guarantee equality of opportunity." See *Equality of Opportunity*, available at http://download.elca.org/ELCA Resource Repository/Equality_of_OpportunityALC66.PDF. The 1964 statement of the Lutheran Church in America (LCA), while supporting the enactment of legislation that guaranteed access to education, employment, and public accommodations, seemed to reject affirmative action in the church, noting that "[i]n the calling of pastors and the employing of staff the congregations of this church should not make the race of the can-

William Rehnquist have rejected affirmative action programs, and the Lutheran Church – Missouri Synod has gone to court to oppose a government affirmative action program imposed on its broadcast facilities.[10]

To drill down to what is at stake in these debates, we might look at the stories of three people who filed lawsuits to invalidate affirmative action programs. Jennifer Gratz, a young white woman, was denied admission to the University of Michigan undergraduate program in 1995. Jennifer "thought she was a shoo-in" to the University and applied to no other colleges, because she had an ACT score in the 83rd percentile, and had worked hard to polish her college resumé as a cheerleader, student body president, homecoming queen, and volunteer.[11] When she received her rejection at Michigan, "[Jennifer was] devastated, angry, and embarrassed all at once. Jennifer thought about all the hard work on her studies, extracurriculars, and application. . . . [She] was sure that something had gone terribly wrong. Her thoughts flashed to a Hispanic classmate who had been admitted to Michigan with lower grades than hers. Finally, Jennifer uttered the first words that came to her, 'Dad,' she said, 'can we sue them?'"

Abigail Fisher, the principal plaintiff in the University of Texas case, similarly claimed, "There were people in my class with lower grades who weren't in all the activities I was in who were being accepted into UT, and the only other difference between us was the color of our skin."[12]

---

didate a qualification for consideration." LCA Statement, *Race Relations* (1964) available at http://elcic.ca/Public-Policy/documents/900.11964-ASocialStatementonRaceRelations.pdf (visited March 28, 2016.) The ELCA "Path to Affiliation" handbook, p. 11, lists the expectation that affiliated social ministry organizations "adopt equal opportunity and affirmative action policies which promote an environment in which racial, ethnic, cultural, and gender diversity is understood, respected and observed." This handbook is available at http://www.lutheranservices.org/sites/default/files/images/pdfs/SMO_affiliation_5.pdf.

10. In *Lutheran Church—Missouri Synod v. Federal Communications Commission and the United States*, 141 F.3d 344 (1998), the LCMS won a challenge to Federal Communications Commission regulations that required radio stations to implement an affirmative action program focused on getting more women and minorities into broadcast businesses. Among other things, it required radio stations—such as KFUO owned by the Missouri Synod, which broadcast from Concordia Seminary in St. Louis—to employ job-recruiting and promotion policies that would increase the numbers of women and minorities in the business. The FCC suggested that hiring policies requiring Lutheran training and classical musical expertise were not relevant to all station jobs, and violated the LCMS's legal responsibilities to recruit minority employees. The Court of Appeals held that the FCC rules violated the equal protection clause.

11. Jennifer's story is taken from Greg Stohr, *A Black and White Case: How Affirmative Action Survived Its Greatest Legal Challenge* 1–2 (2004). In the legal cases filed by Jennifer and her law school applicant counterpart, *Grutter v. Bollinger*, 539 U.S. 306 (2003) and *Gratz v. Bollinger*, 539 U.S. 244 (2003), the Supreme Court considered two University of Michigan affirmative action admissions programs. The undergraduate program awarded significant points toward their total admissions score to applicants who were racial or ethnic minorities, while the law school considered race and ethnicity only as a factor to be weighed with all others in the decision. The Supreme Court upheld the law school plan, but overturned the undergraduate plan which was applied to Jennifer Gratz as a violation of the Equal Protection Clause.

12. Fisher's video statement was again reported in the wake of the Supreme Court's decision in *Fisher v. University of Texas*: Richard Wolf, "Court Calls for Tougher Scrutiny of Affirmative Action," *USA Today*, June 24, 2013, available at http://www.usatoday.com/story/news/

In another seminal Supreme Court case, *Adarand Constructors, Inc. v. Peña*, 515 U.S. 200 (1995), Randy Pech sued the federal government because, under a program for socially and economically disadvantaged persons, it awarded contractors who employed minority subcontractors a bonus that these contractors did not receive if the subcontractor was white. Pech was the only Caucasian owning a guardrail company in the geographical area of a Colorado highway project, and his low bid to furnish guardrails was rejected because of the federal bonus program. Pech thought that "government programs that disfavored White men were gaining momentum." When he heard that he had submitted the low bid but the contract would still go to a minority firm, he said, "I flipped."[13]

For Jennifer, Abigail, and Randy, and those who support their cause, the government's application and contracting policies were unfair because skin color played a partial role in who would be selected to go to Michigan or Texas, and to get a guardrail contract in Colorado. They essentially argue the law should be "colorblind," to use Justice Harlan's language,[14] applying the same standard to every applicant or contractor without paying any attention to his or her racial or ethnic background. A stingy reading of Luther might support their cause: affirmative action programs seem not designed to restrain evildoers in this world, the chief object of the "civil use" of the law.[15] Affirmative action opponents would argue that this sort of evil is fully "taken care of" by mid-twentieth-century civil rights laws prohibiting racial and ethnic discrimination, passed in the wake of shameful and devastating racial apartheid practiced in the United States both before and after the Civil War. In their view, affirmative action either is irrelevant to this kind of wrongdoing, or goes so far that it re-creates the wrong in the other direction, toward innocent white people.

Secular Law Embraces Justice

A reading of the civil use of the law that limits the secular law to

politics/2013/06/24/supreme-court-race-affirmative-action-texas-michigan-roberts-kennedy/2086039/.

13. Pech's story is taken from Joan Biskupic, "High Court to Hear Racial-Preference Case," *Albany Times Union*, Jan. 17, 1995, at A4.

14. In *Plessy v. Ferguson*, 163 U.S. 537, 559 (1897) (Harlan, J., dissenting), Harlan opined, "Our Constitution is color-blind, and neither knows nor tolerates classes among citizens. In respect of civil rights, all citizens are equal before the law. The humblest is the peer of the most powerful." *Plessy* was the seminal case upholding racial segregation by law, and was not fully overturned until the Supreme Court cases leading up to *Brown v. Board of Education*, 347 U.S. 483 (1954).

15. Augsburg Confession 28 describes the chief use of the secular law in this way: "The civil rulers defend not minds, but bodies and bodily things against manifest injuries, and restrain men with the sword and bodily punishments in order to preserve civil justice and peace."

punishing extreme moral wrongdoing seems unduly meager, particularly in a world in which law governs so much more of our social and economic lives than it did in Luther's time. The Augsburg Confession so recognizes by understanding the civil use of the law as not only restraining evil, but also embracing the duty "that charity be practiced in such ordinances [of the State.]"[16] However, Lutheran theology also rejects the claim that the secular law should mimic a "what would Jesus do?" standard to be imposed on all persons, Christians and non-Christians alike. That solution seems to conflate the two kingdoms, push us back into works-righteousness, and misunderstand how Christian freedom engenders what ethicists call supererogatory works on behalf of the neighbor.[17]

If we cannot simply legislate "what Jesus would do" into the secular law of this unruly world, then we are left to consider what justice on this earth entails, and how much we factor in human frailty and sinfulness in building structures that will create more "earth-justice" and less destructive behavior. Jennifer Gratz and Randy Pech believed that earth-justice required their government to assess what they personally had done to earn their places in line for government benefits. They also believed the government should compare it with what others, here racial minorities, had done, according to relevant objective factors like grades and bids. For them and others, consideration of race in awarding these benefits violates the basic constitutional principle of the political equality of all citizens. Put simply, if Jennifer's grades were higher than her Latino classmate's, she believed that she deserved to get in rather than him. If Randy Pech submitted the lowest successful bid on guardrails, then the objective rules of government contract bidding, instituted so that governments can run most economically, should have dictated giving the job to him, he believed.

But those who support affirmative action in these cases call for a longer view of the problem. Rather than assessing each applicant's qualifications as of the application or bid, they would expect government decision-makers to view the historical context of these decisions. Maybe the minority students who got in with lower scores than Jennifer Gratz attended largely segregated schools (as an embarrassingly large number of students still do), and thus did more poorly on the ACT, even if they were actually smarter than Jennifer.

16. Augsburg Confession 16 (5)–(6).
17. The *Stanford Encyclopedia of Philosophy* defines these as "the class of actions that go 'beyond the call of duty.' Roughly speaking, supererogatory acts are morally good although not (strictly) required." The Encyclopedia notes that Lutherans and Calvinists attacked Catholic moral philosophy's development of the idea of acts that are not required though morally good. *Stanford Encyclopedia of Philosophy*, "Supererogation," available at http://plato.stanford.edu/entries/supererogation/.

Maybe their high schools were impoverished, and didn't offer students access to the extracurricular activities Jennifer had accumulated. Similarly, maybe Randy Pech was able to build a low-bidding guardrail business because he had better access to capital from Caucasian business partners who wouldn't fund some of his minority competitors. Or perhaps he got a head start in his business at a time when construction industry discrimination kept them out (as Congress found was the case in extensive hearings on the construction industry).

To follow a metaphor often used to explain the affirmative action position, maybe Jennifer and Randy started the race closer to the finish line because of their advantages. Thus, a true "equal chance to compete" requires affirmative action by government to move their minority competitors up to the same starting line. Of course, affirmative action opponents rightly point out that not all disadvantage correlates to skin color. Yale law professor Stephen Carter famously wrote a book, *Reflections of an Affirmative Action Baby* (New York: Basic Books, 2002), describing how he received affirmative action consideration for college even though his family was far from disadvantaged. And Cheryl Hopwood, a rejected white applicant who won an affirmative action case against the University of Texas, remarked that she too had disadvantages which weren't considered in denying her application: she was the child of a single mother, and struggled to maintain her 3.8 GPA while parenting a severely handicapped daughter and working twenty hours a week.[18] Nevertheless, affirmative action proponents will point out, there remains a significant correlation between race and disadvantage in American society.

Affirmative action advocates will also put forward another fairness argument: affirmative action is an appropriate form of "reparations" for past racial discrimination that we now all acknowledge. Isn't affirmative action the least we can do for someone who has suffered pervasively from social discrimination throughout his life, or whose life-chances have been diminished because of discrimination his parents or grandparents were subjected to? For example, studies have suggested that family wealth disparities between Caucasian and minority families in the U.S. are in part traceable to past racial discrimination in employment and business; that discrimination has limited the ability of minority families to accumulate and pass down money and property to their families.[19] That extra wealth has made it possible for later

---

18. David G. Savage, "'Bakke II' Case Renews Debate on Admissions," *Los Angeles Times,* July 30, 1995.
19. One of the most recent studies of racial wealth disparities in the U.S. shows that the past five years of recession, which have seen continuing discriminatory practices, have deepened the wealth gap between whites and minorities. African Americans possess about six-

generations of Caucasian students to attend better schools, have access to more educational and social opportunities, and even to provide capital for new businesses or ventures.

Affirmative action proponents also argue that racial and ethnic minorities need to make up social and economic ground lost during slavery and segregation (and we need to help them do so), so that we all can take full advantage of their talents and skills. When everyone is provided with the opportunities to maximize his or her gifts, we all benefit. They may cite Justice Blackmun, who opined, "in order to get beyond racism, we must take account of race. There is no other way. And in order to treat some persons equally, we must treat them differently."[20]

Does Affirmative Action Cause Social Evil?

In trying to decide whether Christians should argue that affirmative action is just or unjust, we must also look at what the Supreme Court has said about why affirmative action programs can cause social evil. In a series of cases, most prominently *City of Richmond v. J. A. Croson Co.*, 488 U.S. 469 (1989) and *Adarand*, the United States Supreme Court has invalidated many affirmative action programs because they could not meet the rigid equal protection requirements of "strict scrutiny" analysis.[21] Indeed, in *Adarand*, the Court held that any government program will be "suspect" even when it aims to help racial minorities overcome disadvantage.[22]

What arguments do the Justices make in favor of reading the Constitution this way? Some simply argue that the use of race is wrong per se, "odious," because it is not relevant in any way to a person's merit,

teen percent and Latino Americans about 17% of the wealth of non-Hispanic white Americans. Annie Lowrey, "Wealth Gap Among Races Has Widened Since Recessions," *New York Times*, April 28, 2013, available at http://www.nytimes.com/2013/04/29/business/racial-wealth-gap-widened-during-recession.html?nl=todaysheadlines&emc=edit_th_2013 0429&_r=0.

20. *Regents of the University of California v. Bakke*, 438 U.S. 265, 407 (1978) (Blackmun, J., concurring).

21. "Strict scrutiny" review invalidates racial classifications unless the government can demonstrate that it has a "compelling" purpose for using them, and there is no other "less restrictive" alternative besides using race that could achieve the government's purpose. This scrutiny has sometimes been called "strict in theory, fatal in fact" because it is exceedingly difficult for any government law to survive it, though some justices like Justice O'Connor have suggested that this is not an inevitable outcome of strict scrutiny review.

22. There are few purposes the government has been able to provide for race classifications that the Supreme Court considers "compelling." One legitimate purpose is to compensate minority groups for the government's own clearly identified racial discrimination in the past in the particular program where affirmative action is being afforded. In *Grutter v. Bollinger*, 539 U.S. 306 (2003) and *Gratz v. Bollinger*, 539 U.S. 244 (2003), following Justice Powell's opinion in *Regents of the University of California v. Bakke*, 438 U.S. 265 (1978), most Supreme Court justices agreed that there is a compelling interest in having a diverse student body in higher education. The Court was split on whether student body diversity is a compelling interest in K–12 education in *Parents Involved in Community Schools v. Seattle School District No. 1*, 551 U.S. 701 (2007).

and has been used oppressively in the past to deny citizens both rights and opportunities. Others argue that preferring minorities is bound to cause resentment by majorities who "did nothing wrong," who did not themselves create socially unjust conditions caused by racism. It is a common moral intuition that innocent people should not be punished if they did nothing wrong; that intuition, the justices suggest, counsels that majority applicants (e.g., white males) should not be denied opportunities because of what their forbears did. Moreover, majority resentment will in turn lead to racial division, with its specter of social conflict and even violence.

A third concern of some justices is that affirmative action will reinforce the majority view that racial and ethnic minorities cannot succeed on their own. In other words, affirmative action is seen to perpetuate paternalistic responses that will result in disrespect and stigmatization of minorities, and even more social discrimination against them. Finally, Justice Thomas has argued that minorities will come to see themselves as "entitled" to preferences and therefore refuse to employ their strengths to compete for such opportunities, thereby perpetuating old stereotypes about minorities, e.g., that they are lazy or incompetent.[23]

So the question: Should Christians argue for eliminating race from any consideration in the award of a government opportunity, even if it is intended to benefit previously disadvantaged minorities? Should the answer to this question be largely shaped by human realities including human sin? That is, should the courts invalidate affirmative action programs because they will result in majority resentment of minorities' good fortune, paternalistic or stereotypical treatment, minorities' corrosive sense of entitlement, or divisive political and social blocs based on race? Or should Christians argue for something more like, though never equivalent to, a "Christian" response—i.e., demanding that better-off majorities "lay down their lives" for these others who have been harmed?

Realistic Contextualization and Critical Engagement

While there is no one "correct" Christian conclusion to these questions, Lutherans' views do, I think, provide some guiding insights. I will describe these insights as *realistic contextualism* and *critical engagement* that takes into account our human condition as *creative creatures* and accepts our responsibility to *welcome the other in his need*. None of these

---

23. These arguments can be found in *City of Richmond v. J. A. Croson Co.*, 488 U.S. 469, 492–93 (1989) and *Adarand* at 215–16, 225–30, 240–41.

insights requires a particular commitment to the Christian faith; all of them can be realized through observation and human reason.

First, Lutheran theology would insist on *realistic contextualism*, that we should realistically approach and value the created world as it currently exists, in all of its complexity. On a material level, that means studied attention to the immediate creation that is directly accessible to our senses as well as that which is accessible through the technologies we have available to us. In the affirmative action debate, that means that decisions about what is just for Jennifer Gratz or Randy Pech must go beyond asking whether a particular policy violates a rule and take account of the institutional structures and dynamics that caused these rules to be in place, including racial discrimination that may have played a part in creating these structures.

Realistic contextualism also insists on attention to the history of humankind. Human history, indeed the history of creation, is as much our responsibility to understand and keep in mind when we make moral and legal choices, even though our grasp on the past is limited and our insight into the future even more so. Thus, it seems to me that Lutherans would reject an approach to the affirmative action question that puts on blinders to the past, or dismisses the possible consequences that might flow from having or not having such programs.

Lutherans would also advocate for recognition of our *creative creatureliness*. That we are creatures reminds us of three things. First, we are created in the image of God, and are therefore deserving of others' respect. Second, we are made finite, and thus our finitude must be accepted as God's will, as we understand our vocation in this world. Third, in the big scheme of things, we are property-less: what we have is not ours and not deserved, but God's and undeserved.

The first aspect of our creatureliness—that we are made in the image of God—leads to the insight captured in international human rights law that the human dignity of all persons must be respected. That means, in a particular legal case, respecting the full dignity of those like Jennifer Gratz who bring lawsuits or propose legislation as well as those who will be affected by the outcome of litigation or legislation, even if they are not visibly before the court or legislative body. In secular terms, the idea of human dignity is expressed in a number of ways. For example, the human person is inviolable and certain things may never morally be done to him or her; he or she should never be used as a mere means to an end.

For Christians, of course, recognition of human dignity is an obligation toward God. When we choose not to see the image of God in the other, we are choosing to deny the goodness of God's creative work in the world. We are also refusing to fully employ the moral imagination God gave us to understand and respond to the created world. In recognizing that all human beings are in relationship with the living God and with each other whether they recognize that fact or not, we might turn our attention away from the word "law" that is often the focus of analyzing "the law written on [our] hearts" and toward the words "written" and "hearts." With this change in perspective, we see that the secular law is not a body of abstract precepts "set in stone out there" in the moral universe, rules to be applied according to a formal logic inherent in their precepts. That is, the natural law does not have its own existence and authority apart from the realities of human community. More importantly, it does not have its own existence and authority apart from the constantly creating work of God.

We might more helpfully say that the moral foundation of the law is God's writing on our hearts in every moment, God's constant demand upon us as we encounter the need of every creature in this world. Jewish philosopher Emmanuel Levinas vividly describes reality *as* ethics: "I am met by the face of the Other, who towers over me in his need, demanding that I respond to it. I am literally denying reality if I try to reduce him or his need to fit into a box that I mentally construct in order to deny the fullness of his need or reject his demand on me to meet it."[24]

If the encounter with other creatures itself is the natural law, our moral life—including our secular law—will be shaped very differently than the justice that legal abstractions of fairness or equality will render. At best, principles of justice will serve as helpful prompts, reminding us that we have to pay attention to God's and the other's demanding simultaneous encounters with us. In paying attention to the writing that God does upon our hearts, we open our understanding to seeing the Other in unexpected ways that are much larger and more complex than can be captured by a statute or constitutional principle. We will understand the secular law as a heuristic to enable us to grasp and respond in the moment to human injustice and human need. That response does not ask us to blind our eyes to human desperation, self-aggrandizement, greed, or the desire to inflict pain on others as we write the law. It asks us to confront the other out of our experience, and to co-create structures that make it possible for him to live a dignified life, appropriately accountable for his wrongdoing and appropriately cared for in his need.

That is to say, the natural law asks us to make room to *welcome the*

---

24. Levinas's extended argument from this image is pursued in many of his works, most thoroughly in *Totality and Infinity: An Essay on Exteriority* (Pittsburgh: Duquesne University Press, 1961), 194–201.

stranger in his need, not as an enemy or a competitor, but as one whom we are called to live for.[25] In our welcome, we acknowledge the second aspect of our creatureliness: we are indeed finite creatures, i.e., limited in our ability to respond to the stranger's need by both internal resources and external possessions. When we forget the finitude that accompanies our creatureliness, it is easy to become angry at the need (and the person) that we see, or to despair that we can make any difference, and turn inward to our own concerns and desires.

Remembering our finitude frees us to our vocation to meet the need of the neighbor, of whatever race he or she may be, to respond as we can out of the endowments we have been provided for this daily work. Likewise, as we construct secular law, remembering that we are creatures as much as creators helps us to remember the limits of what it can do, both to restrain evil and to build up community. That reminder helps us to be modest about our fallible judgment, realizing that we will often misunderstand what justice requires, and that secular law must be corrected from age to age. It also helps us to remember that secular law cannot do everything to bring about just communities; we will think carefully about what the state can usefully accomplish and what must be left to other institutions in human life.

Secular Law and Human Need

What this means for the affirmative action debate is that human need, not human sin, must be our foremost consideration in shaping secular law. To simply accept the proposition that the law must succumb to, and be fully shaped by, the reality of human sin seems to subvert the reality of our encounters with others. In the reading of some justices, human beings will inevitably respond to racial preference with resentment, paternalism, and claims of entitlement. Thus, in their view, law must be framed to avoid these outcomes at all costs, even if it means not seeing the effects of historical racism and other sins on others' human need today. Even if it means not seeing them at all. That strikes me as most un-Lutheran. While these sins may not be as damaging tears in the social fabric as murder, rape, or theft, yielding to them without challenge is even more damaging in the long run. To accept such sin as a given, to let it triumph as the chief architect of our secular law without challenging how it disrupts human community, is the precise opposite of our calling as Christians. Instead, we are called to *critical engagement*, to

25. Much of what I have learned about welcoming the stranger I have learned from my friend Patrick R. Keifert; see *Welcoming the Stranger: A Public Theology of Worship and Evangelism* (Minneapolis: Fortress Press, 1992).

challenge the sins surrounding this issue, not only the sins of majorities who take their position for granted, but also the sins of minorities who allow themselves and their lives to be defined by racism, rather than by their Creator.

The third aspect of our creatureliness is that we are property-less. Instead of being owners of our lives and our possessions, we are owned by the One who made us; we are tenants of everything we are and have with all of those who have influenced who we are and what we own from our very conception. The sins that the justices are prepared to give priority to—resentment (by whites disadvantaged by affirmative action) and claims of entitlement (by minorities)—misperceive reality. They accept the presumption that someone like Jennifer Gratz or Randy Pech has earned everything by his or her own efforts, and therefore justly seeks the sought-after reward.

For Christians, that presumption that we are deserving owners of our own lives essentially curses the God who gave human beings every blessing of intelligence, skill, family, wealth, and so on, they have. The sins of paternalizing or stigmatizing minorities, choosing to believe that they are inferior and have gained their advantage undeservedly, similarly refuse to recognize the complex goodness of God's creation in them. But even for non-Christians, it does not take much thought to recognize that what we are and have is a gift that many others have made possible, one that gives the lie to the idea that we have earned anything.

Forging New Paths

But, if we cannot let these sins have the last word in our construction of secular law and cannot demand that everyone live a "Christian" life without contravening God's twofold governing plan, then how can we shape secular law that responds to the destruction caused by the race-sins of both the fathers and the sons? How can we write a secular law of racial equality in a way that realistically accounts for these human sins of pride, resentment, and blindness to the other's need, without having the law be captive to those very sins?

Here is where our recognition of our sin and finitude does not fully define us. As suggested, we are *creative creatures*—God has given us all manner of gifts to try to forge new paths to ameliorate our past and present sins as we encounter and acknowledge them. One of the questions that the Supreme Court justices have asked in the recent affirmative action cases is whether governments have considered other alternatives before imposing race-based affirmative action programs. While this requirement may be and has been applied too harshly at times, its virtue is that it requires lawmakers and citizens to exercise compassionate and creative thinking about the ill effects of racism and what might be the most beneficial ways of addressing those effects. Lawmakers and citizens are invited to imagine paths that may not have quite the same corrosive side effects described by members of the Court.

This nudge by the Supreme Court forces us to candidly acknowledge that one of the reasons affirmative action programs became popular is that they have been a cheap way out for communities that do not want to fully face the effects of institutional racism. Instead of directly and fully addressing such ill effects of racism as unequal education or wealth disparities, which would require those better off in our society to give up more to provide better education or benefits to those who have been "put behind" by racism, it is much easier and cheaper to tell minorities they will get some extra points when they are applying for college or a job. The problem, of course, is that eliminating affirmative action programs is not likely to spur that kind of political sacrifice that truly responds to the original racism. So, racial minorities who have been disadvantaged by discrimination would seem to be left with the crumbs of affirmative action, or, under the recent Court rulings, nothing at all for their injuries, directly experienced or inherited.

So the task of a Lutheran theology is to recognize its prophetic role in the culture, criticizing the ineffectiveness of the alternatives society is currently willing to offer to deal with our sordid racial past, while proposing solutions that account for human finitude and sin that can hinder progress toward a colorblind society.

Christians have an important role to play in focusing citizens' and lawmakers' attention on the full context and the history in which decisions about racial justice are made. We will insist on acknowledgment of the racial sins of commission and omission that have been and continue to be committed, and we will push for political resolve and creativity to respond justly to these problems. Christians can be a healthy leaven in the public conversation about how to further social justice through law without falsely claiming that they have any divinely authorized answer to these difficult problems. In this way, they too can "show that what the law requires is written on their hearts, to which their own conscience also bears witness."[26]

26. Rom. 2:15.

10

The Ethics of Augsburg: Ethos under Law, Ethos under Grace, Objective Ethos

Michael Hoy

What's the relationship between one's faith and how one lives? Are certain ways of living more holy than others? How are we accountable? And to whom? In this chapter, Dr. Michael Hoy examines how these ethical/theological questions (that are still current) were addressed in the Augsburg Confession. Hoy demonstrates how the Reformers' confession of faith with regard to ethics not only distinguished between law and promise, but also articulated the hub of justification by faith alone.

Ethics were controversial in the Reformation era just as they are today. The articles of the Augsburg Confession and its Apology that particularly bear upon this topic are the sixth (The New Obedience), the twentieth (Faith and Good Works), the twenty-sixth (The Distinction of Foods), and the twenty-seventh (Monastic Vows).

Two of these articles—the sixth and twentieth—were in the section of the Augsburg Confession that the Confessors did not think, at least initially, was controversial. In this section, the Confessors thought they were articulating the accepted faith and tradition of the church. Nonetheless, as a result of the "Augsburg Aha" that the hermeneutic of justification was at the root of the church's controversy at the time of the Reformation, the fuller treatment of these articles was absorbed and treated under the fourth article of the Apology.[1] The latter two articles, the twenty-sixth and twenty-seventh, were considered under the section on the "disputed articles and abuses which have been corrected" in the Reformation churches.

The selected title of this chapter is an unmistakable reference to Werner Elert's *The Christian Ethos*.[2] By ethos, Elert means "the established behavior of man which can be judged qualitatively."[3] Ethics is largely a theological-anthropological judgment of each and every human being who is judged for his or her behavior under law and under grace.[4] This treatment of individual ethos comprises the bulk of Elert's analysis. Objective ethos, which Elert treats in his final section, refers to the corporate behavior of the whole Christian community judged by its participation under "the objective criteria of Christianity"—namely, the gospel of Word and Sacraments.[5]

Knowledge of Elert's treatment of ethics is not a prerequisite for appreciating the Reformation perspective on this topic. Elert, though, was deeply influenced by this promising, confessing tradition—and because of that confessional grounding, Elert himself was also influential for his student, Edward Schroeder.[6]

Ethos under Law and Ethos under Grace: AC 6 (The New Obedience) and AC 20 (Faith and Good Works)

One of the enduring contributions of the Reformers to ethics is how they lifted up the matter of accountability. In fact, that is the grounding point for ethical reflection. How are we accountable? And to whom?

For the Reformers, accountability is theological. We are accountable to a God who holds us responsible for the truth of our being. Augsburg confessors in subsequent generations would reflect this understanding.

1. "In the fourth, fifth, and sixth articles, as well as later in the twentieth, they condemn us for teaching that people receive the forgiveness of sins not on account of their own merits but freely on account of Christ, by faith in him." *BoC*, 120 (Apol 4:1). Melanchthon, however, does provide some further treatment of article twenty in the Apology.
2. Werner Elert, *Das Christliche Ethos* (Tübingen: Furche-Verlag, 1949). It was later translated by Carl J. Schindler as *The Christian Ethos* (Philadelphia: Fortress Press, 1957). The book is currently out of print, though there are efforts to retranslate the work.
3. Elert, *The Christian Ethos*, 3.
4. "Law and gospel are addressed to the individual. In fact, they create his individuality by calling him from the crowd and impressing him with the fact that he must appear by himself before his judge. His ethos is qualified by the judgment God pronounces upon him, a biographically unique individual. In technical terminology, ethos is always individual ethos." Ibid., 333.
5. Ibid., 334.
6. Elert's theology was the subject of Schroeder's doctoral dissertation, "The Relationship between Dogmatics and Ethics: An Investigation into the Theologies of Elert, Barth and Troeltsch" (University of Hamburg, 1963). A condensed version of the dissertation was published as "The Relationship between Dogmatics and Ethics in the Thought of Elert, Barth, and Troeltsch," in *Concordia Theological Monthly* 36, no. 11 (December 1965): 744–71.

Elert, for example, would speak of sinners in truth and sinners in fact (or "in reality"). Sinners in fact live with the illusion—the "as if"—that they are not sinners; and in doing so, they cling to a nomological (law-based) existence as their rule of life. Failing to trust Christ as the new truth of their being, they resort to the unfaith of trusting in themselves and their works as the basis of their righteousness. By contrast, those who have a promising encounter with Jesus the Christ are not only sinners in reality, but sinners in truth—that is, they make no pretensions that they are anything *but* sinners. The freedom and boldness to accept that greater truth of accountability is grounded in the faith that dares to trust that Jesus the Christ is the friend of sinners.[7]

Many ethical systems, including many Christian ethical systems and even the system of the Confutators to which the Augsburg Reformers responded, miss the depth of this theological accountability. The classical example of such a flawed system in the model of "sin and grace," for example, construes "sin" as, strictly speaking, a human problem that is overcome by the divine solution of "grace." There is rarely a sense in such a model that God, in holding human beings accountable, is critical of the creature. God is regarded only as the divine embracer of a fallen humanity. In fact, the idea that God could be one who holds us accountable and critiques us is dismissed as being inauthentic to the very nature of God—a nature that is generally characterized only as love.[8] Ethics for such systems, therefore, would lead one to seek to emulate the presumed gracious love that God has for all of God's creatures and creation, but without the cognizance that all our efforts are, because of our sinful nature, necessarily flawed; and without an understanding of justice that probes deep enough to take account of the truly theological accountable meaning of justice. Most of all, there is no real consolation in such a system except the practice of our own works and the ambiguous (at best) encounter with God.

From the perspective of the Reformers, the theological flaw of this approach is that it is subevangelical. It dismisses how and why it is we need a crucified Lord; and ultimately, it does not provide comfort for the consciences of believers.[9] Only when the love of God is deeply

7. Elert, *The Christian Ethos*, 182–88.
8. While not formally presented as such, this is the logical conclusion of Robert W. Bertram's treatment of revelation and universality in his tome, *A Time for Confessing* (Grand Rapids: Eerdmans, 2008), 159–84.
9. These two elements of the honoring of Christ's merits for us, *together* with the comforting of consciences in this grace, is at the heart of the Reformers' grasp of the depth and meaning of the gospel. Cf. *BoC*, 120–21 (Apol 4:2–3). One will see these two elements over and over again throughout both the Augsburg Confession and Apology and always in the same sense of lifting up Christ and applying his benefits to despairing consciences (presuming the accusatory nature of the law where we all are by nature of our sin). Later in Apology 4, Melanchthon would also speak of the gospel in these terms: "strictly speaking, [the gospel is] the promise of the forgiveness of sins and justification on account of

grounded in the death and resurrection of Jesus the Christ can one come to a solution that takes the damning consequences of our sins and crosses them out of existence. This, in fact, is the very starting point of the New Obedience, with the "new" here being characterized by the newness of the gospel itself (AC 6). Through the liberating ministry of the proclamation of the gospel in Word and Sacraments (AC 5), faith dares to trust that we are redeemed from all our sin and reconciled with God. Good works ("good" also defined by the very Source of our faith in Jesus the Christ) are the *yield* of this justifying faith, flowing like the living water that it is from the life of the believer. Indeed, the believer, as with all people, "*must* do such good works as God has commanded for God's sake *but not place trust in them* as if thereby to earn grace before God."[10]

This "must" in AC 6 is reiterated in the Apology and also begins to address the primary concerns of AC 20:

> We openly confess, therefore, that the keeping of the law *must* begin in us and then increase more and more. And we include both simultaneously, namely, the inner spiritual impulses and the outward good works. Therefore the opponents' claims are false when they charge that our people do not teach about good works *since our people not only require them but also show how they can be done.*[11]

The emphasis on this "must," therefore, is not for legalistic or moralistic reasons (which would run counter to the whole claim of the Reformation), but in order to rebut any attempts to downplay the evangelical grounding for good works that the Reformers put forward. Indeed, the Reformers were deeply concerned about the connection of faith and works. They belong together in the life of the Christian. And any attempts to portray the Reformers as separating faith and works

---

Christ." *BoC,* 127 (Apol 4:43). Notice in both of these presentations that the gospel is not just simply talking about Jesus the Christ, nor using Christ moralistically (as a role model), but how Christ is applied promisingly to and for us. This is important to see how Christian theologies (and ethics) not only lift up the name of Jesus the Christ (and some of them, regrettably, do not even do that much), but how they also "*use* him" *BoC,* 131 (Apol 4:69), that is, how he is *necessitated,* evangelically.

10. *BoC,* 40 (AC 6:1). Italics mine. The German text especially has this sense of good works as natural fruit (*Früchte*) of faith, which must (*müsse*) follow faith. In the Latin text, the words for "yield" and "must" are *debeat* and *oporteat,* which implies more a sense of duty, and perhaps hence a greater reliance on the "command of God" (law) than on the working of the Spirit. As it is presented here in AC 6, however, the sense is acceptable, because it follows from the proclaimed Word which creates faith. After 1530, this would become more of an issue between Melanchthon and Luther. Cf. Leif Grane, *The Augsburg Confession: A Commentary* (Minneapolis: Augsburg, 1981), 83. Cf. also Wilhelm Maurer, *Historical Commentary on the Augsburg Confession* (Philadelphia: Fortress Press, 1986), 351.

11. *BoC,* 142 (Apol 4:136). Italics mine. Consider also this later reprisal of this theme in *BoC,* 150 (Apol 4:189ff.): "For good works are to be done because God requires them. Therefore they are the result of regeneration. . . . Thus good works ought to follow faith as thanksgiving to God [and good of the neighbor?]. Likewise, good works ought to follow faith so that faith is exercised in them, grows, and is shown to others, in order that others may be invited to godliness by our confession."

was inconsistent with the confessional writings, as well as the extensive writings of Luther on the subject of faith and works.[12]

It is well known that the fourth article of the Apology, with its accent on justification by faith alone, comprises the largest and probably most important section of the confessional writings.[13] However, the portion of that article dealing with the connection of faith and works (including an extensive evangelical hermeneutics of the scriptures) is actually the larger part of Apology 4.[14]

Why this prevalent emphasis on the proper connection of faith and good works? Because the church had so misunderstood and misrepresented this connection that it had distorted the gospel's own message. "We are debating about an important matter, namely, about the honor of Christ and the source from which the faithful might seek a sure and certain consolation—whether we should place our confidence in Christ [faith] or in our own works."[15]

The Reformers did not claim that faith is necessary to do civil works for the good of the neighbor. On that point, the Reformers affirm that civil works can, in fact, be done by *reason*, apart from faith.[16] Nonetheless, such "reasonable" works can never set us in a freeing relationship with God; and in fact, when works become a system of presumed righteousness (as they did then, and often do today), they become a damning burden—not a consolation—to the people who do them.[17] Works, apart from faith, cannot claim the freedom of being "good works," or "the new obedience," which is the evangelical-ethical accent of the Reformers. In the concluding section, we will want to return to this issue.[18]

---

12. For evidence of Luther's passionate connection of faith and works, consider the sampling provided here: "We say that justification is effective without works, not that faith is without works. For that faith which lacks fruit is not an efficacious but a feigned faith." *LW* 34:176. "When I have this righteousness [of Christ] within me, I descend from heaven like the rain that makes the earth fertile. That is, I come forth into another kingdom, and I perform good works whenever the opportunity arises." *LW* 26:11. "Thus it is impossible to separate works from faith, quite as impossible to separate heat and light from fire." *LW* 35:371. "For we have said often enough that a Christian life is composed of two parts: faith in God and love toward one's neighbor." *LW* 30:47.
13. Apol 4 comprises about one-third of the entire Apology, and about one-tenth of the entire *Book of Concord*.
14. Beginning with paragraph 122, Love and the Fulfilling of the Law, and continuing to the end of Apology 4 in the Response to the Arguments of the Opponents. In some editions of the *Book of Concord*, this section comprises a separate article. This entire section comprises about two-thirds of Apology 4; and the Response to Opponents is about one-half of all of Apology 4.
15. *BoC*, 145 (Apol 4:156).
16. *BoC*, 124 (Apol 4:22–23).
17. With regard to contemporary versions of works-righteous systems, cf., e.g., Rick Warren's *The Purpose Driven Life*, the prosperity gospel preaching and writings of Joel Osteen, and several theologies on all spectrums that promote a so-called biblical ethics, even an ethics of Jesus, without availing the theological benefits of the cross.
18. Cf. *BoC*, 15 (Apol 4:203): "Although good works ought to follow faith in this way, people who cannot believe or establish in their hearts that they are freely forgiven on account of Christ use works for a very different purpose. When they see the works of the saints, they think in a human fashion that the saints have merited the forgiveness of sins by those

Again, in Elert's categories, the difference here would be between an ethos under law (which is the only theological grounding provided by the Roman critics of the Reformation who promulgated a righteousness by works, never fully grasping either the law or the true value of works[19]) and an ethos under grace (where good works are done for the good of the neighbor, freely, and with free conscience).

AC 20 (Faith and Good Works) is included in this trajectory of thought; and to some extent, it provides a bridge to the articles that follow (26 and 27). How so? Because the accent in this article lifts up the truly good works for the neighbor, outlined in the Decalogue, "about which little had been taught before our time. Instead, for the most part childish, unnecessary works—such as rosaries, the cult of saints, joining religious orders, pilgrimages, appointed fasts, holy days, brotherhoods, and the like—were emphasized in all sermons."[20] Hence, there is here a sharp contrast between truly good works that help the neighbor as "commanded by God" vis-à-vis the ongoing practice in the church to do works to try to please God.

AC 20 shows some willingness to make mild concession to the Roman critics for "saying that faith and works makes us righteous before God" (namely, for the Roman critics' inclusion of *faith* and not just works). However, the Reformers go on to say that "such talk may offer *a little more comfort* than the teaching that one should rely on works alone."[21] The Reformers were not conceding that this Roman teaching, therefore, was *ultimately* comforting or evangelical; but that it was better than what had been maintained in the recent past. Nonetheless, the Confutation[22] debunked any real association even with this concession, clinging instead to an understanding of meriting forgiveness of sins through good works. The Confutators' only "use" of Christ was as "an *example* in order that what he did we might also do."[23] The Apology would counter

works and that they are regarded as righteous before God on account of those works. Accordingly, they imitated those works and think that through similar works they also merit the forgiveness of sins. They try to appease the wrath of God and trust that they are regarded as righteous on account of such works." Notice that only when it is understood the works follow faith that Melanchthon uses the adjective "good," not in the cases where faith is absent. Cf. also *BoC*, 56 (AC 20:38–39): "Such lofty and genuine works cannot be done with the help of Christ, as he himself says in John 15[:5]: 'Apart from me you can do nothing.'"

19. Cf. *BoC*, 141–42 (Apol 4:133–36), which explores the "veil" of Moses in 2 Corinthians 3—the "human opinion about the law," which, when removed, "God shows our hearts our impurity and the magnitude of our sin. Then we see that we are far from fulfilling the law" and "we learn how our smug and indifferent flesh does not fear God and does not truly believe that God looks out for us. . . ."
20. *BoC*, 52, 54 (AC 20:2–3).
21. *BoC*, 54 (AC 20:6–7). Italics mine.
22. Following the presentation of the Augsburg Confession in 1530, Catholic theologians (especially their leading theologian, Dr. Johann Eck) prepared their own response known as the Confutation.
23. "Confutation of the Augsburg Confession," in *Sources and Contexts of the Book of Concord*, ed. Robert Kolb and James A. Nestingen (Minneapolis: Augsburg Fortress, 2001), 118. Italics mine.

that there is really only one appropriate use of Christ: as "the *atoning sacrifice* for our sins."[24]

We must also address the matter of Thomistic thought at the time of the Reformation.[25] According to this scholastic tradition, faith was itself divided into two parts—an unformed, "material" faith brought about by grace (*fides informis*) and a faith that found its "formation" in love (*fides caritate formata*).[26] When the human will exercises faith, the latter comes into being. Hence, only the latter "formed faith" mattered in this line of reasoning; the former "unformed" faith was dead without love. The Reformers, however, do not accept this bifurcation of faith. In fact, they dismiss a sense of any such thing as an "unformed" faith.[27] Faith is "the desire for and the reception of the promise."[28] And it is this promise, this *object* of faith (that is, Christ!), that defines it. Because we already *have* our righteousness in Christ through faith (*glaubst du, hast du*, as Luther often said—"Believe it, and you have it."[29]), the works of love can issue freely for the sake of the neighbor and in keeping with God's will.

Objective Ethos: AC 26 (The Distinction of Foods) and AC 27 (Monastic Vows)

These two articles could just as well have been treated in the previous chapter (nine) on church and secular authority, particularly given the way the Confutation responds to them. But the wisdom of including them here in this chapter on ethics provides a venue for us to discern what we mean by "objective ethos." What are the values that the church holds dear? How do these values lead to the faithful kinds of practices in the church's life?

The title of AC 26 is a little misleading. The title is no doubt drawn from the biblical passages that address which foods can and cannot be eaten if one is to be faithful.[30] But the substance of the article is about ecclesiological practices at the time of the Reformation, and why the Reformers had already taken the steps they had taken to do away with such practices and abuses.

The particular practices in question were all ecclesiastical: "new fasts, new ceremonies, new monastic orders," which were being invented by the church and demanded to be followed. (Keep in mind that the use

---

24. *BoC*, 236 (Apol 20:5).
25. Thomistic thought refers to Catholic scholastic theology that follows the insights of Thomas Aquinas. Cf. chapter 1, footnote 6, for more information on scholastic theology.
26. *BoC*, 138 (Apol 4:109).
27. Cf. *LW* 26:269.
28. *BoC*, 164 (Apol 4:283). Cf. Theodore G. Tappert's edition of *The Book of Concord* (Philadelphia: Fortress Press, 1959), 154 (Apol 4:304).
29. Cf. *LW* 35:38.
30. Cf. e.g., 1 Cor. 6:13, 8:1ff., 10:23ff.

of "new" by the Reformers here is not theological but temporal.) "They were fervently and strictly promoted [by the church authorities], as if such things were a necessary service of God whereby people earned grace if they observed them or committed a great sin if they did not. Many harmful errors in the church have resulted from this."[31]

The Reformers' objection is based on three points. First, "the grace of Christ and the teaching concerning faith are thereby obscured." This is the same objection of Apology 4: "we should learn that we do not become righteous before God by our works but that it is only through faith in Christ that we obtain grace for Christ's sake."[32]

Second, "such traditions have also obscured God's commands."[33] The distortion of works in the church was to keep the fasts and ceremonies and to regard these as truly spiritual, while "other necessary good works were considered secular, unspiritual ways of life."[34] Thus, vocations and truly good works for the neighbor were regarded as "a 'secular and imperfect' way of life, while the [ceremonial] traditions had to have impressive names, so that only they were called 'holy and perfect' works."[35] This second objection is closest to the overall ethical theme of this chapter. The Reformation as a whole helped to lift up the vocation of all persons in the world in a way that was a breath of fresh air for the church.

Third, "such traditions turned out to be a heavy burden to consciences." These ecclesiastical traditions had replaced the liberating message of the gospel—and the results were tragic. Many people despaired under the weight of this burden, and some even committed suicide, "because they heard nothing about the comfort of Christ's grace."[36] This deeply evangelical-pastoral concern needs continued vigilance in the church of every age so that we do not resort to moralism and legalism in our preaching of the gospel.

Because of the "dire need" of addressing this matter, the churches of the Reformation abandoned any teaching or practice of these "new" ceremonies, even though they are consciously aware that this runs counter to their own ecclesiastical superiors.[37] Furthermore, the Reformers also indicated what it is that they do observe in their teaching and practice in their churches: that no one can earn grace by observing these traditions for the sake of the gospel.[38]

---

31. *BoC*, 74 (AC 26:2–3).
32. *BoC*, 74 (AC 26:4–5).
33. *BoC*, 76 (AC 26:8).
34. *BoC*, 76 (AC 26:9–10).
35. *BoC*, 76 (AC 26:11).
36. *BoC*, 76 (AC 26:12–13).
37. *BoC*, 76 (AC 26:18–20).
38. *BoC*, 78 (AC 26:21–29).

The rest of AC 26 seeks to rebut false accusations. The Reformation churches, contrary to their critics' portrayals, did observe Christian bodily disciplines to strengthen the faith (such as fasting) and retained "the order of the Mass and other singing, festivals, and the like."[39] But all of this is done because it helps to promote the gospel of Christ, not because it is mandated by the ecclesiastical authority.[40]

In AC 27, the Reformers address the issue of monastic vows. While in an earlier time the idea of leaving monastic life was allowable, in the time of the Reformation it had become as "a prison of their own [ecclesial] devising."[41] Young people who were either dedicated to the monasteries by their parents, or those who were insufficiently able to "estimate and understand their capabilities," were "forced and compelled to remain in such bondage to their vows (most especially here, the vow of celibacy), in spite of the fact that even papal canons would have set many of them free."[42] Even worse, the church promulgated a faulty meritorious message that through such monastic life one was keeping the "commands [or precepts] and counsels" of the gospel; hence, "monastic vows were praised more highly than baptism."[43] Indeed, the merits of monastic life were held in higher esteem than all other vocations and "walks of life."[44]

In response to these dehumanizing practices and theological abuses, the Reformers put forward three corrections. First, "all those who are not suited for celibacy have the power, authority, and right to marry."[45] This is based on God's command, which overrules the ecclesial human authorities that have placed these restrictions on persons in the monastic orders. Second, all vows should be voluntary, not mandatory or forced.[46] Third, all monastic vows are "null and void" whenever they are placed higher than the decrees of God's own command. "For all service of God instituted and chosen by human beings without God's command and authority to obtain righteousness and grace is contrary to God, the holy gospel, and God's decree."[47]

---

39. *BoC*, 78, 80 (AC 26:30–40).
40. It is, therefore, practical adiaphora. It should be noted that the entire Confutation response to this article is a harangue on how the Reformation churches were not observing ecclesiastical authority. It should also be noted that Melanchthon does not provide a specific response to this critique in the Apology (i.e., there is no Apol 26), but does have responses in the Apology that relate to this material in both Apol 15 (on church rites and human authority) and 28 (on the power of the bishops). The Confutation's citing of Luke 10:16 and Heb. 13:17 (*Sources and Contexts*, 132), in response to AC 26, finds an answer from Melanchthon in Apol 28:18–20 (*BoC*, 291).
41. *BoC*, 80 (AC 27:2).
42. *BoC*, 82 (AC 27:5–6).
43. *BoC*, 82 (AC 27:12–13).
44. *BoC*, 82 (AC 27:13). The German word here is *Ständen*, vocations or callings.
45. *BoC*, 84 (AC 27:18).
46. *BoC*, 84 (AC 27:27).
47. *BoC*, 86 (AC 27:36).

At the heart of the Reformers' objections and corrections is a liberating theology which understands that the "state of perfection" is not something that can be earned or merited by monastic life, but only by faith. "For Christian perfection is to fear God earnestly with the whole heart and yet also to have a sincere confidence, faith, and trust that we have a gracious, merciful God because of Christ; that we may and should pray for and request from God whatever we need and confidently expect help from him in all affliction, according to each person's vocation and walk of life; and that meanwhile we should diligently do external good works and attend to our calling."[48]

The value of AC 27, like AC 26, is twofold. It underscores the true liberating authority of the gospel as that which supersedes all humanly contrived systems and practices—even and especially those practices in the church. And it calls people *back into the world*, to embrace their vocations in life, the right to marry, and political work as part and parcel of their Christian calling.

Conclusion: Why Good Works Really Do Matter

Catholic scholar Brad Gregory has recently suggested that the Reformation may be the unintended culprit for many of our contemporary ethical problems. In what is already heralded as an epic historical analysis, Gregory's claim is that when the Reformation overturned the normative ethical ideal of *caritas* (love) in medieval Christianity in favor of an alternate truth claim, *sola scriptura* (scripture alone), it inadvertently opened the doors for rival truth claims to emerge. This eventually gave way to reason and, more recently, consumerism to define the social order. Gregory claims, therefore, that a trajectory from the Reformation to the present demonstrates a societal shift that has led to the ethical chaos of our current secularized and subjective morality as well as consumerist-capitalist and hyper-pluralist society.[49]

Churches of the Augsburg Confession will want to consider the implications of this critique. Clearly, and even Gregory would concede, it was never the intent of the Reformation to abandon ethics to the whims of a society that chooses values not rooted in love for the good

---

48. *BoC*, 88 (AC 27:49). The Confutation, by contrast, claimed monastic life as the "the most Christian form of life" and a means by which persons "acquire perfection." *Sources and Contexts*, 137. The Apology rejects not only this understanding of perfection, but further- more the so-called "merits of supererogation," the system of belief that there are "extra" good works performed by those living in monastic communities that can then be sold to others as meritorious works for salvation. *BoC*, 281 (Apol 27:24).
49. Brad S. Gregory, *The Unintended Reformation: How a Religious Revolution Secularized Society* (Cambridge, MA: Harvard University Press, 2012).

of the neighbor. Luther offered many treatises that spoke out on the social issues of his time, including usury, marriage, and political responsibilities.[50] Nonetheless, insofar as the rise of individualism and its social ills are attributable to the Reformation, repentance is in order.

On the other hand, while Gregory recognizes that medieval Christianity failed both morally and practically in implementing its normative value of *caritas*, he does not seem adequately aware or willing to concede that there was a serious *theological* problem that needed addressing in the church at the time of the Reformation—how we cannot be justified by love, but only by faith.[51] Moreover, however much the scriptures have been and still are twisted and turned by competing rival claims to truth, the Reformers advocated that the real hermeneutic of *sola scriptura* is always *solus Christus*. How is Jesus the Christ and his promising mercy in the gospel being proclaimed over the moralistic and legalistic versions of the so-called biblical truth?

Truth is, the Reformers never really did abandon the value and place of love. If anything, they helped to clarify what love really is; how it is for the neighbor; how the failure to love does not excuse one from divine accountability; how people are to be valued in the gospel beyond their dehumanizing and despairing state of being; and how love itself is re-centered and re-grounded and liberated to risk when it is the fruit of faith.

We can summarize, therefore, some of the key theological-ethical insights of the Augsburg Reformers as follows:

- Accountability is a theological given for all of human life. Our Creator holds us accountable and critiques us for what we do and do not do for others and for the environment.

- People of faith can cooperate with all people of good will and reason who also do works for the good of others.

- Liberating people from dehumanization and despair is an enduring truth of the gospel's promise.

- Vocation in worldly life is to be esteemed for how it helps others.

- Works that truly help others are what matters, not continuing a system of religious merits.[52]

50. *LW*, vols. 44–47.
51. Gregory, *The Unintended Reformation*, 365–87. Gregory indicates that he is not calling for a nostalgic return to medieval Christianity, but still clings to the enduring value of *caritas*.
52. George W. Forell provides this illustration: "If one were to abolish the need for begging by finding useful work for the unemployed, adequate houses for orphans, special care and rehabilitation for the blind, the crippled, and all other handicapped people, one would threaten the whole merit system, which needed both beggars and givers in order to furnish opportunities to perform meritorious 'good works.'" Forell, *The Augsburg Confession: A Contemporary Commentary* (Minneapolis: Augsburg, 1968), 86. While the illustration

- Lastly, but most importantly, under no circumstances can works take the place of faith in setting one in right relationship with God—for their own good, and for all the good that they bring to all human beings and all of creation.

---

is dated, the point is not: charity (as it is so often practiced in churches) is often to make the giver feel good, when what the neighbor really needs is a true measure of justice and equality.

11

A Lutheran Confessional Exploration of Gospel Praxis

Steven C. Kuhl

The Confessors at Augsburg addressed various practices that their evangelical churches had changed in light of the gospel. These changes were necessary, said the Confessors, because practices required by church officials burdened Christian consciences with requirements that contradicted the gospel and obscured the law.

Dr. Steven Kuhl reminds us that these changes serve as examples of the Confessors' concern to have every practice of the church be an articulation of the "hub," that is, the gospel of God in distinction from the law of God. When church practice is shaped and evaluated in this way, by what Kuhl calls the "meta-assumption" of the gospel (as the Augsburg Confession advocates), Christians are freed from the burden of an accusing conscience. They are also freed to act forthrightly, even in compromising situations, not because they are in themselves above the law's accusation, but because they are by faith securely included in the gospel, Christ's victory over the law.

Orthopraxis as Critical Reflection on Practice in Light of the Word of God

The signers of the Augsburg Confession and its Apology divided their confession of the catholic and evangelical faith into two sections: the first being an exploration of what could be called "orthodoxy" (a right confession of the gospel) and the second, what might be called "orthopraxis" (a right practice of the gospel).

In articles 1 through 21, the Confessors addressed the substance of their "teaching" or doctrine, showing it to be a faithful expression of the gospel (aka, the Word of God) for their times, not only when measured up to the scriptures, but also when compared to the teachings of major figures and moments in the Christian tradition. The Confessors claimed that what they taught was not novel or unique to them, but it was disputed in their times—disputed by, of all people, the (secularly) authorized ministers of the church, including the highest ministers: the pope, his curia, and theologians.

In articles 22–28, the Confessors addressed the "practices" that their evangelical church had changed in light of the teaching articulated in articles 1–21. They showed why these changes were necessary and should therefore be "permitted." This, too, was necessary because, of all people, it was the church's own (secularly) authorized ministers who were forbidding such changes.

In this chapter I will analyze the reform measures that articles 21 (on the invocation of saints), 22 (on the reception of both elements in the Eucharist), and 23 (on clerical marriage) of the AC and its Apology deemed necessary to make for the sake of the gospel. I do so in order to get an understanding of "orthopraxis" (as the Confessors understood it) that might be useful today. In this sense, I hope to "update" these articles by teasing out of them their methodology and by showing how that method is related to the modern methodological concept known as "praxis." I hope to do this for the explicit purpose of making these articles useful models of orthopraxis for the church to learn from as it wrestles with its "practice" of the faith today.

The Concept of Praxis Today

In order to connect the Confessors' reform measures to the modern concept of praxis, we need to say a few words about praxis. The term "praxis" is a dialectical concept that can be notoriously flexible in definition depending on the concerns and assumptions of the user. In the areas of sociology, political science, and ethics (how we should live) praxis means evaluating any theory of life in light of the actual living of life. Again, the assumption is that right understanding and right living can be had only when the two finally confirm one another. Short of that, tweaking the dialectic becomes the standard approach to knowing and living. Praxis, then, can generally be described as "critical reflection on the interaction of theory (how we understand things) and practice (how we do things)."

Our definition of praxis might be refined as follows: praxis is critical reflection upon the interaction of theory and practice in light of some overarching meta-assumption. This meta-assumption in the modern concept of praxis, then, is the hermeneutical key that guides the process of critical thinking on the theory and practice, and being clear about it is essential to the exercise of praxis.

This view of praxis fits well with the thinking of the Confessors at Augsburg. They explained why it was necessary for the truth of the gospel to reform the practice of the church as they did with regard to the invocation of the saints (Art. 21), the reception of both elements in the Eucharist (Art. 22), and clerical marriage (Art. 23). The Confessors' praxis can be termed "orthopraxis" because it is critical reflection on the church's practice (activity) in light of the Word of God. In other words, the meta-assumption or hermeneutic that guides their critical thinking on the state of the church's praxis is what they variously call the "gospel" or the "Word of God" or "justification by faith" or the "distinction of law and gospel," depending on what aspect of this meta-assumption is under discussion at any given time.

Whatever one may think of the Confessors' meta-assumption, it is to their credit that they are absolutely clear on what it is and where they got it. In that sense, they are not afraid to submit their meta-assumption to "falsification." Therefore, it is my contention that the AC and its Apology are good examples of the modern idea of praxis turned to the purpose of confessing the faith and reforming church practice. Let us now examine the Confessors' meta-assumption, that is, their understanding of the "gospel," out of which all their thinking proceeds.

The Gospel as the Meta-Assumption

The AC and its Apology do not claim to answer all questions of doctrine and practice. (The Confessors focus only on some areas or articles that are obviously under dispute in their times.) However, the AC and Apology do claim to lay bare *the* meta-assumption of the Christian faith that necessarily guides both the church's teaching and practice on all things: what throughout those confessions is variously titled the Word of God, the gospel, the promise, justification by faith, the distinction of law and gospel. The Confessors often described this meta-assumption as "the doctrine" of the church (and later theologians "the doctrine upon which the church stands or falls").

What they mean by this is that it is the metateaching that informs all teachings. It is the metanarrative that illuminates all narratives. It is the hermeneutical or interpretive key that unlocks the mysterious ways (law and promise) of God's interaction with the world. The Confessors, no doubt, suspected that the gospel as meta-assumption was the issue between them and their critics before the Diet of Augsburg. Nothing confirmed this more than the Roman Confutation and its criticism of the AC. The Confessors saw in that official document an explicit condemnation of their meta-assumption: the gospel.

This explains both the length and tenor of the Apology in contrast to the AC. The AC is rather concise and congenial in tone because in it the Confessors still gave their opponents the benefit of the doubt that they (their opponents) would see and respond reasonably to their (the Confessors') concerns. After all, the emperor called the Diet of Augsburg (1530) in the spirit of concord. However, after the Confutation clearly and matter-of-factly condemned not only the Confessors but the very gospel premise (the meta-assumption) they confessed, all things changed. In the Apology (or defense) of the Augsburg Confession, Philip Melanchthon meticulously examines the dispute at the level of meta-assumptions. This he does by assessing and analyzing his and their assumptions, his and their consistency in argument (or lack thereof), and his and their use (or misuse) of the same sources, both scripture and church tradition. What Melanchthon ultimately concludes is that the gospel itself is at issue and that, in light of that gospel, certain, select, basic reforms in church teaching and practice need to be "permitted" over against the Confutation's "No!"

The most sustained discussion Melanchthon gives of the gospel as meta-assumption is set forth in article 4 of the Apology. Note, the issue is not whether one used scripture as source for one's position—both sides claimed to be scriptural—but whether one read and understood scripture with the lens or the meta-assumption that it was written to proclaim the gospel of Jesus Christ, the good news, the God-promise that we are saved, forgiven, justified before God by grace alone (as a free gift) through faith alone (solely by trusting or relying) in the merits of Christ alone (what he accomplished in his death and resurrection). The problem with the Confutation, according to Melanchthon, is that it supplied an alien assumption in the reading of scripture that distorted, if not obliterated, its message and meaning. Specifically, the Confutation read scripture through the lens of the law and the meta-assumption that our efforts in response to the law were part of the calculus of our salvation.[1]

---

1. See *BoC*, 121 (Apol 4:7).

Understanding the nature of scripture, so as to read it properly, therefore, becomes of central importance. And, according to Melanchthon, the methodological key for interpreting scripture is the proper distinction of law and gospel: "All Scripture should be divided into two main topics: the law and the promises."[2]

The "law," according to Melanchthon, refers to all that is symbolized by the Decalogue. It encompasses all that God "demands" of humanity, requiring both outward civil works, which humanity can do to some measure through the exercise of reason, and true fear, love, and trust in God, which is impossible for fallen humanity to do.[3] Significantly, for Melanchthon, the essential characteristic of the law is summarized in his little catchphrase *lex semper accusat*: "the law always accuses."[4] That catchphrase signals the fact that this "demand" is not simply instruction. Much more, the law is also critique, for it always seeks to expose *humanity's innate lack of fear, love, and trust for God*, what article 2 calls "original sin," humanity's congenital self-centeredness that always opposes the God-centered nature of reality.

Stated another way, the law includes all in scripture and life that points, first, to the *theological* reality of God's anger on sinners[5] and, second, to the *sociopolitical* necessity of cultural and civil restraints[6] in the maintenance of social order and justice among sinners. Like the Enlightenment "principle of critique," the law as God's demanding-and-critical operation in the world permeates everything. The law hardens the heart of the obstinate and crushes the heart of the desperate. The law is experienced in whatever irritates the human conscience, whatever punctures human pride, and whatever "stings" in the reality of death. Although the law brings some sense of social security to the world by restraining sin (the civil function of the law), it ultimately undermines any sense of self-security by exposing sin, revealing wrath, and administering death (the theological function of the law).

The gospel of Christ stands in stark contrast to God's critical, demanding word of law. As we saw in the quote above, one of Melanchthon's favorite words for it is "promise." A promise is an interpersonal affair that is the opposite of law. The promise of God, for example, is characterized by God offering something *to* us, namely, Christ's righteousness, as opposed to the law of God, which demands

2. *BoC*, 121.
3. See *BoC*, 121 (Apol 4:8–9).
4. See *BoC*, 126 (Apol 4:36–38).
5. See article 2 on Original Sin for a thoroughgoing discussion of the human condition. Sinners are those who are turned-in-on-self, thus lacking true fear, love, and trust in God. Werner Elert, in *The Christian Faith* (Philadelphia: Fortress Press, 1957), describes it well as an egocentric existence.
6. See *BoC*, 124 (Apol 4:22).

something *from* us, namely, the fulfillment of our debt or the satisfaction of our wrongs. A promise calls forth trust and is secured by faith alone in the one who promises it. With promise, all the glory belongs to the one who promises, and all the benefit belongs to the one to whom it is promised. For Melanchthon, the essential character of the promise, then, is "mercy," because in the gospel God promises to us what we don't deserve. It is for Christ's sake that God is eager to give us what we can't deserve, namely, forgiveness, justification, and eternal life. What's more, and this is key for Melanchthon, the idea of "promise" emphasizes the fact that the fulfillment or accomplishment of what is promised depends wholly and completely on the one who promises. For that reason, the recipient of a promise by definition lives by faith alone, by trusting the one who makes the promise. As such, the promise structure of the gospel is that we are reconciled with God by mercy/grace/gift alone, by faith alone, in Christ alone.

Of course, as Melanchthon explains, the meta-assumption that is the gospel is not only about *distinguishing* law and promise but also about how they *correlate*. That correlation is seen in the "scandal of the cross,"[7] where the wrath/law of God (on sinners) encounters the promise/mercy of God (in Jesus Christ)—and promise/mercy (Christ) wins. Therefore, Christ is the "end of the law" for all who trust in him. At the heart of the gospel, then, is the assumption that God's promise overrules God's law, that faith in Christ and his merits triumphs over our sin and demerits, and that the sentence of death we deserve is subverted by the promise of resurrected life with Christ. To be sure, in the meantime, Christians live in the battle between promise and law, faith and doubt, death and life, as *simul totus iustus et totus peccator*, simultaneously a total sinner and a total saint.

Therefore, for the Confessors, to maintain this faith it is essential to keep the gospel message not only clear but fresh in the hearing and minds of its recipients. The life of the Christian is maintained only through the ongoing proclamation of the promise of God against the countervailing word of wrath and law. To this end, for the sake of nurturing and maintaining faith, Christ authorized the means of grace.[8]

Helpfully, Melanchthon identifies two criteria for checking if the gospel is being properly distinguished and correlated with law. They can be summarized as follows: First, does the message being proclaimed illumine and magnify the honor of Christ? And second, does the message bring the abundant consolation that devout consciences need?

---

7. See *BoC*, 125 (Apol 4:29–33).
8. See *BoC*, 174 (Apol 7–8:5).

That is, does the message bring authentic relief to consciences terrified by the law?[9]

Edward Schroeder has called these two criteria the "double-dipstick." It is called a "dipstick" because it is the *measuring* stick for both orthodoxy and orthopraxis. The reason he calls this single dipstick a *double*-dipstick is because, while the two criteria are conceptually distinct, they are never methodologically inseparable. For Christ is honored only when he is used to comfort law-troubled consciences, *and* law-troubled consciences are authentically and truly comforted only by faith (the highest form of honor one can give) in Christ.

The Language of Conscience

Before I proceed to show how their gospel meta-assumption works in the practical reform program for their churches, a word is in order on the idea of conscience. In the sixteenth century, the language of conscience was becoming the "modern" way of talking about the essential core of the human person. Even so, there was not one single understanding of the nature of conscience, even as there is not today.

As George Forell has observed, many today assume that "the reformation was based upon the assertion of freedom of conscience"—with conscience defined as "the *autonomous* human conscience against the *heteronomy* of church and state."[10] Moreover, the incident most often cited in support of this assumption is Luther's famous "Here I stand" statement at the Diet of Worms. But as Forell further notes, this assumption is far afield from Luther's way of thinking. While few dispute that "conscience" plays a significant role in both Luther's theology and ethics, there is dispute over what that significance is. Therefore, understanding exactly what Luther and the Lutheran Confessions (which follow Luther's lead in this matter) mean by "conscience" is essential for understanding their dynamic view of the gospel as true consolation for troubled consciences.

Three different views of conscience at work in Luther's time need consideration: (a) the emerging "Enlightenment" view, which has Renaissance humanism as its source, (b) the persisting "scholastic" view, which has the Aristotelian tradition as its source, and (c) Luther's view, which is sourced in his understanding of the Pauline, Augustinian traditions of distinguishing law and gospel. The use of the word "conscience" to describe the inner life of the human person is ancient.

9. See *BoC*, 120, 121 (Apol 4:2).
10. George Forell, "Luther and Conscience" available through the *Journal of Lutheran Theology* online at http://www.elca.org/JLE/Articles/991. Emphasis mine. Note also that much of this discussion on conscience is deeply indebted to this article by Forell.

The word itself has its roots in Greek philosophy[11] and is roughly comparable to what the Semitic tradition, in more earthy terms, called "the heart."[12] The terms are analogous to something like our center of gravity: the conceptual (mathematical-like) point upon which the law of gravity, the essence of our human nature (however it is conceived) is concentrated.

Our English word for conscience is a translation of the original Greek word *syneidēsis* and a transliteration of the Latin word *conscientia*. The words literally mean "co-knower," and are used, generally, to highlight two aspects of human experience. On the one hand, this co-knower could refer to how we come to act (as in, let your conscience be your guide) and, on the other hand, it could refer to why we question ourselves as we do (the conscience as my judge). Interpreting the meaning of this experience of the self in daily life is where the three views of conscience differ—and they differ in accordance with the basic meta-assumptions that govern thoughts about human nature.

The Enlightenment view of conscience is rooted in the optimism with which Renaissance humanism assessed the essential core of human nature. The feature of life that was emerging at the time of the Renaissance that prompted this optimism was the way *individuals* were pushing the boundaries of human knowledge and artistic expression. This development in human progress demonstrated for them that humanity is intrinsically "good" and, ultimately, the master of its destiny. True, this view of humanity, as Renaissance thinkers insisted, was not unprecedented in human history. Classical civilization, they said, was also in possession of this understanding, but it had been lost for a thousand years due to the stifling effects of Christendom, the uneasy marriage of church and state. This new outlook on human nature was called the "Renaissance," then, because they saw it as a "rebirth" of classical culture. They called the thousand years of suppression between the Classical Age and its Renaissance (or rebirth) the "Medieval Era" (or the "Middle Age") because it was a period of deep darkness between classical culture and its rebirth.

The Enlightenment view of conscience, then, is a response to the overreaching power of the medieval church-state arrangement that dominated European life for a thousand years. The Enlightenment view is based on the meta-assumption that the *individual* has personal access to the fundamental truth of existence that gives the individual

11. W. D. Davies, "Conscience," in *The Interpreter's Dictionary of the Bible*, ed. George Arthur Buttrick et al., vol. 1 (Nashville: Abingdon, 1962), 671–76.

12. For example, when the Synoptic Gospels talk about essence of the law as the demand to love God with all your heart, soul, mind, and strength, that list could have easily included conscience. See Mark 12:30, Luke 10:27, Matt. 22:37, and their source, Deut. 6:12.

autonomy with regard to a wide range of issues defined as matters of conscience. The most radical feature of this autonomy implies the right to judge established authorities. As Forell notes, this view of conscience is closely aligned with the Enlightenment concept of reason, and can be defined as the innate capacity in the *individual* to know and to judge truth. Conscience is a kind of sacred repository of truth.

Many humanists heard Luther's "Here I stand" declaration as rooted in this view of the conscience. That it is a mishearing of Luther is evidenced by the disillusionment later humanists felt towards Luther—the most notable example being evidenced in Erasmus's exchange with Luther on the "Bondage of the Will." While the Enlightenment view of conscience may have been an effective "political" argument against the heteronomy of church-state collaboration, in Luther's view, it misses the mark with regard to understanding the gospel.

The scholastic view of conscience was rooted in the Aristotelian notion of natural law as it was reshaped and developed by Thomas Aquinas and his successors. It is rooted in Aquinas's meta-assumption about nature and grace: grace supplies the energy for nature to fulfill God's purposes, that is, the law. Like the humanist view, the scholastic view of conscience is also positive or optimistic about human nature, but with significant differences. For the scholastics, as Forell describes it, conscience is "the guarding or keeping of the natural principles of the moral law [and] the habit of understanding these primary principles or precepts." As such, the conscience grounds humanity's "ability (habitus) to act according to the law," indeed, to keep the law.[13] Also like the humanists, conscience is virtually interchangeable with reason. "A command of conscience and a command of reason are the same thing."[14]

Where the scholastic view differs from the humanist view is in the distinction it makes between revelation and reason and between form and substance. For the scholastics, "in matters of faith the [conscience] is by definition inapplicable since the light of reason does not suffice in matters of faith." Therefore, in matters of faith, one needs an outside authority to command or teach the conscience. That authority was the church or, more precisely, the magisterium. The scholastics also differ from the humanists in that, for the scholastics, conscience does not automatically contain the content of law or knowledge that it needs to act appropriately. It must be "informed." The conscience, then, is the form, the empty bucket, that has the ability to hold the substance of teaching it needs, but it does not supply that substance. That substance is

13. Forell, "Luther and Conscience," paragraph 5.
14. Ibid.

supplied by an external authority ordained by God, namely, the church's magisterium. Therefore, in light of the scholastic understanding of conscience, it is easy to understand the scholastic response to Luther's struggle in his "Here I stand" statement. It is crystallized in the words to Luther by the secretary to the archbishop of Trier: "Lay aside your conscience, Martin; you must lay it aside [and let the church inform it] because it is in error."[15]

Luther's view of conscience (and that of the Lutheran Confessions) stands in stark contrast to both the scholastic and the Enlightenment views of conscience. It is rooted in Luther's understanding of the gospel made clear through the method of distinguishing the gospel from law. Although Luther's understanding of conscience developed throughout his career, by 1521 his basic view was well established, as evidenced in numerous writings from 1521 and after. Against the aforementioned scholastic view, where conscience is deemed a power to act, Luther writes with all succinctness in his 1521 treatise, "The Judgment of Martin Luther on Monastic Vows":

> For the conscience is not the power of acting but the power of judging which judges about works. Its proper work (as Paul says in Romans 2:15) is to accuse or to excuse, to cause one to stand accused or absolved, terrified or secure. Its purpose is not to do, but to speak about what has been done and what should be done, and this judgment makes us stand accused or saved before God.[16]

Unlike the scholastics and humanists, Luther does not have a "positive" view of conscience but rather a "critical" one. The conscience is not a reservoir of "positive" information out of which a person can act confidently, nor is it the "positive" experience of the voice of God within that one can follow with certainty. Rather, the conscience is humanity's unique experience of always being called upon to justify itself. For Luther, the witness of conscience is a purely anthropological phenomenon and consists in the nagging awareness of always being under evaluation, not just by others, or even by God, but *by one's own self*. Luther puts it succinctly when he says conscience "gives witness of themselves to themselves."[17] The character of that witness is not merely informative but evaluative or critical. It is a witness that involves people in a process of "accusing" and "excusing" themselves.[18] This essential critical or "accusing" function of the conscience sets Luther's view apart from the other views.[19]

---

15. Ibid., paragraph 4.
16. "The Judgment of Martin Luther on Monastic Vows," *LW* 26:139.
17. Luther describes it this way: "their conscience gives witness of themselves about themselves." *LW* 25:187.
18. See Rom. 2:15.
19. Forell, "Luther and Conscience," paragraph 8.

To be sure, the phenomenology of conscience is very complex and dialectical in nature. Luther's 1521 Commentary on Romans (2:15) speaks to this point. As an inward dialogue of the self, concerning (the quality of) the self, the conscience is experienced as both a protagonist and an antagonist, a friend and an enemy. Insofar as our conscience assesses our deeds as justified, righteous, or good, we think of ourselves as affirmed or "excused" and our "co-knower" as friend. Insofar as our conscience assesses our deeds as unjustified or unrighteous or evil, we think of ourselves as under attack or "accused," and our "co-knower" as enemy.

As Luther notes, because of humanity's sinful condition (that congenital condition of self-centered versus God-centered) it is easy for us to hear and welcome judgments of conscience that "excuse" us and become "pleased with ourselves." However, it is not so easy to hear and welcome the judgments of conscience that "accuse" us. Indeed, such murmurings of conscience are very troubling, even angst-inducing. As a result, we often try to suppress them or minimize them. In Luther's judgment, this suppression of conscience is also often interpreted (mistakenly, of course) as righteousness. Nevertheless, this wrestling with conscience—a fundamental characteristic of the human person—can be suppressed at times, but not overcome in principle. So accurate is the accusing conscience of the self that Luther has God say of it on the Day of Judgment: "See, it's not I who am judging you, but I merely agree with your own [conscience's] judgment about yourself and acknowledge this judgment. You cannot judge differently concerning your very own self, neither can I."[20] The conclusion Luther draws from all this is that a troubled conscience is a fundamental feature of the human condition. The conscience is the internal struggle where the self must come to terms with itself as it is.

Theologically speaking, the conscience is that conceptual "place" in the human person where God's evaluation confronts the human person in his or her totality—whether as law or gospel. The law is God's word of judgment that comes from outside us and serves to corroborate or stimulate the accusations of the conscience. In the law of God, then, we have a second witness against us, God himself, who confirms and even amplifies the witness of conscience. The troubled conscience is thus the "natural" state of sinful humanity. It can be no different.

Into this hopeless scenario, the gospel of Jesus Christ enters as humanity's only hope. The gospel is a word that contravenes the witness of both the human conscience and the law of God. This it does, not by saying their witness is untrue, but by bringing their witness to an end in

20. *LW* 25:188.

the cross of Christ. In the cross and resurrection of Christ, God overrules and brings to naught the accusations of both, the human conscience and the law of God. Faith in Christ is a troubled conscience taking refuge in the cross and resurrection of Christ.[21] Therefore, when Luther makes his "Here I stand" statement, he is appealing neither to the autonomy of his conscience nor to the alleged prerogatives of the church's magisterium, but to the Word of God itself. "Here I stand" is a declaration of faith in the Word of God.

If one wants to argue with Luther about this, then one must argue with the Word of God, which he pleaded over and over to be done. To be sure, Luther also drew on scripture for support for his declaration. But not because he held a fundamentalist view of scripture. Not, "The Bible says it. I believe it. That settles it." For Luther, the scripture, like his conscience, does not argue for its own autonomy; rather, it too promotes Christ. It argues the Word of God, the Word made flesh, Christ crucified and raised. And it does so by distinguishing God's law and God's gospel.

Augsburg as a Model of Orthopraxis: Apology 21, 22, 23 and Their Relevance for Today

In what follows we will look at three examples of how the AC and its Apology used the *meta-assumption* of the gospel (justification by faith) and the *method* of orthopraxis (law-gospel distinction) to reform three very different aspects of Christian life. The *first* deals with an aspect of the devotional life, the misdirected focus of prayer (Art. 21); the *second* deals with an aspect of liturgical life, the misadministration of the sacrament of the altar (Art. 22); and the *third* deals with an aspect of church discipline, the misguided assumption about marriage and celibacy (Art. 23). In all three of these practical areas of Christian life, the "double-dipstick" will guide the reform: (1) Does the practice respect the honor that is due Christ alone? and (2) Does the practice respect faith alone as the true consolation for law-troubled consciences?

Article 21: The Invocation of the Saints

In the sixteenth century, the importance of the saints in the devotional practice and piety of the church was taken for granted. And in many respects, the AC did not challenge that importance. In particular, the Confessors liked the way the cult of the saints could serve as a means of grace.[22] In an almost boastful fashion, the AC states that in Lutheran

---

21. Ibid. See here Luther's own exuberant and extensive description of this.
22. See how Robert W. Bertram describes this in his article "Mary and the Saints as an Issue

churches the people are taught to "remember the saints" because such practice and piety "may strengthen our faith when we see how they experienced grace and they were helped by faith."[23] Even more, Christians are urged to take note of the good works of the saints and learn how they are particularly fashioned to their life's situation or calling, even as every Christian's good works are so fashioned.[24] In this regard, the Confessors unambiguously "honored the saints" because their lives, rightly understood, met the criteria of the "double-dipstick": they magnified the saving role of Christ alone and they demonstrated the all-sufficiency of faith alone as the foundation of a conscience that is at peace with or "certain" of its standing before God.[25]

However, one aspect of the medieval cult of the saints, in the Confessors' view, proved to be poisonous to the honor of Christ and the sufficiency of faith—and this would prove to be the fault line between them and their Roman Catholic opponents. Somehow smuggled into this otherwise good piety was the idea that the lives of the saints do not simply *demonstrate* or reveal or honor the work of Christ as redeemer, mediator, or propitiator, but that the lives of the saints *add to* or complete Christ's work.

Much to the Confessors' dismay, their opponents condemned the Confessors' idea of "honoring" the saints as too limited. Instead, they "required" the add-on, specifically, that the honor due the saints include the idea of the "invocation" of the saints for help in the attainment of salvation. That "requirement," in the Confessors' view, was a nonstarter precisely because it both (1) dishonored Christ as sole redeemer of humankind and (2) burdened human consciences with requirements contrary to the gospel, that is, the meta-assumption of justification by faith and its orthopraxis of distinguishing law and gospel. The opponents' add-on makes the saints into more than mediators of intercessions (as all Christians are). The saints become mediators of propitiation, a role that belongs to Christ alone.[26] By insisting that the invocation of the saints is a "requirement," the Confessors' opponents rob the conscience of its certainty (faith in Christ alone). Human (in this case, the saints') works and not Christ's work alone become the promised foundation of salvation. Indeed, this is precisely what has already happened, as they point out "popular opinion" among the people that they "imagine Christ is more severe and that the saints are

in the Lutheran Confessions," available at http://www.crossings.org/library/bertram/Maryand theSaints.pdf.
23. *BoC*, 58 (AC 21:1).
24. Ibid.
25. *BoC*, 239 (Apol 21:17).
26. *BoC*, 239 (Apol 21:14–15).

more easily conciliated, and so they rely more on the mercy of the saints than on the mercy of Christ. Thus, they flee Christ and turn to the saints."[27]

As new forms of devotional practice and piety enter serendipitously into Christian life and practice today, we would do well to think about them as the Confessors thought about the invocation of the saints in their day. The double-dipstick is still the best tool at the church's disposal for doing this. While identifying and evaluating the various new popular forms of "Christian" devotional practices that are emerging today is a subject for another article, it seems to me that devotional practices that emphasize mindfulness, centering, and meditation are continuing to be in vogue in postmodern Western culture. What is significant about these current practices is how different they are from the practices of medieval Christendom. The cult of the saints (especially with regard to the idea of the invocation of the saints, criticized by the AC) has its roots in tribal ancestral piety, a type of piety and belief system that still exists among numerous immigrant groups today, such as the Hmong community.[28] The predominant focus of the Western mind is not about how to secure the help from the ancestors or the saints, but self-fulfillment through self-awareness and mindful living.

Whether these practices can be redeemed for Christian purposes (the way, for example, the Confessors thought the cult of the saints could be) is still an open question. Robert Bertram wrote an insightful article using the double-dipstick criteria (if not explicitly, at least, implicitly) with one early form of self-fulfillment thinking: transactional analysis. His conclusion:

> For the most constructive use of Transactional Analysis I would propose two alternatives. We should either demythologize TA's soteriological pretensions and then employ it for a very limited purpose of secular behavioral change [that is, utilize it in the service of the civil function of the law], or we should radicalize it with the anti-Gnostic secret of the Christian Gospel and then use it for the Kingdom unabashedly and outright. Of these two, my preference is the second.[29]

Article 22: Concerning Both Kinds in the Lord's Supper

To be sure, the history of liturgical practice is messy and the actual

---

27. *BoC*, 239 (Apol 21:15).
28. I am somewhat familiar with the Hmong ancestral worship belief system and practices from a former student in one of my courses at Lakeland College who practiced it and from my limited connection to the ELCA Hmong Ministry Network, which is concerned about how to respect the ancestors and worship Christ alone.
29. Robert W. Bertram, "Transactional Analysis: Redeemable for Christian Purposes?" available at http://www.crossings.org/library/bertram/transactionalAnalysis.pdf. I highly commend this article to the reader.

liturgical practices undertaken throughout the church diverse, and often arbitrary. Still, liturgical practice has its intended purpose and its distinct accountability. It exists to serve the one gospel and sacraments so that saving faith may abound, and its distinct accountability is to the Christ who accomplished our salvation and who instituted the gospel and sacraments so that he might find faith on earth. Note, purpose and accountability here are simply another way of talking about the double-dipstick. Liturgical practice is "orthopraxis" when it (1) honors the preaching of the gospel and the administration of the sacraments that Christ instituted (2) for the purpose of creating saving faith—faith that unburdens law-troubled consciences.

In the sixteenth century, it had become not just common practice, but the church's regulation, to withhold the wine from the people. It is that quality of "requirement" and the reasons for it (or more accurately, lack thereof) that raise the concern of the Confessors. In the Confutation, the opponents list the various councils that set forth this regulation, but, as Melanchthon notes, they never give a theological reason "why" they do it—and that is a clue to the problem. The church's magisterium has come to think of itself as Lord over the sacrament. For this reason, the AC and its Apology accentuate the fact that Christ instituted the Lord's Supper and that the church has no right to change what God has instituted through Christ.[30] In essence, the practice of communing in one kind is a case of the church's magisterium elevating itself over the Christ to whom it owes obedience and service. The practice dishonors Christ and his sacrament. Even here, though, a distinction needs to be made. The very idea of attaching the notion of "requirement" to the sacrament is to dishonor it and the Christ who instituted it.

For the Confessors, the Lord's Supper does not fall into the category of "requirement." Rather, it is a "testament" or "promise" given by Christ to the church that says: here, in eating and drinking the bread and the wine Christ gives you his very body and blood for the forgiveness of sins for the "consolation and encouragement of terrified hearts."[31] The institution narrative clearly summarizes the double-dipstick: Christ alone is the giver and the content of the sacrament, and consolation for law-troubled consciences is the sole reason he instituted it. To mess with that is to dishonor Christ and to burden Christian consciences.

Of course, there is one other aberration that has been smuggled in through this distortion of sacramental practice. The practice of giving one kind (bread) to the people and both kinds (bread and wine) to the clergy was pure clericalism. As Melanchthon says, "This is the chief

30. *BoC*, 245 (Apol 22:2–5).
31. *BoC*, 246 (Apol 22:10).

reason for defending the prohibition of one element [for them], namely, in order to exalt the status of the clergy more highly by some religious ritual."[32] But even this pales in light of the charge that the magisterium has, by its presumption to "regulate" the sacrament, elevated itself over Christ.

As new forms of liturgical and sacramental practices emerge in the contemporary church, we should evaluate them in light of the double-dipstick as the Confessors did in their day. As we do, it's important to remember that when the Confessors criticized the Roman magisterium for changing what Christ instituted, they were not advocating either a literalistic or a historical-critical approach to the Bible for settling such matters. To read them in light of that contemporary debate would be the worst kind of anachronism one could perpetrate on them. Rather, the Confessors used the meta-assumption of the gospel (justification by faith) and orthopraxis of law-gospel distinction. The issue is making sure the content and purpose of the sacrament remains as Christ intended it. I can imagine circumstances where the administration of the sacrament might accommodate the needs of the recipients, including giving the sacrament in one kind or adapting the elements. The point to remember is that it is the *Lord's* Supper, not the church's magisterium or its laity, and that it is given for the purpose of comforting law-troubled consciousness—not simply to look hospitable. The temptation to distort the sacraments to fit our purposes is the perennial temptation.

Article 23: The Marriage of Priests

In the sixteenth century no single institutional practice was more vigorously defended than the practice of clerical celibacy. That's because, as Melanchthon astutely noted, "the real purpose of the law [of clerical celibacy] is not religion but domination, for which religion is just a wicked pretext."[33] And so, when the AC came out in full support for the marriage of priests on theological grounds, the writers of the Confutation were "astounded." In Melanchthon's assessment, so "silly," "trivial," and "ridiculous" were the arguments of the writers of the Confutation that "it only required as judge a person who is honest and fears God" to see through them.[34] Still, as Melanchthon also noted, the magisterium's addiction to dominance was buttressed by a theology that was contrary to the gospel and that needed exposing for two reasons: so that priests could enter into marriage and so secular authorities could

---

32. *BoC*, 246 (Apol 22:9).
33. *BoC*, 256 (Apol 23:60).
34. *BoC*, 248 (Apol 23:6).

defend these marriages with a good conscience.[35] Note, marriage, including the marriage of priests, is a secular matter, not a spiritual matter. It concerns life in the old creation, not the new. Therefore, Melanchthon marshals a theological assault that is a masterpiece in orthopraxis: the art of properly distinguishing and recoordinating what the Confutation had thoroughly confused: law and gospel or, more accurately stated in this context, the secular and the spiritual.

As a secular matter, marriage is described by Melanchthon as a "divine ordinance" or command.[36] Those words should not be heard as "legislative" requirements issued to this or that person but as a statement about reality itself, "an order divinely stamped upon nature."[37] God created humanity as sexual creatures in order to procreate and to be attracted to one another in a sexual, natural way. Given that fact about creation, the right to contract in marriage is both a divine (established by theology) and a natural (established by the jurists) right. As such, the church has no right or authority to overthrow the established order of creation. Such an idea fails to properly distinguish law and gospel, the secular from the spiritual. In addition, because concupiscence, which is sin, has become a major feature of the human species since the fall, the natural affection between the sexes has been complicated and corrupted by lust. Therefore, marriage has also become, after sin, a safeguard or remedy for limiting the consequences of this sin-affliction for both the individual, who is enflamed by lust, and the security of human community, which is endangered by lust. Sinful human beings can know that to live in marriage is a natural good even though they are not good—except by faith in Jesus Christ alone. As such, for the church to forbid priests to marry is to deprive them of God's natural help against lust and to expose them and the world to great danger.[38]

Melanchthon charges the Roman magisterium with advancing superstition, theological error, and historical falsehood—all, I might add, confusingly intertwined—in defense of clerical celibacy. The superstition the magisterium advanced is the idea that the grace of ordination can bestow the gift of celibacy. Melanchthon does agree that celibacy is an "extraordinary" gift and that it should be honored wherever it exists. Nevertheless, it is a gift that is given by God alone and not by the power of the church or its ministry.[39] The theological error rests in thinking celibacy is what makes priests "pure," whereas marriage defiles.[40] Both marriage and celibacy can be described as "pure" insofar

---

35. *BoC*, 257 (Apol 23:71).
36. *BoC*, 249 (Apol 23:7).
37. *BoC*, 249 (Apol 23:12).
38. *BoC*, 254 (Apol 23:51).
39. *BoC*, 254 (Apol 23:50).

as they are callings approved by God, with marriage being the more common calling and celibacy the more extraordinary calling. But neither marriage nor celibacy makes us "pure" before God. Purity before God is "purity of heart," and that comes only through faith in Christ. What the magisterium fails to see is that the gospel allows marriage for those who need it, including priests, and that it does not compel marriage for those who have the gift of celibacy. There is no conflict between being "pure of heart" (faith in Christ) and being in a secular calling, such as marriage or any other station in life.[41]

It is worth noting the historical falsehood in the assertion that, throughout Christian history, councils and tribunals (like the ones against Jovian) have required celibacy of priests because of the purity required of priests in the carrying out of their ministry.[42] Of course, says Melanchthon, the facts, let alone the present practice in the Eastern Church, do not bear this out. However, because Melanchthon was not given a copy of the Confutation, he was not able to address its particular historical claims point by point.[43]

In our changing culture, new ideas about sexuality have emerged due to the way the "jurists" of our day are thinking about (in a deep scientific, psychological, and sociological way) the nature of God's creation and the human species. What is being discussed in light of this thinking is vexing both our culture and our church, leading to culture wars and church schisms. A prime example is the recent controversy around the decision of the Evangelical Lutheran Church in America to allow the possibility for clergy in same-sex relationships to remain clergy in good standing. The decision was so controversial that it precipitated the formation of the North American Lutheran Church in protest of the decision.

Should clergy in same-sex relations be allowed to continue in those unions and remain clergy or should they be forced to choose between celibacy and their homosexual inclinations? A detailed exploration of this issue is beyond the scope of this study. Nevertheless, it seems to me that Apology 23 provides helpful insight into how to reform church practice in this matter in a way that does magnify Christ and console law-troubled consciences.[44] Is homosexuality an "extraordinary gift"

40. *BoC*, 251 (Apol 23:26).
41. *BoC*, 252 (Apol 23:28–35).
42. *BoC*, 257 (Apol 23:67–69).
43. *BoC*, 257 (Apol 23:68).
44. Within the Crossings Community, Robert W. Bertram and Edward H. Schroeder have each offered a way of thinking about this issue that utilizes the orthopraxis approach of the Augsburg Confession and its Apology. What we see here is that the law-gospel outlook is not a template to give us the "right answer" to knotty secular matters, but a way of securing a "right heart," a heart focused on the gospel, and a clear conscience, one that finds its certainty in faith, as we live in this knotty world. For examples of Schroeder's thought, see Ed Schroeder, "Gay Is OK. An Argument from the Lutheran Confessions. What!?," *Thursday Theology* #685, July 28, 2011 (http://www.crossings.org/gay-is-ok-an-

(what science might call a genetic/natural trait or others an orientation) like celibacy? If so, might not something like marriage be appropriate for gay and lesbian people for the sake of their own struggle with lust and the stability it brings to social relations? If, on the other hand, homosexuality is not an extraordinary gift, but, say, a deeply and mysteriously held "choice" related to humanity's *incurvatus in se* (curved in on one's self) nature, then what does that mean? Need homosexuality be rejected at this time as a dangerous aberration or might it come under the category of polygamy as in the time of Abraham and Jacob? Melanchthon himself argues like this: "It may happen that the heart of a husband, like Abraham and Jacob, who were polygamists, was purer and burned with less lust than the hearts of many celibates who are truly continent."[45] Might that be the kind of law-gospel orthopraxis thinking we could apply to today's issue of homosexual committed relations?

Whatever the ethical or policy choice, Melanchthon reminds us that the church's concern is always about hearts made pure by the gospel (faith in Christ alone) so that people can make decisions in questionable matters with a good conscience. Of course, as Melanchthon notes, pure hearts and good consciences always have as their character "the whole [reality] of repentance,"[46] defined not by outward appearance or conventional moral behavior but by denial of self and inward reliance on God's mercy alone.

Conclusion

We have sought to "update" (make useful for today) the reform measures of the Augsburg Confession and its Apology by explaining the method of thinking the Confessors employed for the issues of their time. That method has *at its center* the meta-assumption of the gospel (justification by faith) and *in its exercise* the proper distinction and correlation of law and gospel. We also showed how this method fits within the modern idea of praxis. There is no need to make a sharp divide between sound theological thinking and sound philosophical thinking. What is needed is an honest recognition of the meta-assumption upon which we think and the reasons we hold them. For the Confessors at Augsburg, that meta-assumption is the person and event of Jesus Christ himself: God's unique, historic encounter with the world to save the world from God's

argument-from-the-lutheran-confessions-what/) and "Augsburg Confessional Theology and the ELCA Sexuality Debate" (http://www.crossings.org/augsburg-confessional-theology-and-the-elca-sexuality-debate/). For an example of Bertram's thought, see Robert W. Bertram, *The Divorce of Sex and Marriage: Sain Sex*, ed. Michael Hoy (Chesterfield, MO: Crossings Community, 2012).

45. *BoC*, 256 (Apol 23:64).
46. *BoC*, 256 (Apol 23:64–65).

own condemnation of it. Church reform, therefore, is always about the art of (1) using or magnifying the good news of Jesus Christ (2) to bring consolation to law-troubled consciences: the double-dipstick.

12

Mission

Jukka Kääriäinen

Even though the Augsburg Confession does not include an article explicitly dedicated to "mission," Dr. Jukka Kääriäinen argues that mission is the inevitable implication of the gospel articulated in the Augsburg Confession. In this chapter, Kääriäinen discusses how the Lutheran confessional distinction between law and gospel preserves the gospel as promise. He then shows how the Lutheran notion of God's hiddenness can serve as a bridge between the confessional gospel as promise and today's world that often asks, "Why Jesus when there are so many other religious choices?" Finally, Kääriäinen illustrates how this gospel as promise addresses our "skeptically suspicious, religiously pluralistic postmodern world."

Introduction: Defining the Problem and Setting the Stage

Readers of the *Book of Concord* will be struck by something remarkable. "Mission" is not mentioned even once! The *Book of Concord*'s index goes straight from "mirror" to "mixture." "Mission" is missing, absent. How is that possible? For laypeople, pastors, and theologians passionate about God's mission in Christ, that's quite a problem to have indeed! This is why Lutheran theology[1] has been criticized as missiologically deficient.

---

1. The distinction between Luther's theology and that of the Lutheran confessional writings as expressed in the *Book of Concord* is important. However, I believe Luther's theology and that of the *Book of Concord* are best understood as offering fundamentally complementary, rather than alternative, positions, centered on the notion of the gospel as promise.

"If Lutherans want to engage in missiological reflection and mission practice," this line of critique goes, "they must look outside of their own tradition." Such has been the prevailing wisdom.

How can this problem be addressed? An important starting point is to recognize the significant chasm—societal, cultural, and theological—between the Reformation context and today's postmodern context. One of the Reformation's main agendas was to "Christianize Christendom," centered on internal reform of the church, rather than engaging other religions in mission and dialogue.[2] This is significant for two reasons. First, the issue of religious pluralism and the need to theologically address it never arose for the Reformers. In his lifetime, Luther probably met fewer than twenty people who were not baptized Christians. Luther, in step with the church of his day, viewed Muslims primarily as "infidels" and a political threat to the Holy Roman Empire, rather than as prospective converts to Christianity.[3] This means, second, that a mission theology, or theology of religions, simply was not on the Reformers' intellectual horizon in the same way it is in our pluralistic context today.

I have been given the unenviable task of demonstrating how, for a classic Lutheran theology arising from core insights of the Augsburg Confession and other Lutheran confessional documents, "mission" is an inevitable implication of the gospel. Such an argument from silence is no easy task. However, similar to the term "Trinity" missing from the scriptures, the fact that the term "mission" is missing from the Lutheran Confessions does not minimize their missional vigor and usefulness. What it means is that these resources are not self-evident, and that their identification, retrieval, and application to our context necessitates a creative process. In other words, these "hidden treasures" need to be unearthed and dusted off. In this chapter, I will outline how I believe this can be done in a theologically faithful and fruitful manner. Before describing my approach, two obstacles—an internal one pertaining to

2. For a fuller treatment of this point and an excellent overview of the various Christian agendas at play in the Reformation era, see Scott Hendrix, *Recultivating the Vineyard: The Reformation Agendas of Christianization* (Louisville: Westminster John Knox, 2004). Hendrix addresses Luther's specific context and concerns in chapter 2.

3. Some inflammatory statements and prejudicial writings by Luther regarding Muslims and Jews in his later years are well known and documented. Perhaps the best-known such work is "On the Jews and Their Lies" (1543). I readily acknowledge such problematic writings and condemn them as unacceptable hate speech. Luther's problematic outlooks and hermeneutical assumptions regarding other religions are partly attributable to their being rooted in his limited life experience with those religions. I wish to claim that such statements do not render Luther's theology missiologically useless, but rather that the fruitful missiological resources within that theology are retrievable and applicable in today's pluralistic context, his inflammatory writings notwithstanding. When it comes to Luther's potential as a missiological resource and thinker, I will be cautioning us not to "throw the baby out with the bathwater." For a balanced, insightful study of Luther on these matters, see Adam Francisco, *Martin Luther and Islam: A Study in Sixteenth-Century Polemics and Apologetics* (Leiden: Koninklijke Brill NV, 2007).

the church and an external one pertaining to wider culture—need to be identified and addressed.

Two Obstacles

First, an internal obstacle relates to the very concept of mission. "Mission" has become a slippery symbol, a concept with many competing definitions. Is mission gospel proclamation, evangelism, common witness, the work of the triune God (*missio Dei*), human liberation and flourishing, work for peace and justice, prophetic dialogue, enculturation, or contextualization?[4] The late Stephen Neill, commenting on such diversity, notes, "If everything is mission, nothing is mission."[5] The same concern applies to the gospel itself: if everything is gospel, nothing is gospel. In a situation where Christians disagree on a common definition of such a core concept, confusion abounds.

Not only does the church face the challenge of more deeply understanding the nature of mission but, second, it faces an even more daunting challenge from the culture at large. What academics and intellectuals call by a fancy name, the "hermeneutics of suspicion," we might designate a suspicious and skeptical attitude toward not only truth and authority claims in general, but also the possibility of making and keeping promises. Our postmodern world has lost confidence in even the very possibility of making promises.

One need not be a postmodern skeptic or agnostic to appreciate the immensity of this challenge. To some degree, all of us have experienced this struggle or have loved ones who wrestle with it. Can the promise, "Till death do us part," be trusted when half of all marriages in the United States end in divorce? Seemingly no significant relationship of trust—husband-wife, parent-child, teacher-student, clergy-congregant, doctor-patient, therapist-client, lawyer-client, public official-citizen—is immune from the epidemic of broken trust, misconduct, and exploitation, as evidenced in scandals involving infidelity, greed, and abuse (spiritual, emotional, physical, and sexual). In such a world of betrayed trust and broken promises, is there any promise that remains truly unbreakable and trustworthy? It's no wonder our culture views any promise, perhaps especially the promise of the gospel, with understandable doubt and skepticism.

4. David Bosch lists at least thirteen different elements of an "emerging ecumenical missionary paradigm," namely, mission as: the church-with-others, *missio Dei*, mediating salvation, the quest for justice, evangelism, contextualization, liberation, enculturation, common witness, ministry by the whole people of God, witness to people of other living faiths (including dialogue), theology, and action in hope. Bosch, *Transforming Mission* (Maryknoll, NY: Orbis, 1991), 372–76.
5. Stephen Neill, *Creative Tension* (London: Edinburgh House, 1959), 81.

Overcoming both of these obstacles (confusion regarding the nature of mission and postmodern distrust of promises) is indeed a daunting task. But I believe our Lutheran theological heritage bestows upon us some invaluable resources for meeting these challenges. What might these be?

Every heir of the Reformation legacy knows the three "*solas*" (onlys) of Reformation theology: *solus Christus* (Christ alone), *sola fides* (faith alone), and *sola gratia* (grace alone). These three axioms have been indispensably foundational for clarifying how sinners can have a saving relationship with God (soteriology). Yet they have not provided much help in guiding followers of Christ in their desire to share and witness (missiology) to the saving truth encapsulated in these three Reformation slogans. How can today's church bridge this gap between soteriology and missiology? Is there a theological "GPS" that can help get us from "here" to "there"? I believe there is.

Just as Reformation theology was built on the three-legged stool of Christ alone, faith alone, and grace alone, likewise a relevant, fruitful, contemporary Lutheran missiology can, indeed ought, to be built on the three pillars of the gospel as *promise*, the *law* as accusing yet connecting us to the Creator, and the *hiddenness of God* as a universal feature of religious experience. Just as each of the three "*solas*" was indispensable for preserving the unique, salvific work of Christ, similarly each of these three elements (promise, law, and the hidden God) is crucial for Lutheran missiology starting from and ending in the right place. If you remove one leg from a three-legged stool, you render it useless. Oswald Bayer captures well my strategic use of these three elements as he discusses the "three, irreducible ways in which God encounters us": (a) in the conflict with the law that judges me, that convicts me with regard to my sins, that accuses me, and that delivers me over to the final judgment of death; (b) in the promise of the gospel, in which God himself speaks by means of Jesus Christ on my behalf, indeed takes my place; and (c) in the assault of the hiddenness of God, which cannot be understood merely as the effect of the law and which so radically contradicts the gospel in an ... incomprehensible way.[6]

In continuity with the rest of this book, I will employ a theology of the cross, utilizing the hiddenness of God, as a concrete bridge from our Lutheran heritage to our skeptically suspicious, religiously pluralistic postmodern world.

The remainder of this chapter will unfold in three parts. First, I will examine how and why the law-gospel distinction is crucial for preserving the gospel as promise, including the critical role the law

---

6. Oswald Bayer, *Martin Luther's Theology: A Contemporary Interpretation* (Grand Rapids: Eerdmans, 2008), 105, 42.

plays in our Lutheran tradition. This step is foundational. Next, I will explicate how the hiddenness of God, demonstrated in a theology of the cross, connects our theological heritage with a religiously plural world. Finally, a brief concluding section will offer some practical suggestions for missional engagement.

The Law-Gospel Distinction Preserving the Gospel as Promise

Does God have one or two missions in and to the world? You may find this question strange, even absurd, but it is actually crucial for starting and ending in the right place. The gospel as promise gives Christian mission a distinctively dual shape. God's mission, while unified in a single economy of salvation, inevitably manifests itself in the dual form of law and gospel, sin and grace, wrath and promised mercy. Luther described these two divine missions in terms of God's "alien work" (*opus alienum*) in service of and directed toward God's "proper work" (*opus proprium*): "Thus an action that is alien to God's nature results in a deed belonging to his very nature: God makes a person a sinner so that he may make him righteous."[7]

The law-gospel distinction, while safeguarding the gospel as promise, ultimately serves as a hermeneutical map for constructing a missiology arising from the gospel as promise. In contrast, the majority of contemporary missiologies arising from the basis of *missio Dei* (mission of God) proceed from the conviction that—since the term *missio Dei* itself is singular—the *one*, triune God pursues *one* mission of speaking and bestowing *one* Word, a word of loving grace to all. Such an approach runs the risk of marginalizing the Spirit's important work of revealing and "convicting the world of guilt in regard to sin and righteousness and judgment"[8] and of necessitating Christ. It is precisely the deep reality of sin and brokenness, and the corresponding necessity of Christ overcoming divine wrath toward sin, that constitutes a central aspect of the "all truth," which the "Spirit of truth will guide you into."[9] Such is the classic Lutheran claim.

Gospel as Promise in the Classic Lutheran Tradition

"For God does not deal, nor has he ever dealt, with us except through the word of promise. We, in turn, cannot deal with God except through faith in the word of his promise. . . . These two, promise and faith, must necessarily go together."[10] In memorable words, Martin Luther placed

7. *LW* 31:51.
8. John 16:8.
9. John 16:13.

the theme of the promise of God (*promissio Dei*) at the center of his Reformation theological agenda. I believe it should also take center stage in today's missiological agenda.

The classic Lutheran tradition offers the gospel as promise of God *par excellence*, concentrated in Jesus Christ as the Promise incarnate, as *gift and promise* to both church and society. For Lutheran theology, "gospel" and "mission" are essential to Christian self-identity and vocation. In addition, "promise" is the best, most fruitful vehicle for relating the two, since the nature of both the gospel and Christian mission are grounded in the promises of God. In other words, "promise" not only holds fidelity to the Christian tradition and relevant contemporary engagement in mission together, but is able to do so precisely because "promise" illuminates a fundamental dimension of both the "gospel" and "mission."

The logic of my argument unfolds in three claims: (1) For the classic Lutheran tradition, the nature of the gospel is pure promise. (2) The nature of the gospel should determine the nature and shape of Christian mission. (3) Therefore, promise becomes a central category for shaping Christian mission. The gospel promise is trustworthy because "the promise [is] made in the name of one who has already satisfied the condition of death and therefore has all the future in his gift."[11] As the late Robert Bertram put it, "*Promissio* is the secret of *missio*."[12]

Claiming the gospel as promise has significant, far-reaching implications in at least six areas: (1) appreciating the nature and character of God as a faithful, promise-keeping God; (2) a view of human nature as fundamentally "trusting creatures"; (3) the nature of Christian faith as trust in the divine promise of mercy for Christ's sake; (4) pastoral concerns of comforting troubled consciences and applying the benefits of Christ; (5) the creative, reality-shaping nature of God's Word; and (6) the law-gospel distinction as safeguarding both the nature of the gospel as promise and that of the law as accusatory. God's dual speech of law and gospel, wrath and promise, creates a relational matrix between God and humanity, confronting and challenging people to respond in faith by trusting the gospel promise of mercy rather than "wasting" their trust on lesser promises.[13]

10. *LW* 36:42.

11. Eric W. Gritsch and Robert W. Jenson, *Lutheranism* (Philadelphia: Fortress Press, 1976), 44.

12. Robert W. Bertram, "How a Lutheran Does Theology: Some Clues from the Lutheran Confessions," in *Lutheran-Episcopal Dialogue: Report and Recommendations*, ed. William G. Weinhauer and Robert L. Wietelman (Cincinnati: Forward Movement Publications, 1981), 87.

13. Robert Jenson has demonstrated that the category of promise, rather than having an exclusively christocentric focus and application, has fruitful potential for application to many other facets of Christian theology: to Israel and the church as the communities of promise, to Jesus as the fulfillment of the promise and the divine promise incarnate, to the content of the gospel as the forgiveness of sins and promise of mercy, to Christian ethics and discipleship, to God the Father as the God of promise, to the Holy Spirit as the

The Law-Gospel Distinction Defined

In classic Lutheran theology, the law and the gospel are diametrically opposed. In stark contrast to the law, which accuses and leads to a knowledge of sin, the gospel comes to us as a "second, decisive, final, [utterly] different Word of God,"[14] one in which God speaks on our behalf and for us (*pro nobis*), being on our side.

The law-gospel distinction seeks to capture and preserve this tension of God's concrete speech to humanity, God's specific dealings with humanity, as well as the deeply interpersonal nature of the divine-human relationship. How does this distinction help clarify the divine plan (economy) of salvation?

First of all, the law-gospel distinction corresponds to the New Testament testimony concerning the dual, twofold nature of divine revelation. A few brief examples are in order. As the prologue to John's Gospel puts it: "For the law was given through Moses; grace and truth were given through Jesus Christ."[15] In Romans 3, Paul contrasts the nature of the gospel as a gift of righteousness, appropriated by faith, as distinct from the law bearing witness to it: "But now a righteousness from God, apart from law, has been made known, to which the law and the prophets testify. This righteousness from God comes through faith in Jesus Christ to all who believe. There is no difference, for all have sinned and fall short of the glory of God."[16]

Such a twofold revelation has been variously described as "natural" knowledge of God versus faith's knowledge of God, the law of creation vs. the gospel of Christ, and the distinction between revelation and salvation.[17] The significance of this distinction for the purposes of revelation is that it affirms genuine, divine revelation throughout creation and in the world's religions, while insisting on Christ's singularity as God's instrument of salvation for all. In doing so, this distinction holds in creative tension the universality of revelation, on the one hand, and the uniqueness of Christ, on the other. As Carl Braaten puts it, "Jesus Christ is sole Savior, not the sole revealer."[18]

presence of the promise, and to the world as the arena of God's promise, etc. Jenson, *Story and Promise: A Brief Theology of the Gospel about Jesus* (Ramsey, NJ: Sigler, 1989).
14. Bayer, *Martin Luther's Theology*, 61.
15. John 1:17.
16. Rom. 3:21–23.
17. Various Lutheran theologians have subscribed to this basic schema of revelation in varying forms, including J. C. Hoffman, C. H. Ratschow, Nathan Söderblom, Oscar Cullmann, Paul Althaus, Paul Tillich, Wolfhart Pannenberg, Carl Braaten, and Edward Schroeder, to name but a few. It should be noted that, while all subscribe to the formulation of distinguishing revelation from salvation, some (such as Pannenberg) object to the law-gospel distinction as the most helpful articulation of this distinction. Pannenberg's concerns center on his view that the law-gospel distinction has become outdated and is no longer relevant in the postmodern world, assuming a sense of guilt that postmodern people largely dismiss.

Second, law and gospel are diametrically opposed realities. As such, law and gospel are deeply resistant to coordination as two different phases of a historical sequence (the law pertaining to the Old Testament, but now superseded by the gospel in the New Testament). Nor can law and gospel be cast in a complementary relationship. Even though in scripture the concept "revelation" is used of both law and gospel, they are not identical or complementary and therefore not contradictory in their message and function. As Werner Elert puts it, "The term revelation cannot eliminate the contrast between law and gospel, cannot even bridge it, even when understood exclusively as the becoming revealed of God."[19] Instead, both law and gospel are enduring realities that have applied to the divine-human relationship through all ages, whereby people live life either under the law or under the gospel.[20] As two opposite revelations, law and gospel stand in substantive, dialectical opposition to each other, saying opposite things about the same subject: "When the one is revealed, the other is veiled; and when the second shines forth, the first one is darkened."[21]

Third, in each of these two words, important, opposing realities in both God and humanity are correlated, affirming the inevitable, mutual engagement of God with humanity: "Wrath and grace become revealed in God, sin and faith in man. . . . The revelation of God's wrath corresponds with the revelation of man's sin, the revelation of his grace with the revelation of man's faith. . . . This also demonstrates the contrast between law and Gospel . . . two things become manifest both in God and in man, which contradict each other, wrath and grace in God, sin and faith in man. With regard to both we must thus speak of a twofold revelation."[22] We now move to examine the nature and function of the law more thoroughly.

A Lutheran View of the Law

Lutheran theology makes a fundamental distinction between the first use of the law (the "civil" law which all must obey or face punishment) and its second, properly theological use of illuminating knowledge of sin and accusing of sin.[23] Such a fundamental, twofold understanding of the

---

18. Carl Braaten, *Justification* (Minneapolis: Augsburg Fortress, 1990), 77.
19. Werner Elert, *The Christian Faith* (Columbus: Lutheran Theological Seminary, 1974), 87.
20. In his various writings, Werner Elert contrasts these two states of being as "ethos under law" versus "ethos under grace." Elert, *The Christian Faith; The Christian Ethos* (Philadelphia: Fortress Press, 1957); *Law and Gospel* (Philadelphia: Fortress Press, 1967); and *The Structure of Lutheranism* (St. Louis: Concordia, 1962).
21. Elert, *The Christian Faith*, 88.
22. Ibid., 87–88.
23. From its earliest days, Lutheran theology has debated whether or not there is a "third use" of the law: whether the law, in the form of moral guidance, applies to Christians, or whether its use is restricted to convicting the sinful self of sin. While traditionally Luther-

divine law leads Lutheran theology to affirm the divine law as a universal existential, permeating all creation. This means that a certain kind of naming of God makes sense universally across all human experience: identifying God as applying pressure against humans ambiguously with judgment in the midst of promise.[24] While contemporary people do not recognize the divine law as such, its influence is an inescapable feature of life. As Oswald Bayer describes it:

> Our contemporaries do not experience the law anymore as the law of God. Rather, the law is experienced as anonymous, or, in the best case scenario, as the "categorical imperative." A sense of inescapable duty weighing heavily on every human heart is revealed to us by this anonymous law. Duty becomes deadly when the law coincides with the gospel, when they are not distinguished from each other.[25]

The divine law itself constitutes a further, threefold structure in describing three, distinct orders through which God and humanity interrelate. These three connective spheres can be described as the orders of creation, the moral order, and judgment, wherein God relates to humanity as its creator/preserver, legislator, and judge, respectively.[26]

First of all, by virtue of creation, God is the creator, source, and manager of our lives, whether or not people acknowledge God as such. As our creator, God gives us the gift of life and places us in specific contexts of space and time, plunging us into a multitude of relationships we did not choose, which are simply given to us.

Second, God as the author of the moral order and "legislator" conveys expectations, commands, and guidelines for how we ought to live our lives as God's creatures. This places humanity under obligation to God, to fulfill such divine expectations and obey such commands. As Luther

ans have affirmed the necessity of the third use of the law, Werner Elert (among others) has vehemently rejected the third use of the law. Elert insisted that the title of the *Formula of Concord*, article 6, "Third Use of the Law," misrepresented the true intent and affirmation of that article. Instead, Elert asserted that, while the law rightly applied to and accused the "old sinful self" in Christians, the "new self" in Christ could and should only be governed by the gospel. Elert understood the ethical imperatives in the New Testament as "grace imperatives," as invitations to live the Christian life in its radical freedom. For a fuller treatment of Elert's view, see his *The Christian Ethos*, 294–303. This debate continues within contemporary Lutheran theology.

24. I am cognizant that this claim is made from within a framework of "confessional ultimate reality." Catherine Cornille describes its nature well: "The natural tendency of any religious tradition is to situate the origin or basis for interconnection between religions in their own particular conception of ultimate reality. Religions indeed presuppose that the fullness of truth is concentrated in their own conceptions of ultimate reality and that whatever form or degree of truth is found elsewhere will be derived from or oriented toward this truth. . . . This is an inevitable condition of the irreducible particularity of all religious perspectives. It is the recognition that . . . each engages the other from within their own hermeneutical framework, which forms the basis for the balanced and sincere exchange that occurs in genuine dialogue." Cornille, *The Im-possibility of Interreligious Dialogue* (New York: Crossroad, 2008), 127, 132–33.

25. Oswald Bayer, "Justification as Basis and Boundary," *Lutheran Quarterly* 15 (2001): 285.

26. Elert, *The Christian Ethos*, 49–56.

put it in his Small Catechism: "For all of this [the gifts of creation] I owe it to God to thank and praise, serve and obey Him."[27] The law as God's legislation reveals a vast web of expectations and obligations, grounded in the broader context of creation, to which humanity is inextricably bound.

Extending beyond these two spheres, the third order connects God to humanity as its final judge, delivering an ultimate, total verdict upon our lives.[28] As the language concerning forensic justification makes clear, God as judge passes a sentence and verdict upon our lives. This juridical sphere reveals to sinners the ultimate value and worth of their lives: "God's law makes sin manifest. It makes man guilty."[29]

Long before humans explicitly learn about the divine law and its functioning within these three spheres, they have already encountered its reality in the universal human experience of not being in control of their lives, of an external "other" opposing and controlling them, frustrating their plans by applying pressure upon their lives. Rather than naming it the divine law, contemporary people refer to this force by various names: destiny, fate, karma, one's lot in life, and so on. The revelation of divine law enters this experiential matrix, unveiling, specifying, and naming this ambiguous, elusive force as *God's* creative law exerting pressure. In addition, our self-assertive resistance and protest against this pressure is further revealed as rebellion and sin against God's very self.

Highlighting and Accessing the Benefits of Christ

Having clarified the law-gospel distinction and the functioning of divine law, we now turn to examine its intrinsic relationship to the gospel as promise. Before doing so, it is helpful to clarify the interrelationship between the gospel, promise, and faith. As Luther's earlier quote on promise makes clear, Lutheran theology posits an intrinsic relationship between the categories of gospel, promise, and faith, which is this: the gospel is a promise that requires faith (trust) in order to be received, in order for the benefits of Christ to be applied to one's life.

Just as faith as trust is needed to make full use of the benefits of the gospel as promise, analogously, the law-gospel distinction is needed to read scripture (that is, the biblical history and the history of Jesus) in such a way as to properly "use" that history for its intended purpose and not waste it. Philip Melanchthon charges his opponents as doing

---

27. *BoC*, 355.
28. Elert, *The Christian Ethos*, 49–56.
29. Elert, *The Christian Faith*, 183.

precisely this. By obscuring the *sola fide*, they let biblical history go to waste. When the *sola fide* is thus obscured, the biblical history as the history of God's promises is wasted and there is no need for Christ. The law-gospel distinction helps ensure that scripture is read and understood as the history of God's promises overcoming God's law, as the history of the God who freely promises to justify the ungodly.

Melanchthon, in Apology 4, emphasizes the importance of which source one chooses as one's starting point in reading scripture, the law or the gospel. "Of these two topics," he says, "[our] opponents single out the law . . . and through the law they seek the forgiveness of sins and justification."[30] His concern is eminently practical: to preserve the gospel promise so that consciences be comforted and Christ be used and glorified. If one starts with the law, one will inevitably lose and bury the gospel promise. Only if one starts with the principle of promise can one properly appreciate, recognize, and utilize both law and promise.

Edward Schroeder clarifies what is at stake in these competing hermeneutical approaches: "So a promise-centered hermeneutics opens up both the legal and the promissive material in Scripture. A Law-centered hermeneutics actually destroys both. Not only does it bury the promise, but in burying the promise it makes impossible the keeping of the Law as well. Thereby both words of God are wasted. In Melanchthon's recurrent phrase, they are 'in vain.'"[31]

Melanchthon's answer to his opponents, by utilizing the law-gospel distinction, is to "recover within that [biblical] history its basic 'need' of having happened at all: Jesus Christ, God's promise kept, who is ours only by faith."[32] Only in this manner is the goal of the entire scriptures, especially the benefits of Christ, realized and appropriated.

How the Law-Gospel Distinction Undergirds the Gospel as Promise

A more systematic articulation of precisely *how* the law-gospel distinction is indispensable to the gospel as promise is now called for. Seven main points clarify what is at stake in this relationship.

First, the law-gospel distinction protects and preserves the gospel as unconditional promise. It addresses the central issue of whether the promise is being highlighted, promoted, and used, on the one hand, or whether it is being marginalized, hidden, and unused, on the other.

Second, not only does the distinction preserve the purity of the gospel;

30. *BoC*, 121.
31. Edward Schroeder, "Is There a Lutheran Hermeneutic?" in *The Promising Tradition: A Reader in Law-Gospel Reconstructionist Theology*, 2nd ed. (St. Louis: Concordia Seminary in Exile, 1974), 117.
32. Robert Bertram, "The Hermeneutical Significance of Apology 4," in *A Project in Biblical Hermeneutics* (St. Louis: Concordia, 1969), 124–26.

it also preserves the law and ensures that it always carries out its theological function of accusing of sin. The law always accuses (*lex semper accusat*). A failure to practice this distinction inevitably distorts the gospel into law, while maintaining the distinction serves to clearly preserve the promissory, gratuitous nature of the gospel. Furthermore, the distinction prevents the law from being eviscerated and shrunk into legalistic moralism. As Melanchthon reiterates, "For the law always accuses since we never satisfy the law" and "the law always accuses them and brings wrath with it."[33]

Third, this dynamic is indispensable for identifying the benefits of Christ. As Melanchthon notes, "For one has to distinguish the promises from the law in order to recognize the benefits of Christ."[34] Helping ensure that these benefits of Christ are utilized and used rather than wasted, the law-gospel distinction directly addresses the pastoral concern that the benefits of Christ be put to use. Such identification and use of the benefits of Christ is not merely a one-time event, but rather a defining, enduring feature of the Christian life. In a classic Lutheran view of the structure of existence, Christians need to continue to use Christ as mediator, they "need to learn how to let both the Law and the Promise move into the Christian life—the Law to expose those areas where idolatry is still thriving, the Promise to have Christ take over those areas and have them function as sectors of redeemed creation."[35]

Fourth, this distinction helps clarify the nature of justifying faith. As the law forces us to give up on our own efforts and righteousness, the gospel directs us to faith and trust as the only means by which we "have" Christ and "use" him for what he was and is—the very Word and Promise of God.

Fifth, the law-gospel distinction facilitates the comfort of troubled consciences. As mentioned earlier, "With the help of this distinction these consciences can sustain themselves in their greatest spiritual struggles against the terror of the law."[36]

Sixth, as mentioned earlier, the law-gospel distinction is an indispensable hermeneutic for ensuring that the scriptural history and the history of Jesus are read in such a way that they come out as the good news of promise, of God justifying the ungodly.

Finally, as a practical application of the preceding six reasons, the law-gospel distinction enables Lutheran theology to properly commend good works without losing the promise. As Melanchthon puts it, "We

---

33. *BoC*, 148, 151, 154.
34. *BoC*, 149.
35. Schroeder, "Is There a Lutheran Hermeneutic?" 117.
36. *BoC*, 581.

must see what Scripture attributes to the law and what it attributes to the promises. For it *praises and teaches good works* in such a way as not to abolish the free promise *and not to eliminate Christ.*[37] Clarifying the role of the law-gospel distinction in relation to the gospel as promise lays the necessary groundwork for elaborating its missional implications.

The Law-Gospel Distinction in the Classic Lutheran Tradition

In a classic passage from *The Freedom of the Christian*, Luther elucidates both the irreducible difference between law and gospel and how this distinction actualizes the gospel, through faith in the promise, in Christians' lives:

> [T]he entire Holy Scripture is to be divided into two words: the commandments or the law of God and the assurances or the promises. The commandments teach and prescribe for us various good works.... They indeed do give direction, but they do not help; they teach what a person ought to do, but furnish no power to make something occur.... When the human being learns about and has discovered his own powerlessness on the basis of the commandments.... He does not find anything in himself by means of which he can be righteous. Following upon this comes the other Word, the divine assurance and promise, which says: If you want to fulfill all the commandments . . . look here, believe in Christ, through whom I promise you all grace, righteousness, peace, and freedom. If you believe, you have it; if you do not believe, you do not have it: For what is impossible for you . . . is made simple and easy for you through faith.... This is what the promises of God provide, what the commandments demand; they fulfill what the commandments demand, so that everything is from God himself, both commandment and fulfillment. He alone commands; he alone also fulfills.[38]

What is true of Luther also applies to the Confessions as a whole: the theology of the Lutheran Confessions is permeated by the "chromosomal structure" (Bayer) of the gospel as promise in contrast to the law. For instance, the Formula of Concord article 2 contrasts the preaching of the law with the preaching of the gospel:

> [T]hrough the preaching of the law [people] feel real terror, regret, and sorrow in their hearts. Through the preaching of the holy gospel of the gracious forgiveness of sins in Christ and through meditating upon it, a spark of faith is ignited in them, and they accept the forgiveness of sins for Christ's sake and receive the comfort of the promise of the gospel. In this way the Holy Spirit, who effects all of this, is sent into their hearts.[39]

37. *BoC*, 150.
38. *LW* 31:358ff.
39. *BoC*, 554.

Having demonstrated the centrality of the law-gospel distinction for the gospel as promise and its missional importance for God's dual mission, we now turn to elaborate how the hiddenness of God connects this foundation with the wider, religiously plural world.

Hiddenness of God in the Lutheran Tradition

Luther's classic expression of God's hiddenness in the cross, expressed in the Heidelberg Disputation of 1518, is worth quoting:

> He deserves to be called a theologian . . . who comprehends the visible and manifest things of God, seen through suffering and the cross. . . . The "visible things of God" are placed in opposition to the invisible, namely, his human nature, weakness, and foolishness. . . . Nor is it sufficient for anyone, and it does him no good, to recognize God in his glory and majesty, unless he recognizes him in the humility and shame of the cross. . . . For this reason true theology and recognition of God are in the crucified Christ. . . . He who does not know Christ does not know God hidden in suffering. . . . God can be found only in suffering and the cross.[40]

God's "alien work" of judging human sin in the event of the cross (the law) serves God's "proper work" of justifying and reconciling sinners (the gospel). Such a theology of the cross is thoroughly paradoxical:

> In Christ, God works in a paradoxical mode *sub contrariis*. His wisdom is hidden under folly, his strength under abject weakness. He gives life through death, righteousness to the unrighteous; he saves by judging and damning. The Hidden God is God incarnate, crucified, hidden in suffering.[41]

The notion of God's hiddenness (*deus absconditus*) articulated here will serve as a bridge between a Lutheran theology of the gospel as promise and the broader context of religious pluralism. As a theology of promise, a Lutheran proposal for mission is best able to establish a point of contact and dialogue with other religions when it seriously engages them through the category of God's hiddenness.[42] In doing so, such a Lutheran missiological proposal makes a distinctive contribution to interreligious dialogue, raises important questions for others and itself

---

40. *LW* 31:52–53. I would nuance Luther's assertion by affirming that while, for Christians, God's loving mercy is most clearly manifested or concentrated in the cross, this certainly does not mean that God's gracious, merciful presence is exclusively limited to the cross. God may be found uniquely, but not solely, in the cross and in suffering.
41. Brian Gerrish, "To the Unknown God: Luther and Calvin on the Hiddenness of God," *Journal of Religion* 53 (1973): 268.
42. Given that divine hiddenness is most readily understood in monotheistic traditions such as Judaism and Islam, my proposal is most directly applicable to dialogue with these fellow "religions of the book." However, while nontheistic religions like Buddhism, Taoism, and Confucianism do not recognize a personal God whose hiddenness can be intelligibly discussed, I contend that this category may potentially be translated into the framework of these religions in a meaningful, intelligible manner.

to consider, and opens itself up for genuine dialogue with and questioning from other religious traditions.

The hiddenness of God is a helpful category for navigating the ambiguity of natural human experience. It is a useful tool for Lutheran missiology in at least three ways: (1) it facilitates an intra-Christian approach toward religious pluralism, (2) connects Lutheran missiological discourse with the wider, theological/philosophical discourse, as well as (3) offers, in the gospel, a hopeful word in the midst of ongoing distress and angst.

While all religions have hopeful words to say, they also wrestle with whether such words of "grace" will indeed be the final word. The most important similarities and overlaps concerning human religious experience are best described, not by categories of being (ontology) or existence (anthropology), but rather as the paradoxical relationship between divine wrath and promise, sin and grace, law and gospel, human brokenness and divine healing. Because human religious experience *is* ambiguous, left to our own devices, we don't really quite know how to "read" or interpret nature. The "hidden God" whom nature ambiguously reveals requires unveiling, in and through the revelation of Christ, if humanity is to have a gracious relationship of trust with this God. As Edward Schroeder comments on the formulation, "There is grace, and there is grace," by Melanchthon, "the 'grace' we encounter in our daily experience of God's creation is something other than the 'grace' that comes in Jesus the Christ."[43]

Luther's emphatic claim, "The cross alone is our theology,"[44] directs us to focus our attention on God's paradoxical absence and presence, hiddenness and revelation, wrath and loving mercy, as those realities are conveyed in and through a theology of the cross.[45] Other religions and philosophies have their own strategies for dealing with questions of divine hiddenness and human suffering, but Lutheran theology nonetheless humbly invites them to a meeting at the foot of the cross.

Christian theology has always affirmed the mystery of God's inner being as hidden, transcending human speech and categories: there is

43. Edward Schroeder, "Encountering the Hidden God," in *Areopagus—A Living Encounter with Today's Religious World* (Hong Kong: Tao Fong Shan Christian Center, 1993), 2.
44. *LW* 25:287.
45. I am acutely aware of the immensely complex nature of issues related to the hiddenness and unknowability of God, apophatic and negative theologies, theology of the cross, and theodicy. While this brief chapter does not allow for more in-depth treatment of divine hiddenness and unknowability as they have been classically articulated by such early Christian theologians as Gregory of Nyssa, Maximus the Confessor, Pseudo-Dionysius, and Meister Eckhardt, nor theologies of the cross of such contemporary theologians as Jürgen Moltmann, Eberhard Jüngel, Douglas John Hall, and others, my aim is very modest: simply to suggest how the hiddenness of God, interpreted within the framework of a theology of the cross, can serve as a missiologically fruitful topic for interreligious dialogue. Such a focus in no way minimizes or negates an emphasis on a theology of the resurrection.

an "excess" to God's being which no human language can fully capture. Commenting on the notion of God's "hiding place" (Ps. 18:11), Luther speaks of at least five modes whereby God is hidden: in the darkness of faith, in light inaccessible, in the mystery of incarnation, in the church and Mary, and in the Eucharist.[46]

Having addressed the law-gospel distinction and divine hiddenness, we now turn to delineate significant, missiologically relevant aspects of the divine hiddenness in the cross. We readily affirm God's universal presence and action, but we also ask the question, "Which God is already at work in a given context: God hidden or God revealed?" as a more helpful diagnostic tool for what God may be doing in any context. The Lutheran distinction between God's two realms serves as the next step toward engaging religious others in mission and dialogue.

The Reign of God and the Two-Realms (Kingdoms) Distinction

This distinction between God hidden (*deus absconditus*) and God revealed (*deus revelatus*) is firmly grounded in Luther's distinction between two realms: God's care for and preservation of creation, on the one hand, and God's mercy in and through Jesus Christ, on the other hand. Luther saw God's various gifts and blessings in creation as distinctly different in quality from God's gifts and blessings in Christ. The first and second articles of the Creed are distinct and offer different connections to God. Let us let Luther describe the difference between these divine gifts, blessings, and works in his own words, first describing the gifts of creation:

> [God] has given me and constantly sustains my body, soul, and life, my members great and small, all my senses, my reason and understanding, and the like; my food and drink, clothing, nourishment. He makes all creation help provide the benefits and necessities of life. . . . Moreover, he gives all physical and temporal blessings—good government, peace, security. . . . It inevitably follows that we are in duty bound to love, praise, and thank him without ceasing.[47]

In sharp contrast to such created gifts and blessings, Luther describes the divine gifts offered in and through Jesus Christ:

> Here . . . we see what we have from God over and above the temporal goods mentioned above. . . . It means that he [Jesus Christ] has redeemed and released me from sin, from the devil, from death, and from all misfortune . . . he who has brought us back from the devil to God, from death to life, from sin to righteousness, and keeps us there.[48]

46. *LW* 10:119–20.
47. *BoC*, 432–33.

The created world, fallen through sin, is a qualitatively different realm from God's "new creation" in Christ, and God has two related, but distinct, strategies for managing each: creation care and preservation versus forgiving, reconciling mercy in Christ.

Much contemporary missiology deems "traces of grace and truth" in other religions as manifestations of God's reign. Luther, though, would locate matters of peace, justice, and creation care—matters often viewed as "values of the kingdom"—in his explanation of the fourth petition of the Lord's Prayer (pertaining to daily bread) rather than in the second petition, "your kingdom come."[49] In contrast, the second petition focuses solely on the spiritual petition that God would "rule us as a king of righteousness, life, and salvation against sin, death, [the devil], and an evil conscience."[50] In other words, the two-realm principle emphasizes the proper distinction between ethics and salvation—and the proper realm for each. God interacts with the world "ambidextrously," with two different, although related, agendas carried out in two different realms.

On the one hand, God's "left-hand" rule and agenda entails caring for His creation, including this-worldly blessings of peace, justice, and everything Luther includes under the fourth petition of the Lord's Prayer for daily bread (see his *Large Catechism*). On the other hand, God's "right-hand" rule entails redeeming creation into a "new creation," forgiving mercy, and all other spiritual blessings through Christ. "One cares for creation, the other redeems it. . . . One is ethics *coram hominibus* (before people), the other salvation *coram deo* (before God)."[51]

Only the costly love of God, demonstrated and mediated through the cross, can mediate (offer) the *peace* with God that undergirds our human work for peace, the *mercy* of God that motivates our human work for mercy, and the *justice* of God that alone can justify and energize our human work for justice. The two-realm principle thus aims to safeguard the uniquely "good" and "new" aspects of Christ's work.

Hiddenness of the Gospel and Christ's Benefits

Luther used "hiddenness of God" in varying ways,[52] but two meanings are particularly relevant for our purposes. First, what is "hidden" beyond and indiscernible among God's manifold blessings within creation is God's mercy and favor toward sinners. What gets revealed in and through Christ is not general divine benevolence or goodwill, but rather

---

48. *BoC*, 434.
49. *BoC*, 450–51.
50. *BoC*, 446.
51. Edward Schroeder, "Second Look at the Gospel of Mark," *Currents in Theology and Mission* 33, no. 4 (August 2006): 294.
52. Gerrish, "To the Unknown God," 267.

something very specific: God as merciful on account of the crucified and risen Christ. Second, not only does God's mercy in Christ require revealing, but this mercy is further hidden or "'covered' under what looks like the opposite." God's mercy is hidden in the paradox, shame, and defeat of Christ crucified, in the God who is "incarnate, crucified, hidden in suffering."[53]

Luther argues for the Holy Spirit's work as *unveiling and delivering* the hidden gifts of God, namely Christ and his gospel benefits, through the oral and sacramental gospel:

> But since this grace [the works, suffering, wisdom, and righteousness of Christ] would not be useful to anyone if it were to remain hidden, and could not come to us, the Holy Spirit comes; he also gives himself to us utterly and completely. He teaches us how to recognize this wonderful deed of Christ... helps us to receive and maintain it, how to use it and share it. ... This he does internally as well as externally: internally through faith and other spiritual gifts, but externally by means of the gospel, by means of baptism and the Sacrament of the Altar.[54]

Not only does the "hiddenness of God" in the cross underscore the distinction between God's law and God's promise, it also provides, in my view, a better theological basis for interreligious dialogue than other approaches offer. Luther, employing the hidden God, comments in his explanation to the third article of the Apostles' Creed:

> These articles of the Creed, therefore, divide and distinguish us Christians from all other people on earth. All who are outside the Christian Church, whether heathen, Turks, Jews, or false Christians and hypocrites, even though they *believe in and worship only the one, true God*, nevertheless do not know what his attitude is toward them. They cannot be confident of his love and blessing ... *for they do not have the Lord Christ*, and, besides, they are not illuminated or blessed by the gifts of the Holy Spirit.[55]

Emphasizing the possessive verb "have" throughout his explanation of the Creed, Luther makes the crucial distinction between having a natural, *first-article relationship* with God, grounded in creation, versus having a *second-article relationship* with God through Jesus Christ. All people have the former relationship, by virtue of creation; only Christians can be confident of having the latter, by virtue of the proclaimed gospel. As Melanchthon eloquently states: "To know [have] Christ is to know His benefits." Luther views the gospel, God's revelation of mercy through Christ, as adding something significantly "good" and "new" to what sinners otherwise, by nature, do not have.[56]

---

53. Ibid., 268.
54. *LW* 37:366.
55. *BoC*, 440. Italics added for emphasis.

Therefore, a Lutheran approach affirms that, while all people may worship the one true God, albeit anonymously, their worship, apart from Christ, lacks important benefits, such as awareness of and confidence in God's benevolent attitude toward them, as well as the comfort arising from trusting the offer of divine, loving mercy in the cross. This distinction is meant to emphasize the crucial connection between the God one explicitly "has" and the benefits that God bestows. That is why Luther, commenting on the sailors in Jon. 1:5 ("All the sailors were afraid and each cried out to his own god"), asserts, "These men in the ship all know of God, but they have no sure God."[57] In other words, "The office of Christ is to make us certain of God."[58]

Practical Application for Engaging in Mission

William E. Lesher expresses our intra-Lutheran struggle with mission articulately, "What does our faith community believe about people of other faiths? What gifts do we have to contribute? What gifts might we receive? What obstacles prevent us from participation in interreligious engagements? What compels us to reach out?"[59]

Based on the distinction between the hidden and revealed God, a classic Lutheran missiology offers several hunches about the lived, faith experiences of the religious other.[60]

First, nobody's daily religious experience is one of only or primarily grace. Second, to ground a theology of religions or interreligious dialogue on how various religions articulate their experiences of grace (for example, Raimon Panikkar's Christophanies) leaves vast areas of religious experience untouched, ensuring that the promise of mercy on account of Christ will become marginalized. Third, the grace of God in Christ is not simply an unexpected, undeserved experience of diffuse "goodness." Rather, it is a surprising word of mercy from our Creator whom we chronically mistrust and to whom we owe an unending debt. Fourth, should not the fact of Christian sinfulness—our lack of faith—serve a central role in dialogue? Christians admit to being "simultaneously saints and sinners" and echo the father's desperate cry in Mark, "Lord, I believe, help my unbelief!"[61] Fifth, Christians are no better in their moral virtue than others. Their claim is not about

56. Edward Schroeder, "Luther's Commentary on the Third Article as a Clue to His Theology of Other Religions," *Missio Apostolica* 7, no. 1 (May 1999): 7.
57. Oswald Bayer, *Theology the Lutheran Way* (Grand Rapids: Eerdmans, 2007), 75.
58. Ibid.
59. William Lesher, "Intra-Lutheran Perspective on the Interreligious Movement," *Currents in Theology and Mission* 33, no. 3 (June 2006): 208.
60. I am indebted to Edward Schroeder's articulation of these in "Encountering the Hidden God," 4–5.
61. Mark 9:24.

themselves, but rather about a gracious Word of promise they have heard and received, giving them hope against all evidence to the contrary. Sixth, to the extent that Christian theology is not enriched by listening to the experiences of God's hiddenness in other religions, to that extent Christian theology remains impoverished.

Suggesting that mission, especially interreligious dialogue, include and elaborate humanity's common experience of divine hiddenness may seem pessimistic. However, such an approach has four distinct advantages. First, it is a radically inclusive approach, inviting the input of all regardless of education or theological sophistication.[62] Second, this approach centers on lived experience rather than theological belief, on praxis rather than only doctrine. Third, obstacles in traditional forms of academic, interreligious dialogue—Christian doctrines of Jesus Christ's divinity, the Trinity, and so on—are moved from the center to the periphery. Fourth, this approach facilitates a narrative approach to proclamation and dialogue by offering the story of Jesus, especially the narrative of his paradoxical experience of God's presence and absence on the cross, as a contribution and letting it speak for itself.

Conclusion

Is the postmodern skeptic right? Are promises "inauthentic simply because they are promises"? Should promises not be made, because they cannot be kept? Is Christian mission, traditionally understood as gospel proclamation and faith active in love aimed at conversion, simply outdated and a relic of the past? We think not. The One who came to fulfill the law on our behalf (Matt. 5:17), taking upon himself its curse by becoming a curse for us (Gal. 3:13), promises to take away our guilt, shame, and condemnation (Rom. 8:1), to give us deep soul rest (Matt. 11:25), and to fulfill our life (John 19:30). Christ crucified and risen promises to fulfill, not only the Jewish demand for signs and Greeks' search for wisdom (1 Cor. 1:22), but also the restless, skeptical postmodern heart.

While skeptical concerning the missional content of Lutheran theology, David Bosch urges that Christian engagement in mission occur in a spirit and attitude of "bold humility." Lutheran theology is well poised to do just that. How so?

On the one hand, we can be *bold*, confident that "no matter how many promises God has made, they are 'yes' in Christ" (2 Cor. 1:20), especially "the promise that our life will be fulfilled by Christ."[63] Not only are we

---

62. One of the criticisms of interreligious dialogue as it has often been practiced is that it has been elitist, engaged in by theologians, academics, and intellectuals.

promised the forgiveness of sins, mercy, new life, and all divine gifts on account of Christ, the risen Christ himself even promises to go with us as we go in mission, in his name, to share the gifts of the gospel in word and deed (Matt. 28:20b).

On the other hand, we go *humbly*, ever mindful of Michael Oleksa's sage exhortation: "The Christian, while knowing where Christ is, can never be certain where He is not."[64] We expect to meet the God of grace revealed in unexpected ways and hidden places. We expect to receive as much, perhaps more, than we give.

Coming to grips with the hidden mystery of God, Lutheran theology insists, entails recognizing not only the mystery of divine, loving grace, but also the mysteries of divine wrath and mercy, law and gospel, God's hiddenness and revelation. In this recognition, we hold in tension the promise of reconciling mercy *in* Christ (2 Cor. 5:19) with the eschatological promise of uniting all things *under* Christ (Eph. 1:10). Within a "mission shaped by promise," the hiddenness of God serves as a bridge between our Christian faith and other faiths. It also serves as a humble invitation to consider the promise of God's eschatological victory over sin, death, and the devil—a victory based on an "eschatological promise whose fulfillment will come only as a stunning and undeserved gift."[65]

---

63. Gritsch and Jenson, *Lutheranism*, 38.
64. Michael Oleksa, "Orthodox Missiological Education for the Twenty-First Century," in *Missiological Education for the Twenty-First Century*, ed. J. Dudley Woodberry, Charles van Engen, and Edgar J. Elliston (Maryknoll, NY: Orbis, 1996), 86.
65. Joseph Dinoia, *Diversity of Religions* (Washington, DC: Catholic University of America Press, 1992), 170.

Afterword

I am surprised, yet honored, to have been asked to write the Afterword for this book. I am not a theologian, an academician, or a scholar; and I don't consider myself a colleague of the ten distinguished writers of this book. What I am is a good listener and an eager learner, and maybe someone who recognizes deliriously wonderful, seemingly too-good-to-be-true News when I hear it—and then can't stop dancing for joy as a result. These special ten writers, starting especially with Ed Schroeder, have been the ones who have proclaimed and explained, clearly and decisively, *why* having a crucified and risen Messiah makes all the difference in the world.

After reading the first three chapters, you may have felt the same way I did: Sigh, such a shame Schroeder didn't get the whole book written. But then, after reading the chapters written by the other nine, I couldn't help but marvel how they all continued Schroeder's approach, that is, how they all started with the "hub" of justification by faith, then articulated a specific "spoke" of Christian doctrine using the law-gospel distinction.

I do have a hunch as to why Schroeder didn't finish his book, that is, a reason *in addition* to the one given. The given reason is that the history of the Lutheran Church—Missouri Synod, culminating in the creation of Seminex, totally sidetracked him. And for sure, that's true. But it's also true that Schroeder became so busy teaching the "Augsburg Aha" to students *and* layfolk, he simply didn't have time to write ink-on-paper books anymore.

People became the books Ed "wrote" on—correction, *imprinted*, with Luther's law-gospel insights. *People*—like the other nine writers and all the other seminary students. *People*—like me and myriads of other layfolk I could list. If you were to add us all up, I do believe we'd be a spilling-over *library* full of books! (Just between us, I think God's gotta be chuckling over the cleverness of this all, but that's changing the subject.)

About that last bunch, us layfolk, and my hunch: it was the phenomenon of Seminex that drove Schroeder, together with his colleague Robert Bertram, mentioned often in this book, to reach out beyond seminary walls (because, bluntly, there were no longer any walls) to us layfolk. And *voila!* Look at the gift that resulted! They may never have realized how large a gift they gave, but I, for one, am immensely grateful for it.

The special gift Robert Bertram and Edward Schroeder have given us is a way to read the Bible that is faithful to the Bible's central message. It's a way to read the Bible that allows us to hear God's word of promise even in the face of God's own word of law. They gave us a simple process for using Luther's law-gospel distinction—as spelled out in this book. They also created a *community* of learners (mostly layfolk) who can *apply* this law-gospel process to our everyday lives. We call the process the Crossings six-step method, and those who make use of it the Crossings Community. Our community has existed for forty years already and is still humming along to that Augsburg whirling-wheel refrain. We're always delighted to have others join us.

Crossings' goal is to cross scripture and daily life doing exactly what Luther did, that is, to use the law-gospel distinction to "diagnose" to the deepest depth our human problem (our condition before God) and then to "prognose" (as in totally cure) that problem with a crucified and risen Messiah. Does that sound like the Augsburg Confession or what? You can find Crossings on the web at http//www.crossings.org.

As I mentioned, I am surprised and honored to be the one who gets to utter the *last words* about this book. But do you get it? What Ed Schroeder, the other nine writers, and now Crossings, articulate and help people like me *get*—take to heart, trust, rejoice about—is that *God's* last word about me/us is that God cares so deeply about us that God—*God's own self!*—became one of us in order to *handle-absorb-destroy* all the muck, desperation, and, yes, let's say it out loud, *God's own* law-critique-judgment. And in return God offers us forgiveness, life, hope—and all the joy that comes with it. Luther called this the happy exchange; Bertram, Schroeder, Crossings call it the "sweet swap." I call it mercy-beyond-belief, and it's changed me forever.

I'm grateful for Ed Schroeder and these gifted nine because what they do, so clearly and vividly—like John the Baptist, like Luther the Reformer, like the confessors at Augsburg—is point *away* from themselves, *away* from the law (as a means of salvation), always *toward* Jesus the Christ, the incredible sin-absorber and absolver (the wheel hub). *He's* the one who makes all the difference in the world. God's *gift* and *promise* is that God has come to our rescue, via Jesus, that *He'll* get us through *both* our lives and our deaths. I trust that. I hope this book helps you, too, dear reader, to trust, and then share such amazing mercy-news.

So, I yield *my* final words to *God's* final words. (Is there any possible comparison? Of course not!) After all, God's final word, *His* "Afterword," is the one that counts. It's the Promise that keeps promising, the Gift that keeps gifting. Aren't you glad?

Catherine Lessmann
Chesterfield, MO

Index of Names and Subjects

Index of Scripture